SYSTEMS OF FAMILY THERAPY:
An Adlerian Integration

by

Robert Sherman

and

Don Dinkmeyer

with chapters by

James Robert Bitter
James W. Croake
Steve Hirschorn
F. Donald Kelly
William H. McKelvie

BRUNNER/MAZEL, *Publishers* • New York

Library of Congress Cataloging-in-Publication Data

Sherman, Robert, 1928–
  Systems of family therapy.

  Includes bibliographies and indexes.
  1. Family psychotherapy. 2. Adler, Alfred,
1870–1937. I. Dinkmeyer, Don C. II. Title.
[DNLM: 1. Family Therapy—methods. WM 430.5.F2 S553s]
RC488.5.S494 1987   616.89′156   86-29897
ISBN 0—87630—457—9

Copyright © 1987 by Robert Sherman and Don Dinkmeyer

Published by
BRUNNER/MAZEL, INC.
19 Union Square
New York, New York 10003

Contents

Acknowledgments

The authors wish to acknowledge the work of the scores of professionals who were not specifically cited in this volume but to whom we are indebted. We especially recognize our teachers at the Alfred Adler Institute of New York and the Alfred Adler Institute of Chicago. They have contributed to the body of knowledge and discipline known as Adlerian psychology from which we obtained many of the ideas for this book. Most of these ideas are generally accepted and recognized in the field and were internalized by us as we read and studied the literature of Adlerian psychology over the course of our professional lives. The ideas became an integral part of our beings. We then used them as a foundation upon which to incorporate our own contributions and refinements.

We tested many of the ideas described in this book in our own families. We are grateful to our wives, Judith and E. Jane, and to our children, David, Allen, Ora, Don Jr., and Jim, for teaching us in real life the true meaning of love, closeness, commitment, encouragement, selective subjective perception, cooperation, social interest, individual motivation in the family, and conflict resolution.

We especially recognize the major contributions to this work by our colleagues who contributed chapters. Each was willing to take on the major challenge of integrating Adlerian psychology with one of the major schools of family therapy. For a seminal contribution to the field of family therapy we recognize Jim Bitter, James Croake, Steve Hirschorn, Don Kelly, and Bill McKelvie.

We are also indebted to our editors Natalie Gilman and Ann Alhadeff for their invaluable assistance. Every author hopes for a good editor. We are among the fortunate authors.

Robert Sherman
Don Dinkmeyer

Preface

Alfred Adler probably developed the first sophisticated professional models for couple and family counseling and family education; these were used extensively in 31 Child Guidance Centers in Europe from World War I through 1934. The model was then spread throughout the world with the dispersion caused by the rise to power of the fascist regimes in Austria and Germany.

Adler emphasized people's creativity in relationships, social interest, wellness, purposiveness of behavior, the holistic nature of both person and social system, and everyone's capacity to learn and to change. He stressed the interactive nature of behavior. He viewed therapy as an educative process that facilitates change and growth. He had great faith in the willingness of people to help one another.

Adler's concerns, ideas, and methods cut across what today are called structural, strategic, communications, experiential, behavioral, cognitive, multigenerational, and ego psychology approaches to the family. He called his theory *Individual Psychology,* referring to the essential unity of the person and of all persons within the social system.

The development of Individual Psychology did not stop with Adler's death in 1937. Talented people in many countries who identify themselves as Adlerians have advanced new ideas and techniques and incorporated the sympathetic concepts generated by other theories into their models and practices. One such development is the evolution from family counseling and family education to family therapy.

We believe there is a need in the field to differentiate in a clear way between Adlerian family counseling and Adlerian family therapy and to set forth the parameters of Adlerian family therapy. At present there is no book that puts together the most recent thinking about Adlerian family therapy per se. In writing this book we undertook that specific task.

We also believe that there is a need in the field of family therapy to develop integrative models in order to synthesize the many good ideas and techniques emerging in the many theories of family therapy now available to us. Recent journal articles and professional conference presentations have discussed this point. The alternative to integration and synthesis is eclecticism, which we think presents other problems and is a less desirable alternative.

Looking at the concepts of the various theories, we were convinced that Adlerian psychology contains an excellent base upon which to form such a theoretical synthesis and in fact Adlerian therapists have been increasingly doing so in their practices. Individual Psychology is an open system theory which opts for inclusiveness rather than exclusiveness and values differences as an opportunity for synthesis and growth. Obviously Adlerian theory is based on its own epistemology and world view, which differ from those of some of the other theories. But there is a great deal of similarity to the majority of specific concepts and techniques used in those theories. This overall idea of presenting Adlerian family therapy as an integrative theory which will enable the clinician to make use of the new ideas and techniques generated in different theories within an internally consistent framework is offered in Chapter 5. To back up this presentation we asked five distinguished contributing authors who are skilled in both Adlerian theory and another theory to make a detailed comparison of the two to see the degree of similarity and difference between them. Such an analysis was made with five popular family therapy theories presented in Chapter 6 to 10. Our thesis that there is a high degree of similarity was borne out. There are, however, vital differences among the theories as well.

We hope that the reader will find in this book a useful articulation of the theory and practice of Adlerian family therapy and find the theory an effective model for incorporating many of the concepts and techniques available in the field at large in a unified way. The reader should also note that for the sake of simplicity, the therapist in this book is typically referred to as "she" and the client as "he."

SYSTEMS OF
FAMILY THERAPY:
An Adlerian Integration

1

Understanding Human Behavior

INTRODUCTION

The Adlerian approach has its origin in the methods developed by Alfred Adler and Rudolf Dreikurs. We begin by providing a short overview of Adlerian psychology as developed by Adler, Dreikurs, and those who studied and worked with them.

Adler was a psychiatrist who worked in Vienna during the first quarter of the century. He was a social psychiatrist who understood dysfunctional behavior in terms of discouragement rather than illness. He believed it was essential for each individual to restore faith, hope, and belief in his potential. He saw that most individual problems were really social in nature and an outgrowth of poor human relationships.

Adler was for a period associated with Sigmund Freud in the Psychoanalytic Society. They ended their relationship because of certain theoretical differences, illustrated by the following very brief comparative list:

Adler	*Freud*
We are social beings	We are biological beings
Motivated to find a place to belong and to complete oneself	Motivated by instincts and drives, particularly the sex drive
Indivisible, total personality (holism)	Personality divided into polar forces of id, superego, ego

In 1922 Adler organized the first Child Guidance Center within the community. Eventually 31 such centers were in use. (Dreikurs, 1959) Adlerian family counseling as conducted in these centers is the predecessor of family therapy from an Adlerian point of view. The counseling, done in public, in front of families, became very popular. The

3

centers remained open until 1934 when the fascists came to power in
Austria.

Rudolf Dreikurs, a student of Adler, emigrated to Chicago in 1937.
Soon thereafter he established the Child Guidance Center at Abraham
Lincoln Center. Dreikurs encouraged other centers and eventually trained
counselors from many parts of the world in the method of Adlerian
family counseling. These centers are now found in a number of places
throughout the United States and in many other countries.

Dreikurs systematically organized the techniques of Adlerian psychology. He was a master teacher and demonstrator of the process. For
example, he developed a system of identifying the purposive nature of
behavior in children into four goals of misbehavior. Dreikurs was perhaps
the dominant influence on the Adlerian family counseling approach in
the United States. A more recent exposition of this model is the work
of Christensen and Schramski (1983) and McAbee and Grunwald (1985).

Adlerian psychology was formally founded by Adler in 1912. The
seminal nature and influence of Adler's early work are revealed in its
impact on a variety of schools of therapists. Certainly Harry Stack
Sullivan, Karen Horney, and advocates of Rational Emotive Therapy
and Reality Therapy all acknowledge Adler's contributions. Adler's
central concepts have also influenced countless therapists even though
they may not consider themselves to be Adlerians.

Adlerian thinking has also had a significant impact in the areas of
parenting and school counseling. The Adlerian approach to parent
education has already been adopted by millions of parents who have
studied STEP (Systematic Training for Effective Parenting), STEP/
Teen (Systematic Training for Effective Parenting of Teens), or Children: The Challenge. Further, school counselor literature features many
references to Adlerian thinking (Dinkmeyer, 1964, 1968, 1972, 1981;
Dinkmeyer & Carlson, 1984; Dinkmeyer & Dinkmeyer, 1982, 1983;
Dinkmeyer & McKay, 1976, 1983; Dinkmeyer, Pew, & Dinkmeyer, 1979;
Dreikurs, 1950; Dreikurs, Grunwald, & Pepper, 1971; Sweeney, 1981).
In this book we show how Adlerian concepts can also become the base
for integrating the various theoretical orientations to family therapy.

The cornerstone of Adlerian psychology evolves from the belief that
people are indivisible, social, creative, decision-making beings whose
beliefs and behavior have a purpose. Thus the individual is best understood holistically as a total being whose thoughts, feelings, and beliefs
are unfolded in a consistent and unified pattern of actions.

Those who study and work in the field of family therapy can quickly
see how a phenomenological theory which works with the social, purposive nature of transactions is a significant theory for the family

therapist. The major principles of the theory can be separately identified for the purposes of understanding, but they function together in an intimate whole, each carefully interrelated and integrated with the others. Because of this, there is some repetitiveness in our effort to describe the major principles.

PSYCHOLOGICAL PRINCIPLES FOR APPLICATION TO FAMILY THERAPY

All Behavior Has Social Meaning

Each individual is socially embedded in an interacting social system. This embeddedness and the interactions within these systems influence each person's behavior. Any movement in the individual, the family, or the environment (the larger ecosystems), and the cosmos instantly creates movement in all the other components. In turn, the family atmosphere and the family constellation help fashion the social meaning of behavior. The family atmosphere consists of all the family forces. The family constellation refers to the birth order of the children and each person's place in the family's organization now and multigenerationally. Strong credence is given here to positional psychology, the meaning a person gives to his position in social systems.

Human relationships require effective interpersonal behavior. Social interaction is not an option in life, but a requirement. We believe that family therapy can teach practical procedures for relating within the family and then within the larger systems of school, work, and society. Family therapy thus provides an opportunity to either learn or relearn. The family therapist will often prescribe the technique of a regular family meeting as a homework assignment and as a process for increasing the opportunities for positive interaction between members of the family.

Humans are social beings. Their behavior is always best understood within social context. As humans, they exist within a milieu that presents regular social demands. The basic desire of each person is to find his place in the group, to "belong." Often misbehavior, inappropriate behavior, and failure to cooperate are a result of faulty perceptions of ways of belonging.

All Behavior Has a Purpose

A basic tenet of Adlerian psychology is the purposiveness of all human behavior. Behavior is goal directed. It is teleological movement toward a goal. This movement, action, and direction of the individual reveals the individual's purpose and intentions.

Goals are created by the individual. Once the family therapist understands the goals and how they are used within family relationships, they can be employed to understand and modify behavior. Thus behavior that at first appears to be inexplicable or confusing becomes understandable once a goal is known. The family, too, as a unit develops its goal and moves intentionally toward it.

The therapist always observes transactions and involvement and tends to offer tentative hypotheses. The basic assumption here is that as we influence the members' goals and beliefs, we come to influence their behavior. The striving then is to influence subjective goals and mistaken perceptions of each family member and the family as a unit. If the goal is valued and useful, the next step is to examine the means and to find more satisfactory ways of moving toward the goal. The therapist therefore looks at the direction of transactions and offers some guesses or hunches, such as "Could it be . . . ?" or "Is it possible . . . ?" (alluding to a goal). Bringing the goal to awareness enables the participants to consider it as chosen and to consider alternatives. It is important to remember that psychological goals are usually unconscious, subjective, and not always in an individual's awareness.

The family therapist can become aware of goals by examining her feelings or by having the members involved in the transactions examine their actions and reactions. For example, in a parent–child conflict, the parent feels annoyed and the parent devotes much time to the child. It may be the child is attempting to seek the parent's attention. However, if the parent feels challenged and would like to prove that the child cannot do that, it is likely that a power struggle will ensue. And if the parent feels hurt, the child's desire to get even will be apparent. Feeling utter frustration or the need to rescue, the parent will know that although the child is capable, he is displaying inadequacy in order to cause the parent to give in and do for him.

It is critical to recognize that this is differentiated from a causal orientation. Adlerians believe that the goal itself, because it gives direction and meaning to any striving, can be regarded as the final cause— finalistic causality. The goal is forward, not behind, and feedback reinforces continuing behavior toward the ultimate goal. The goal in turn is related to significance and belonging, which is discussed in the section called "Striving for Significance."

The understanding of each family member's beliefs and goals has a strong effect on understanding all the meanings that occur in the relationship. Once beliefs and goals which mediate behavior are identified, it is then possible to predict behavior in a given social setting.

Unity, Pattern, Holism

Adler viewed people holistically, believing that the conscious and unconscious, the physical, mental, and emotional, were all part of a unified system moving toward the same psychological goal. We believe that the individual cannot be understood except as a unified whole. We need to understand all aspects of the client's beliefs and perceptions in relationship to his unique goal. The basic question for the family therapist is how each member of the family uses each of these attributes in moving toward or relating to the same goal of the family. Dreikurs stated this well (1950): "The doctrine of the unity of the personality gave Individual Psychology its name. This name, which is so often misunderstood, is derived from the Latin word 'individuum,' which literally means 'undivided,' 'indivisible.'" Life style is based on the premise that each person is a unified organism whose experience moves in meaningful patterns toward a goal. Thus beliefs, perceptions, and goals are interrelated. Similarly, the family is a unified whole organized around its goals.

Therefore, isolated events are understood in relation to the total pattern, and the relation of any of this movement to the goal. Adlerians believe that our movement is intentional, that we create it, and that we are responsible for it. There is no matter of blame since in terms of the internal logic of the person or system, we are doing the best we can to achieve goals that we perceive as appropriate to the circumstances.

Striving for Significance

All behavior is designed to overcome feelings of inferiority and attain feelings of superiority. As humans we have inferiority feelings which emerge in childhood. These are often a part of our obvious dependence on adults for survival. Then, as we develop, we become aware that we are truly insignificant when compared to the universe. This brings about our continuous striving to overcome the challenges of life. The striving in itself is not a problem. However, when the individual loses the courage to continue to strive, to move forward despite discouragement, this interferes with the person's effective functioning.

We believe that the striving to meet the varied challenges of life— work, social, sexual, self, and spiritual—is the basis for motivation. We are motivated by our continuous desire to overcome our feeling of inferiority, to compensate through striving to achieve. We continuously work from a minus to a plus.

The inferiority feelings are based on our faulty subjective self-evaluations. They come out of a competitiveness which tends to make us believe "I am not as much as I should be. I can't live up to others' expectations. I'll never do as well as I should." These faulty, fictional perceptions of self, the world, and human relationships result in discouraged persons.

The person sometimes makes the faulty choice of attempting to overcompensate and prove that he is superior. However, he seldom tends to get even a sense of satisfaction when he does achieve. This is involved in the continuous striving toward the goal of becoming more than others. Hence the direction of striving is from perceived inferiority to the desired goal of superiority.

Adlerians see the solution to this problem in helping people to learn that it is possible to be both equal and significant, to strive for excellence rather than domination, to act in cooperation with others instead of competing. The goal is to actualize and complete the self, the community, and the species.

We believe that the master motive is to be competent and to belong, while creating a unique identity. The striving, then, can clearly move toward significance, which might be established in intellectual, athletic, financial, social, or other accomplishments that also contribute to the community.

A person's behavior, perceptions, attitudes, ways of relating, all illuminate how that person believes he fits into the social milieu. How each of us seeks to achieve significance is clearly reflected by how we seek to be known. We are creative beings deciding our actions based on our subjective perceptions, not merely reacting. We actually often elicit responses that help us maintain negative self-perceptions. An understanding of the behavior that persons move toward or away from provides useful clues to identifying alternative behaviors.

It is in the family of origin that we first work out the issues of belonging and significance, and then again in the procreative family.

Behavior Is a Result of Our Subjective Perceptions

It is essential that the therapist understand the perception of the family members. Each person develops and is responsible for his or her subjective view of life. People give all of their experiences meaning. This process has been described as follows: Each person writes the script, produces, directs, and acts out the roles. We are creative beings deciding our perceptions, not merely reacting. We actually often elicit responses which help us to maintain our self-perceptions, including negative ones.

Adlerian Psychology Is a Psychology of Use, Not of Possession

How a person has decided to use his capacities is deemed to be more important than determining his potential. The focus is on motivation, not just possibilities. In analysis of family relationships, it is often easy to assume that problems exist because of what one member of the family has or lacks in potential abilities. However, Adlerian family therapists are most interested in how each person chooses to use whatever abilities and potential he has.

How people use their abilities depends on their subjective impression of the situation and the goals toward which they strive. The objective is to meet the challenges of life and to overcome problems. When we are directed toward overcoming people, it leads to a power struggle.

Family Atmosphere

The Adlerian system places great importance on family processes. It is primarily during childhood that the family exerts an influence on the development of personality. The conjunction of all the family forces—the climate of relationships that exist between people—is termed family atmosphere. This atmosphere is a function of the way parents relate with each other and the resultant attitudes, relationships, and behaviors parents practice in the home. The person's sense of self, human relationship, and how he relates to the world emerges in the family atmosphere.

The learning that comes from observing and interacting with the parents' model often has a profound impact on the development of personality. Parents also express their system of beliefs and values, some of which they hold in common or about which they have come to working agreements, whereas others may be a source of conflict. There are many assumptive values incorporated in the parents' way of life of which they are unaware or only dimly aware. In turn, children may incorporate these values as they subjectively interpret them or rebel against them.

Things around which values tend to exist include education, athletics, religion, money, achievement, caring relationships, and compliance or obedience. These values will have a clear-cut influence on the child. It is clear that attributes the children share, such as musical ability or athletics, are frequently the result or reflection of family values. When traits are not shared by siblings, it is often the result of competition within the family. One child becomes so talented in a field that the others become discouraged in that area and give up. The others may demonstrate that although they are not best, they can be the worst. But they may also excel in other areas rather than compete.

Values and beliefs are often expressed in the form of expectations. Unmet expectations are sources of conflict. The one holding an unmet expectation is likely to try to train the others to comply.

An essential ingredient in family atmosphere is the manner in which the members communicate. Who speaks with whom? Do they tend to be hostile, critical, commanding, direct, indirect, attentive, preoccupied, active, passive, cooperative, competitive? Are they warm, caring, and able to negotiate differences? Do they utilize double messages, create double binds, or depend on magical thinking? Is there a feeling of openness or rigidity, fear or seriousness? Is there a sense of tension, challenge, or ease?

The child has to learn to negotiate the family system in which he finds himself. He is a full member of the family and by his actions also helps to create the family atmosphere. A nonsleeping, colicky baby may contribute to a considerable amount of tension in the family atmosphere.

The Family Constellation

The family constellation refers to the birth order of each child. The child's position in the family constellation provides a unique perspective on social relationships and one's abilities. Adlerians think that the meaning a person gives to his position and that of each other in the family is of greater importance than the ordinal or chronological age. In other words, positional psychology is the more potent in affecting behavior.

The family constellation position is influenced by factors such as emotional ties between family members, age differences, sex of siblings, size of the family, characteristics of each sibling, alliances with parents, the relationship between the parents, and the absence of a parent.

Family positions are never static but are constantly changing. They are a function of each sibling's interpretation of his or her position. The family therapist uses information about the family constellation to develop a better understanding of each family member's perception of the world and what he can do with it.

The family constellation position can have a variety of effects. An only child often is treated like an adult and may experience a more adult world than a child born into a family with two or three children. The only child may act responsibly in adult life even at an early age.

Firstborn children enjoy a favorite position. However, when firstborn children undergo the experience of being dethroned, this advantage of position may only be temporary.

The second child may feel that he is in a constant "race." It is not unusual for the second child to develop personality characteristics which are opposite those of the first child, particularly if there is little age and no sex difference between siblings.

The second child may believe that he or she can be first only by excelling in certain areas. The first child may be surpassed in a number of areas by an ambitious second child.

The youngest of three is treated like the "baby," receiving special favors, and comes to exhibit relatively little autonomy and ability to do things for himself. But being the lesser increases his ambition to catch up.

The difference in the way in which parents treat the only and the youngest child, for example, may have tremendous repercussions on the development of their personalities.

The Life Style

Life style refers to the person's basic orientation to life, the set of patterns or themes which run through the person's existence. Life style is influenced first by family constellation and family atmosphere. However, formative experiences within the family context help to crystallize and establish the set of guidelines for understanding life which eventually comprise the life style. Most children start to establish the life style, which will provide a feeling of belonging and acceptance, in the first five or six years of life.

The central goal of the life style is often termed the fictional goal. This goal influences and organizes our experiences and behavior. Life style then becomes an organizational pattern which directs some of our behavior. Although formed in early childhood, it is continuously influenced and reinforced through selectivity. Life style is self-consistent, coherent, and unified.

Family therapists need to be aware of the life style as demonstrated by varied members of the family. As these life styles become evident, it is important to see how they mesh and interrelate with each other to form a family life style or intrafamilial conflict.

Social Interest

Adlerians put a great value on the social context of all behavior. Behavior is always understood as a function of the person's perception and social milieu. Since people are continuously striving to belong, and this is a universal phenomenon, many of our problems stem from our failure to achieve belonging. Belonging, however, involves more than merely acceptance; it involves contributing to and feeling a significant part of the group.

Adler believed that social interest was the measure of mental health, insofar as it reflected the individual's capacity to give and take, the willingness to participate and cooperate for the common benefit of the group. In the family, it is important to ascertain how much social interest is involved and the family's willingness to work with each other, to give up their personal preferences for the family good. Social interest thus is a measure of the individual's sense of belonging. Adler also used the phrase "social feeling," by which he meant that the socially developed person really cares about his fellows, is attentive to their needs, and takes appropriate action to join with them.

A person with social interest works with people, agrees to participate, not necessarily to conform, and shows a care and concern for others, a sense of community. It is a major component of family loyalty and cohesiveness and the family's participation in the larger community.

Understanding Behavior by Following the Line of Movement

Adlerians are particularly perceptive of psychological movement, pur-posive behavior, and transactions between family members. Since be-havior is goal directed, these transactions between family members are always purposeful. Thus we believe that behavior never lies, though talk and verbalization may be misleading.

In cause and effect modalities, movement is from the past leading to a present consequence. In the circularity models common to general systems theory, self-reinforcing movement is a repetitive, self-regulating loop that acts to maintain the balance or status quo. For Adlerians, the movement is a proactive continuum toward accomplishing the goal. It is not caused by the past. It is decided upon in the present in anticipation of the future. The goal is to move from a minus to a plus rather than to keep things as they are. Avoidance behaviors have a similar purpose. Their goal is to protect and safeguard from harm, but always in an effort to complete the self or move to a better or superior position.

The chosen line of movement is the way in which power is typically expressed.

Adler (1963) defined power as a continuing line of movement or actions directed toward a goal. They are based on our private logic which makes subjective sense when derived from our beliefs about self and the world. The goal is always consistent with the person's inner belief system.

"Each person creates a line of movement. It is the essence of one's way of coping with and striving within the world" (Sherman, 1983). Because power is conceived of as a continuing line of movement in repeatedly expressed behavior, a therapist can observe and identify the direction and probable goal and make predictions about what kinds of behavior are likely to occur.

Positive power is experienced when the direction of power is outward from the individual toward others and toward the environment. Adlerians call this positive power "social interest" or "social feelings."

In the analysis of movement, look for the use of power between family members, the movement to control, and the desire to get power over others either actively or passively. Observing the direction of the movement and the subsequent behavior of others helps us identify the goal and purpose of the behavior.

Adlerian psychology provides a pragmatic theory that can integrate the theories which address family therapy. The theory is especially well fitted to family therapy because of its emphasis on the social purposiveness and the meaning of all behavior. Adlerians consider transactions and interactions to be the basis for understanding behavior. The emphasis on family atmosphere and family constellation are basic to working with families.

REFERENCES

Adler, A. (1963). *The problem child.* New York: Putnam.

Christensen, O. C., & Schramski, T. G. (Eds.). (1983). *Adlerian family counseling.* New York: Hawthorn.

Dinkmeyer, D. (1964). Conceptual foundations of counseling. *School Counselor, 11*(3), 174–178.

Dinkmeyer, D. (1968, May). Contributions of teleoanalytic theory and techniques to school counseling. *Personnel and Guidance Journal, 46*(9), 898–902.

Dinkmeyer, D. (1972, November). Use of the encouragement process in Adlerian counseling. *Personnel and Guidance Journal, 51*(3), 177–181.

Dinkmeyer, D. (1981). Adlerian family therapy. *American Journal of Family Therapy, 9*(1), 45–52.

Dinkmeyer, D., & Carlson, J. (1984). *Training in marriage enrichment.* Circle Pines, MN: American Guidance Service.

Dinkmeyer, D., & Dinkmeyer, J. (1982, June). Adlerian marriage therapy. *Individual Psychology, 38*(2), 115–122.

Dinkmeyer, D., & Dinkmeyer, J. (1983, June). Adlerian family therapy. *Individual Psychology, 39*(2), 116–124.

Dinkmeyer, D., & McKay, G. (1976). *Systematic training for effective parenting.* Circle Pines, MN: American Guidance Service.

Dinkmeyer, D., & McKay, G. (1983). *Systematic training for effective parenting of teens.* Circle Pines, MN: American Guidance Service.

Dinkmeyer, D., Pew, W. L., Dinkmeyer, D., Jr. (1979). *Adlerian counseling and psychotherapy.* Monterey, CA: Brooks/Cole.

Dreikurs, R. (1959). Early experiments with group psychotherapy. *American Journal of Psychotherapy, 13,* 882-91.

Dreikurs, R. (1950). *Fundamentals of Adlerian psychology* (p. 56). Chicago: Alfred Adler Institute.

Dreikurs, R., Grunwald, B. B., & Pepper, F. C. (1971). *Maintaining sanity in the classroom: Illustrated teaching techniques.* New York: Harper & Row.

Dreikurs, R., & Soltz, V. (1964). *Children: The challenge.* New York: Hawthorn.

McAbee, H., & Grunwald, B. (1985). *Guiding the family: Practical counseling techniques.* Muncie, IN: Accelerated Development.

Sherman, R. (1983). The power dimensions in the family: A synthesis of Adlerian perspectives. *American Journal of Family Therapy 11*(3), 43–52.

Sweeney, F. J. (1981). *Adlerian counseling.* Muncie, IN: Accelerated Development.

2

Family Organization and Dynamics

The principles of Adlerian family therapy described in Chapter 1 function in our conception about how a family is created, organized, and how it functions dynamically. In this chapter we examine the individual's contribution to the family system, how a new family is created, family constellation, the model of the ideal family, and family dynamics. We begin by considering how some of those principles contribute to our understanding of the five major areas of family organization listed above.

THE INDIVIDUAL'S CONTRIBUTION TO THE FAMILY SYSTEM

What does each self-determined individual bring to the creation of a family system? We think that each person plays a fully equal part in the system regardless of age and intelligence based on his impact on the system which must accommodate his presence and existence. The emphasis is on the word *plays* because a member can change place or behavior at any time, eliciting new responses in others or efforts to force conformity. A family is a natural system, not a machine that must maintain an arbitrary homeostatic mode. Both individuals and families are proactive problem seekers as well as reactive problem solvers. They are constantly moving toward and becoming.

The individual has some measure of choice and free will. Based on his goals and perceptions he chooses his behavior in the family. His actions are much influenced by family history, expectations, and demands, but not determined by them. He can conform, modify, or rebel. The degree to which he is in agreement with family rules and goals contributes to loyalty and cohesiveness. The degree to which his behavior differs places a demand on the family for negotiation of a new way of

15

being together. If the family is stuck in a repeating pattern of conflict, the conflict itself may be a family rule to fulfill some goal such as providing excitement and drama or helping the members connect in an otherwise disengaged family system. In any case, by his choice of behavior, his inputs, the individual each day helps create the dynamic family system.

Therefore, it is also possible for the therapist to help change the family by working with one person as long as she is thinking about the family system as a whole. The disadvantages are that the therapist is dealing with only one person's subjective perception of how the family functions. Seeing the entire family in action may present a very different picture. Also, when working with an individual only, she cannot assist directly in negotiating new agreements and shifts in roles with the other members.

CREATING A NEW FAMILY

The family is indeed a wondrous act of creation, but there is no certain beginning or end. History, anticipation of the future, and present desires and actions are all part of the fabric. Arbitrarily, let us begin with a couple coming together to form a marriage and found a new family unit, the process of coupling. In this society coupling is usually a matter of choice by the two participants who typically believe that to some degree they are in love. Love is not entirely a matter of magic or chemistry. It probably consists of some combination of attraction, attachment, affection, intimacy, excitement, and a sense of commitment.

The Dimensions of Love

Briefly, attraction is a desire to pay attention to the other person and a feeling of excitement generated by the other. Attachment consists of the bonds between the two in terms of expectations such as availability and division of labor in the relationship. Affection reflects one's interest in and liking for another. It may be a function of looking into your eyes and finding that I am good there. Intimacy is the degree of emotional and physical closeness developed by a couple. It includes attentiveness, sensitivity toward the other, trusting the other, and sharing life experiences, information, and feelings (entrusting oneself to the other). Excitement consists of the elements of surprise, change, and development in the relationship. Commitment is the sense that each is dedicated to the relationship in a continuing way and it will not be terminated by whim or mood. It includes a feeling of security about the other person and the relationship.

The degree to which each partner wants to be engaged in each of those dimensions of love depends on the subjective needs and desires of the partners and their private language of love. We bring our family legacy, life style, needs, and goals into the relationship. We then try to teach our partners how to behave to confirm our subjective views and to meet our subjective needs. A partner who does not conform to critical needs generates tension. Thus a partner who pays too high a degree of attention may be regarded as infringing on my independence like my mother did. One who rarely tells me how much he cares and appreciates me leaves me feeling unimportant and abandoned.

The differences between the partners are negotiated in daily inter-actions leading to deepening feelings of love or, if unsuccessful, to bitterness.

Each person has a private, idiosyncratic language for experiencing and expressing love. The language is related to the goals of the life style to overcome inferiority and to seek an improved situation. The person therefore wants to continue to receive a great deal of something that was very special in meeting his needs or to get something very important that he feels has been sorely lacking in his life. Because these are so vital to him, he generally gives the same things as his gifts of love to others. An individual who thinks that he was largely unattended to growing up will feel much loved by someone who gives him a great deal of attention. However, he may not know how to handle it, even though he wants and demands it. Another who has become very significant in his family by helping and serving others will express love by helping and serving and will feel loved when someone does that for him.

Loving behavior is therefore valued according to one's subjective goals. On a mythical scale of 1 to 10, with 10 the highest, if my wife puts fresh flowers on my desk she rates herself 9 in the expression of love, whereas for me it is a 4 or 5 in feeling loved. It is very nice to receive the flowers and appreciated. But a hug would be a 9 for me. I value physical closeness more than aesthetics. The problem is that hundreds of 4's do not equal one 9 or 10. If I do not get some 9's or 10's in my own language, I will not experience being properly understood and loved. Reciprocally, if I do not express love to my wife in the language of aesthetics, her language of loving, she will not feel understood and loved in terms of her needs.

Assumptive Values

Assumptive values are a second major influence in creating a family. They are ways of being, believing, and doing things that are absorbed from the family multigenerationally, uncritically, and often unknowingly. They are just there to be learned and practiced in context and are not particularly either affirmed or questioned. Some examples follow. Men are supposed to do repairs around the house. Women keep close contact with the extended family. Children receive religious instruction. The neighbors don't have to know our business. Sunday is family visiting day. A man shows love for a woman by often bringing flowers and other romantic gifts. We will sacrifice anything for our children's education. The only way to get ahead in this world is by luck or pull. Children must comply with a parental demand immediately and without question. Drink a lot of alcohol when you want to feel better or celebrate.

Such values absorbed in the family of origin are converted into powerful expectations in coupling and marriage. They become assumed rules for the couple and the new procreative family. The difficulty is that they are assumed and unquestioned. The partner may not even be informed that they exist, yet compliance is expected. For example, "I expect my wife to make all the social arrangements for us and I don't understand her complaints that I never take any initiative. I take care of the bills and work. She takes care of the kids and the social engagements. What's the big deal?" However, the couple never discuss such a division of labor.

An assumptive value may not even come into play until later life stages such as allowing a child to leave home before marriage or the correct way to deal with aging parents. Discovering the assumptive values and negotiating differences around them is a major task in coupling and founding a family.

Family Guiding Lines

Among the values available are the historical distribution of complex systems of roles and attitudes which prevail over generations. For example, alcoholism and how a family organizes around it; appropriate vocational categories such as learning a trade, acquiring a profession, or establishing a private business; the proper role of husband, wife, child, sex partner; and the customary stance toward education, religion, and politics. The couple bring such guiding lines into the marriage. The guiding lines form powerful expectations of self, partner, and family.

The degree to which we are aware of those values as expressed by family members influences our choice of the degree to which we will conform or rebel. A woman who has experienced a supercritical mother may swear never to treat her children that way. Typically, if she feels very strongly about it, she will go to the opposite extreme and become very permissive. However, family patterns of behavior are deeply ingrained as habits and we often see the second generational mother strongly advocating permissive beliefs while actually acting very critically toward her children and partner just like her mother did.

Priorities

Obviously, not all values are of equal importance to the individual. To assess values we assign greater weight to what a person actually does than what he says. We place greater trust in the movement. How much energy and what resources is he willing to commit? A few highly generalized values form the center of one's philosophy of life and life style. For example, a person who feels he is an inferior being may develop a priority of seeking to become superior by dominating others, including his partner. At first the partner may experience this as strength and be "turned on" by it, but even a masochist rebels against oppression by getting back at the oppressor somehow.

The person will act in the service of the priority values in competition with the other values held. The person will also do his best to elicit those behaviors from his partner which support his priority strivings.

The Couple

Two individuals come together with their history, assumptive values, guiding lines, beliefs, and priorities. They join, interact, and form a new entity in the world separate from each of its partners—a couple. A couple evolves its own identity, myths, rules, customs, and traditions. There is a division of labor in which each member plays a subordinated part to the couple as a whole. Neither member can have complete independence of action without taking the partner into account, for then the couple would cease to exist. Other people think of the couple as a unit, as well as two different individuals. Any recently divorced person can speak eloquently about the difference between being single and being a member of a couple. Similarly, in a remarriage, if the partners do not clearly establish themselves as a couple, one of them is likely to remain an outsider in the family and patterns of conflict and disengagement are likely to be the norm. To be a couple they must negotiate a common way of being in the world together.

The Marriage Contract

Entering into a marriage is a different entity from being lovers or living together. It is a contract sanctioned by the state, community, and usually an institutionalized religious faith. It carries with it the expectations and myths of those institutions. The couple relationship is now sealed in a bonded contract. The relationship is embodied in the law of the land with all kinds of defined rights and obligations. Not least of all, the two extended families are now also bound together as in-laws, a term which describes a legal relationship. Such bonds now can be severed only through legal means.

The Extended Family

A major part of establishing the couple as a separate entity is the manner in which they relate to their families of origin. They need to establish boundaries of decision making and control as well as the pathways of connection and engagement. The couple as an entity and one's partner become a higher priority than the family of origin in our culture. The process is one of separation-individuation of the couple entity on the one hand and recognition that the couple is also a part of the extended family systems on the other hand. The extended families will now have to develop some kind of relationship, however close or distant. They too have become relatives.

Among the issues that arise are the following: How frequently do we visit or call? Where do we spend holidays? How are differences and conflicts expressed, and who handles them with whom? And what kind of help is solicited by whom from whom? What do you do if you want less help or criticism?

Founding a Family

Founding a family is again very different from having a lover. Just as a marriage is a new entity specifically recognized by the community, a new family represents the historical continuity of both families of origin physically, their sense of identity within their culture and faith, their values and traditions, and their hopes for the future. These constitute a set of expectations placed upon each generation to carry on. Each member of a couple is aware of many of the specific expectations as they choose one another and as they form a new unit. If the partner chosen appears to violate or interfere with important family expectations, the choice will create strain in the family system.

Among the more common causes of tension are choices of a partner from a different faith, ethnic group, socioeconomic background, level of educational attainment, level of aspiration, or willingness to have children. Choosing a homosexual partner is another source of disappointment; in addition to other possible objections is the concern for the continuity of the family line.

The Birth of a Child

When a child is born, the system reorganizes to accommodate the addition. The child immediately acts upon the system by its presence and by its demands. It asserts its own needs and wishes, which the couple must now take into account in guiding their couple relationship and personal lives. The child also learns that he has to adapt to or contend with the ways of his parents. The negotiations already begin either with the desire to conceive or with conception. The birth of the child holds separate special meanings for each partner and for the couple.

There are many reasons for having a child, including the fulfillment of one's sense of femaleness or the proof of one's maleness, the assurance of one's mortality or continuation of the family legacy, evidence of significance, attempts to save a failing marriage, nurturance and development of another human, or replacement of a dying or deceased parent. Some alienated persons want to create a being whose task will be to love them rather than be loved.

Some children are unwanted accidents, seen as an unfortunate burden. Children born with serious disabilities may generate anger or guilt in their parents.

Each parent has a fantasy of what the child *ought* to be like and how it would be to have such a child. Of course the child is a real being with a mind and will of its own. It does not conform fully to anyone's fantasy.

The birth of the child establishes new identities and new roles— parents. Parents have a particular sanctioned status in society embedded both in culture and in law. Assuming the place and identity of parent involves new interests, concerns, and skills. One looks differently at one's self and the world. New expectations, goals, and rules are developed. "Which of us will take care of the child when he awakes at night? We must start saving money for his future. Is this the right neighborhood in which to bring up a child? We have to find a way to earn more money."

Defining the Nuclear Family

It is at this point that the nuclear family is born, as we tend to think of it in our society. It consists of one or more parents with one or more children in an organized unit in which they function somehow together sharing a common identity. They distribute roles, divide up the labor, solve problems, strive toward goals, and create a unique style of life. They share a common heritage and create a common history. Yet each member continues to function as a discrete entity within the family structure, both influencing that structure and being influenced by it. The family pressures each member to assume a functionally subordinated position that will contribute to the existing family pattern and goals. Simultaneously, each member chooses his own behaviors and goals which act on the family pattern and help to create it daily.

As each additional child is born or leaves or other additions and losses in the family organization occur, the family reorganizes and reidentifies to accommodate the changes.

Common Issues in Creating the Family

Any number of issues could occur. We briefly describe eight that seem to appear most frequently in our practices.

1. *Readiness to move from couple to family.* Some couples have children before they work out some of the developmental issues in establishing themselves as a couple. This leads to confusion in identity, boundaries, and common goals and procedures. Some have not yet attained the social interest to nurture another being and feel resentful or overwhelmed by the need to care for a child.

2. *Conflict about having a child.* The couple is not always in agreement about the decision of whether or when to have a child. The decision, or ultimately the child itself, may become a continuing source of conflict for the couple. Should they have the child, it is possible that one parent will then ally with that child against the other parent.

3. *Difficulty in conceiving.* If the couple encounters difficulty with fertility, the process of attempting to conceive often interferes with the spontaneity of their sex lives and creates strain and distance between them. They may also engage in blaming one another for the difficulty. Or one accepts the blame and feels guilty and inferior to the partner.

4. *Integrating the child into the couple relationship.* The intimate relationship between mother and child during pregnancy and birth may lead the father to believe that he is being displaced by the child in his wife's affections and certainly her attentions. This belief is further

reinforced by the neediness of the child if the mother remains the primary child care person for a substantial period after birth. It is even more aggravated if the child is chronically ill or suffers a disability for a substantial period of time. The couple may no longer feel free to engage in their usual routines together or have as much time together as before. One or both parents may feel overwhelmed by the additional responsibility and create either sickness or conflict as a means of coping.

5. *Deciding who should care for the child.* It is no longer taken for granted that mother will be the sole caretaker. Even if she assumes the role of primary caretaker, she is likely to expect some division of labor, which may lead to conflict. Most marriages today involve dual-career couples. It is the intention of both to continue with their careers. Who then will care for the child? One or more of the couple's parents, a hired worker, or an institution may be involved to assume an important part of that responsibility. How will that person or institution be engaged and supervised? What place will the person or agency have in the life of the family? Is it acceptable to both parents that an outsider will be so involved? There are many possible sources of conflict and blame in this whole process.

6. *Agreeing on child-rearing practices.* Each parent has a somewhat different model of how to raise children based on their experiences in their families of origin. Each is likely to think "I am right." Further, if they cannot settle other problems between them as a couple, they might find it easier to fight about the children.

7. *Resolving differences in temperament and style among parents and child.* We know that some people are quick and ready while others are slow and steady. Some are easily aroused and dramatic while others are placid. Such differences in temperament can be exasperating. Imagine a quick and ready mother whose slow and steady child seems always to be dragging behind in his thoughts and actions. The mother may even believe that he does it deliberately to get at her. After a while, the child may indeed adopt such a strategy.

Similarly, people have different styles for learning and coping. They respond more favorably to material received through one sense organ than through others and may better express themselves through a preferred sensory mode. For example, one may enjoy "hands-on" experiences, whereas a second is better with "words" and a third has to see "it." We all prefer different levels of light, sound, and heat for our comfort. And we all develop our own unique cognitive style. Parents

Make a Questionaire for self

and child need to be tolerant of their differences and find ways of working together efficiently.

8. *Agreeing on family goals and aspirations.* What kind of traits do we want our children to have? What do we want to do economically? Should one or both of us work longer hours to make more money or should we have more time together and with our child? How can we best manage dual careers? Do we want our children to have a particular religious training or education? The child will be affected by the answers to these and other questions and by his own behavior will influence the answers.

Looking at all the factors that go into creating a family system might cause us to wonder how so many of them are able to be reasonably successful. Social feeling, love, sensitivity and understanding, commitment of energy, common background and the ability and willingness to benefit from or resolve differences are the major tools for success in creating and maintaining a family.

FAMILY CONSTELLATION

The patterns and themes of family organization and interaction are the materials included in the family constellation. Constellation is the Adlerian term used to describe how the family is organized and functioning. Such factors as birth order, gender, generation, values, and guiding lines are considered in the context of the family's multigenerational history and culture. Significant events are identified. The degrees of cooperation and competition, closeness and distance, and who is allied with whom are assessed. Which members are moving in what directions is also observed.

Since the creation of the genogram, the pertinent factors can be plotted on a family map which visually depicts all those relationships and events.

Following is a brief discussion of some of the factors included in the family constellation.

Birth Order

Adlerians have done a great deal of work on birth order. So many variables influence behavior that we cannot make accurate predictions. However, there are definite observable modal tendencies which characterize each position.

The eldest child receives much attention prior to the birth of his fellows. He rapidly develops age-appropriate competencies. With his greater age and competency parents rely on him to undertake more responsibility than his siblings, to model "good behavior" for them, and perhaps to take care of them. He learns to become a high achiever, responsible, conforming, and a leader. He may sometimes complain about his burdens but is unlikely to give up his position. Eldest children are greatly overrepresented in the ranks of the helping professions.

The middle child is often described as the black sheep or sandwich filling. He sometimes feels that way. He believes that he does not share the privileges of either the eldest or the youngest. He learns to relate to peers both above and below him and so he becomes highly sensitive to others and develops strong interpersonal skills. He carefully observes the eldest, but usually chooses a different path to follow. He becomes independent, more distant than other family members, creative, and less conforming to family and adult values.

The youngest child begins life as the least competent and less than the others. His task is to run to catch up. He becomes very ambitious and sets very high standards for himself. In spite of many caretakers and probable pampering, he feels the most vulnerable. He fears he will somehow not be accepted or be good enough and he will be left alone. He therefore wants more closeness than the others. His need to keep running leads to an interest in many activities and a desire to explore.

The only child lives primarily in an adult world. He receives much attention and develops competencies early. He becomes a high achiever, self-confident, self-reliant, responsible, and independent. Since he has no siblings to share with, he values his possessions and space.

Among the many variables which influence place in the family are expectations, the gender of each sibling, the number of years between births, and the roles assumed by the parents. For example, if one parent is inadequate or chronically ill, one of the children may assume a pseudo-parental role. Or if the parents cannot work out their differences, each may ally with one or more children against the other.

Sibling Rivalry

Rivalry is a normal part of family life. It is based on differences among the members and the striving for personal significance. It can help the participants sharpen competencies or strike out to find new, innovative pathways. Severe fighting among the children is more likely to reflect a power struggle in the entire family system to determine who will get the most, who will be the sickest, most noble, most helpless, most independent. It is a drive to overcome other people rather than solve problems. Often when the children fight, it is for the benefit of the parents and to gain the parents' attention. In most instances, when the parents refuse to become involved, the fighting is reduced. The type and goal of the fighting are determined by the behavioral expression of power in the family; direct physical aggression, verbal aggression, withholding, withdrawing, lying, and keeping secrets are often seen.

Gender

Sex role guiding lines are established in the extended multigenerational family. Expectations of how a male or female is to behave are both modeled and asserted as rules. Each member accepts or reacts to the model presented and either imitates it to some degree or rejects it. Changes in cultural values about sex roles influence the family and may cause some confusion about how one ought to behave. It can also lead to sharp conflict between parents and child, extended family, and neighbors.

THE IDEAL FAMILY

Implicit or explicit within every theory of family therapy is some notion of how a family ought to function and a consequent definition of dysfunction.

Democratic Process

Adlerian psychology is firmly based on a philosophy of democratic living. It is therefore expected that a well-functioning family will be adhering to many democratic principles and processes. The assumption is that people are created equal, but not the same. Each has a different place and different roles to perform to contribute to the whole. Positions and functions are subject to change as time goes on and as a result of negotiation among the participants. Each person has a voice in and some influence over those things that concern him. To facilitate discussion and decisions the couple holds meetings around their interests and the family conducts meetings to discuss family issues. Parents are the leaders of the family and are responsible for guiding it. Children are to pursue their age-appropriate tasks and responsibilities.

Growth and Development

The family is dedicated to the growth and development of itself as a unit and of each member. Actualization and improvement are constant goals. The members strive for excellence but have the courage to be imperfect. They are optimistic in dealing with the challenges of life. They recognize that the need is to solve and overcome problems, not people. They seek to join with other people to solve problems. They realize that actions involve risks and that mistakes will be made. It is their intention to profit from their mistakes as a means toward further improvement. They take responsibility for their actions as a family and as individuals.

Social Interest and Social Feeling

Although there are many needs which tend to bind the family together, such as physical survival, economic necessity, and legal sanctions, we believe that in the well-functioning family it is social interest that provides the important bonding. It is feeling for and caring about one another. The parents begin with a well-developed social interest about the family and the world and model this for the children in their beliefs and behavior. They set the tone. They are constantly sensitive to one another without being symbiotic. Interpersonal behavior is marked by respect and courtesy. Each person is accepted and affirmed and knows that he counts and his opinions and needs count. Parents model listening carefully and empathically and understanding the other's point of view. Respect for others also means that tasks are delegated and the responsible person within limits is allowed to do it his way and to make a reasonable number of mistakes. This encourages creativity, responsibility, and diversity.

Social interest also enjoins us to attend to the boundaries of individuality, personal property, and privacy. The individual does not get lost in the collective. Children are taught concern for others and commitment to the common good. They are taught to engage and participate.

Rules, Discipline, and Consistency

Beyond the level of unaware assumptive values, family rules are arrived at by discussion and agreement. Children can begin to participate in rudimentary ways by the age of two. An agreement is a contract that can be changed only by renegotiation. Where children are acting out to bully and overcome their parents, the parents will not allow this. Bullying is disrespectful and undemocratic and shows a lack of social interest. Rules are firm and followed through. The parents establish natural and logical consequences so that the effect of the child's behavior acts as a natural corrector. If the child fails repeatedly to come home in time for dinner, the table is cleared and the next meal is breakfast. There is no argument or recriminations. Apology is made that dinner is over and it is most unfortunate that he missed it. It is hoped that he'll join the family in time for dinner tomorrow. This enables children to learn from the consequences of their acts without punishment.

For more information on child-rearing practices and programs see Chapter 12.

FAMILY DYNAMICS

In observing a family, we are concerned with both structure and function. Structure involves place and how the family is put together. Function deals with how the family interacts or performs. There is, of course, a constant interplay between structure and function. We will label this interplay family dynamics. There are many dynamic interaction categories that one could identify. They are closely interrelated. We believe that nine are most pertinent: power, boundaries and intimacy, coalitions, roles, rules, complementarities and differences, similarities, myths, and patterns of communication.

Power

The power dimension involves the lines of movement through which the family and each of its members strive toward goals (Adler, 1966; Sherman, 1983). It includes the mechanisms for negotiation and decision making, assertiveness, aggression against others, and efforts to control, influence, and manipulate. The family seeks to obtain compliance with its rules and values. Individual members or subsystems put forward rules and seek compliance from the others.

Differences of opinion are often converted into fights or power struggles. The objective of a power struggle is to win over another person rather than solve a problem. A continuing conflict therefore becomes a problem in the relationship. If none of the actors can succeed in getting what he wants, there is a balance of power between them. It usually appears otherwise, that one is more assertive or aggressive than the other. However, the initiator is effectively stymied by the one who withholds. The person who controls through weaknesses like crying, getting depressed, pleading inability, or withdrawing may indeed be very powerful.

In a conflict each person has reason to believe that he is right and the other is wrong. His wishes are reasonable and if the other loved him, he would surely comply. He is not trying to be the boss, only to do it right. He also has a right to expect that someone who is "supposed" to love him would be smart enough and cooperative enough to do the right thing. With the introduction of moral expectations, rightness is converted into righteousness and the other person is now not only wrong but also bad and, perhaps, unlovable. The bad one is hurting him. It is now permissible and morally justified to strike out at the bad one, either to teach him or to win revenge.

Peter watches his wife, Audrey, very carefully. He constantly tells her what to do and corrects what she is doing. He is convinced that his judgment is correct and that she is both lazy and incompetent. Therefore, he is furious with her, scolding and nagging her. Audrey feels discounted and a nonperson. If he loved her, how could he do this to her? She gets even by procrastinating, forgetting, and not completing tasks. This infuriates Peter. The power struggle is in perfect balance even though Peter appears to be the stronger. They are both convinced of their moral righteousness.

The therapist will help the family clarify their expectations, identify the power play, defuse the power play, redirect the use of power, experience being powerful, develop respect for differences, and learn to utilize problem-solving and negotiation skills.

Unresolved differences in the following eight areas of dynamics will result in power plays among the members.

Boundaries and Intimacy

This category is concerned with the degree of physical and emotional closeness and distance among people and who is included or excluded. How much separateness does a person require to be independent and how much connectedness to feel close? How much privacy of space, feelings, activities, time, and responsibilities are needed and granted? These are very subjective matters based on cultural factors and personal needs and goals of a given family. The amount of distance and closeness may also vary according to different situations. Traditionally men in our culture tend to like to *do things* together, whereas women prefer to share intimate feelings and *be* together.

Who are included in the definition of a given nuclear family? In a remarried family are noncustodial children members of the nuclear family group? When a child misbehaves, is it your child or our child? If grandmother lives in the same residence, is she a member of our family or is she your mother? What about a live-in boyfriend?

Adlerians are strong advocates of equality in the family. However, each generation in the extended family is seen as having its own place and tasks. Violation of generational boundaries would be seen as a form of inequality and as being inappropriate. It deprives both of their proper place and function. A teenager who is bossing his parents cannot assume the responsibilities of a teenager; nor can his parents do an effective job of parental leadership. Similarly, involving a third person in the middle between two others would be seen as dysfunctional for all three. Each pair needs to have its own dyadic relationship. Boundaries also involve who is supposed to do what with whom in the family and with those outside of the family. Similarly, who speaks to whom or who protects whom are boundary issues. When Adam wants to use the family car, does he ask mom or dad for permission?

There are many ways of creating distance: One can add people in the middle or overwork, overeat, or overinvolve in anything. One can withhold or withdraw or trigger a fight. Of course, if people are not able to connect in other ways, fighting and colliding with one another can be a very important form of connection. Anger and hatred can also substitute for love as a means of maintaining some measure of attachment and connectedness.

Intimacy involves such factors as paying attention to, being sensitive to, responding to, engaging with, trusting and entrusting oneself to, and sharing together.

Coalitions

Coalitions are two or more people who join together as a subsystem either to support one another in some important ways or to attack one or more other people. They can be open alliances or hidden collusions. Such coalitions have a profound influence on the distribution of power in the system. When a family comes in for therapy, presumably seeking change, it is likely that if change is brought about, existing power arrangements will be disturbed, leading to some form of resistance. People are often reluctant to give up power and privilege. The therapist can ally herself with different subsystems to help bring about a more equal family system or to upset the existing dysfunctional balance of power. For example, if a child is out of control, it may be necessary to help strengthen the parental subsystem. If a parent and child are in collusion against the other parent, the therapist may seek to remove the child from that coalition.

Jane is 26 and the eldest of three daughters. She lives at home, has a responsible job, but does not date. Her sisters have left home. She and mother generally do things together. Mother and father live in the same house together but share little. There is much bitterness between them. They rarely talk. Jane and the other girls believe it is father's fault and have little to do with him. Jane has become mother's partner and protector. Mother rebuffs all efforts of her husband to join with the family or with her. As long as Jane remains mother's partner she cannot seek out a relationship of her own and the parents make little opportunity to work out their couple relationship.

Roles

Roles are the reciprocal characteristic patterns of social behavior that each member of the system expects of one another. To some degree the place in the system will influence the roles undertaken. Each person has many roles. Some are explicitly labeled. Others are implicitly assumed. Examples of some roles for one person might be husband, father, male, lawyer, financial provider, house repairer, lover, child disciplinarian, the logical one, scorekeeper for observance of family rules, and family historian.

In each role father tends to behave in reasonably consistent ways each time, which in turn tends to elicit a fairly consistent pattern of behavior in the other members. We begin to predict what the other one will do and assume it even before it is done. We often then jump ahead of the action and take the next steps as if the others had already done what they were expected to do. This can be very efficient or it can short-circuit any possibility of change in the process. If I believe that someone will treat me badly, I behave as if they had already treated me badly, then the other person reacts negatively, thereby confirming the validity of my original opinion and the action that I took.

A sense of moral entitlement is attached to role behavior. If I work hard in school, the teacher is "supposed" to give me a good grade, regardless of the quality of the work. If I love my children, they "should" obey me. Failure of the other to perform as expected is not just a difference of opinion; it is a violation of moral entitlement.

A change in the customary pattern of interaction is a surprise. When the new behavior is more highly valued than the old, it is more readily accommodated. Higher value does not in itself mean better liked. It may somehow be more useful to the priority purpose.

The therapist brings about change by redefining the place or the role of one or more members; by helping them to assume new roles, places, or role behaviors; by reversing roles; and by negotiating agreements about roles. The therapist can dramatically characterize symptomatic behavior as a role: family hero, boss, tragedy queen, switchboard, stan-

dard bearer, loser. A simple example involving changing roles is the
father who has to wake his son for school each morning. The therapist
characterizes father as his son's alarm clock. When father objects to
being an alarm clock, the therapist suggests the father buy the son an
alarm clock to get himself up in the morning. In a role reversal, the
very serious compulsive parent can be put in charge of family fun and
the looser, less responsible parent can be put in charge of work and
discipline.

Rules

The family rules determine what is or is not allowed and what behavior
is to be included or excluded from given roles and what roles are
acceptable or necessary. Rules provide for stability in relationships.
Some rules are explicit; others are implicit and closely related to assumptive values. Examples of explicit rules in one family are (1) members
of this family are to be high achievers; (2) no one is to be disturbed
when working; and (3) every member is to obtain a higher education.
Implicit rules in the same family might be: (1) it is important to
compete with others successfully; (2) we have to be perfect; and (3)
make your parents proud of you.

When one or more members hold a specific expectation and demand
compliance with it, they are putting forth what they intend will be a
rule. If it achieves compliance, the rule is established. If rejected or
ignored, disappointment or conflict ensues. Rules are closely related to
individual and family value systems. Like values, rules are organized
in a hierarchy of priorities. For the P. family, the highest priority rule
is that we must provide for our security by working hard every minute
to earn a living. Fun and pleasure are far down on the priority list.
Much of the behavior and much of the conflict in a family will be
organized around high-priority rules.

Complementarities and Differences

Since roles are reciprocal patterns of behavior, it is evident that much
of that reciprocity will be of a complementary nature. There can be no
inside without an outside and no up without a down. Similarly, there
cannot be a leader without a follower, a rescuer without a victim, or
a pursuer without a distancer. For any role to be maintained, there
must be cooperative reciprocity. Members assume roles to help complete
the whole. When one member is very disorganized, another is likely to
be highly organized to compensate. When one parent is very soft and
permissive with the children, the other may be more rigid and stern

with them. When both want to assume the same role, they are likely to alternate in its complementary role. So if both want to be dependent, they may take turns being dependent and caretaker.

Ideally, these kinds of differences among people add excitement and options for new behavior to the system. Dreikurs (1953) points out that each puts forward his differences providing opportunity to sharpen knowledge and skills and to learn new ideas and methods from each other. The interaction of thesis and antithesis can lead to the development of a new synthesis. The active person helps the passive one to mobilize his resources and become more assertive. The active one learns that it is all right to relax sometimes and let things happen.

The opposite occurs when the members try to overcome each other instead of taking advantage of their differences: Each intensifies what he is already doing and the system becomes increasingly rigid. Since all behavior is directed to move from an inferior to a more enhancing position, the positions taken reflect an underlying need of the system and the individuals. The assumed roles thus reflect life style positions, needs, and goals.

Often the needs of two subsystems in conflict are very similar even though they may be expressed in a different vocabulary. For example, the husband wants more appreciation and the wife more warmth and closeness. Both need more positive attention. If there is too much emphasis on differences, the therapist may wish to help the family identify the many ways in which they are similar and to appreciate their differences as an asset.

Similarities

Similarities are those things which the members think, feel, have, or do in common, the ways in which they are alike. Similarities are the major ingredient in cohesiveness and family identity. Common history, faith, level of education, political affiliation, and goals bond the members together. Similarities provide them with common perceptions of experience and a shared vocabulary.

However, if they are too much alike, there may be a lack of excitement, new ideas, and new options for problem solving. The therapist may wish to help this kind of family to identify, emphasize, and value their differences.

Mrs. Jones screams that her son Arthur is terribly emotional just like she is. The therapist agrees that they are both very intense, caring people. "However, did you notice that you tend to become upset and withdraw, while Arthur is more assertive and fights for his point of view?"

Myths

NB •

Myths are the family's subjective interpretations of how things are, came to be, and ought to be. They are representational models of reality. There are myths about what is a man, woman, child; what is a marriage; what is a family; and what kind of a family are we. Consider some examples of family myths: in our family we are all for one and one for all; we are an oppressed lower-class family; we must all protect mother so she won't get depressed; this is a family of scholars.

Myths give birth to rules and roles. If this is a family of scholars, then each person must become a scholar and undertake a scholarly occupation. You must read and study a great deal, achieve well in school, and perhaps write and teach. To do those things, there must be many books available. We have to live near a good library. The children must attend good schools. Failure to do or provide those things is a serious aberration.

The best way for a child to upset his parents is to violate a major myth or rules pertaining to it. Of course, a myth may be a poor or mistaken representation of reality. The family will still operate to force conformity to it.

For example, we have seen families with a "depression mentality," that is, a family that still operates as if the socioeconomic conditions of the 1930s were in effect even though the family has been relatively affluent for the past 30 years. The children must be spoiled and get and do everything the parents missed or the family must watch every dollar as if it is the only thing that stands between us and starvation.

Myths are not always shared. Each partner may have a different myth about what marriage is supposed to be and each acts as if that partner's myth is known to and shared by the other. This could lead to serious disappointment and conflict as each tries to impose rules based on his or her myth. The husband may bring a family myth that the family is a permissive place in which each person is free to try out his wings with the least possible interference from others, even if there are some serious negative consequences. The wife believes that children need firm rules and guidelines to help them develop safely and responsibly. The clash between the parents is predictable.

Patterns of Communication

Interactions obviously involve some form of communication, verbal and nonverbal. If what the communicator intends is received as intended, then sender and receiver both know where they stand, whether pleasing or not. However, there are many types of communication that lead to misunderstanding.

Withholding information, giving partial information, overgeneralizing, giving incongruent information, forgetting, and lying are ways of exercising control over others. Magical thinking is another form of withholding. It involves the expectation that others will know what you mean symbiotically without your having to inform them. Having to tell them means they are not tuned in and don't really care about you. Having to tell spoils the whole situation. They are supposed to know.

Projection is assuming that what you think the other person is thinking is what he is thinking and then acting as if he is indeed thinking that way. There is no effort to check it out. Behaving in relation to what you think he is thinking then often elicits from him precisely the behavior expected. This is a source of many errors in communication.

Giving double messages creates difficulty because the receiver does not know which message to attend to as the priority message. Body language or tone of voice may convey anger while the words are very positive. Also the verbal content may include two opposing parts. "Yes, but . . ." messages are a frequent example. "I know you are old enough to make your own decisions, but be home by 10 o'clock." "You look very nice, but what a horrible tie you're wearing."

The double bind is a particularly troublesome form of double message. It sets up a negative paradox so that no matter what the receiver does he loses. Mother shouts at Sam to grow up and clean up his room. He cleans up his room and mother says, "You only did it because I made you, not because you wanted to." Further, if he listens to her, he is dependent and compliant. If he doesn't listen to her and strives for more independence, he is a bad boy.

We each have our own private languages and wavelengths. Tuning in to the language of another requires attention, sensitivity, and the ability to learn and use the other's vocabulary. This point was discussed earlier in the chapter in the section called "The Dimensions of Love." Based on our personal needs and goals, we develop our own ways of expressing and experiencing love. The same is true for anger, sorrow, hurt, joy, and fun. The communication needs to be sent in the proper language to have the full impact intended. Behaving protectively toward someone who is striving hard to establish a greater sense of individuality and independence may be a poor expression of love toward that person, even though the sender is in fact very loving.

The therapist assists the family to observe their interactions, to clarify their intentions, to discover their respective private languages, and to learn basic communications skills. We cannot here go into all the many basic communication skills such as positive listening, acknowledgment, making direct positive statements about what is wanted, speaking for oneself, checking out perceptions, and a host of others available. The therapeutic process itself models effective forms of communicating.

In Chapter 3 we will discuss how some of the organizational principles and dynamics presented in this chapter can be applied to diagnosis and the strategy for the initial interview. In Chapter 4 they will be applied to the process of change and the strategy for conducting the four major stages of therapy.

REFERENCES

Adler, K. (1966). The psychology of power. *Journal of Individual Psychology,* (22), 166–170.

Dreikurs, R. (1953). *Fundamentals of Adlerian psychology.* Chicago: Alfred Adler Institute.

Dreikurs, R. (1970, February 21). *Conflict solving.* Unpublished address, Nanaimo, British Columbia.

Sherman, R. (1983). The power dimension in the family: A synthesis of Adlerian perspectives. *American Journal of Family Therapy. II,* (30), 43–52.

3

Structure of
Adlerian Family Therapy

INTRODUCTION

The structure of family therapy we describe here is based on our experiences first in being trained as students of Adlerians and then as trainers of family therapists. Among our original Adlerian trainers were Kurt and Alexandra Adler, Danica Deutsch, Rudolf Dreikurs, Harold Mosak, Helene and Ernest Papanek, and Bernard Shulman. These Adlerians did not write or speak much on the topic of family therapy. They were primarily therapists working with individuals or in group therapy, or in Family Education Centers. They were not practicing family therapists in the sense in which family therapy is now understood.

However, Alfred Adler was a social psychiatrist concerned with educational approaches to the normal challenges of life and the dysfunctional or negative strategies employed by some to meet these challenges. In his practice as a psychiatrist, Adler became aware that many of the problems he encountered in adults resulted from improper training in childhood. In 1922 Adler organized his first Child Guidance Center within the community in Vienna. This center met with such enthusiasm and success that the movement eventually grew to 31 such centers. They were usually located in public schools and conducted by people trained by Adler. The centers were open to the public. They provided opportunities for parents, teachers, social workers, and all others interested in childhood education to observe the process. This open family counseling was the first move that Adler made into family therapy. These centers were closed in 1934 when the fascists came to power in Austria.

Rudolph Dreikurs, one of Adler's students, opened the first Family Education Center in the United States in 1937 in Chicago. Soon other

37

centers were opened. Dreikurs trained counselors from many parts of the world in Adlerian family counseling, and today we find many Adlerian-Dreikursian Family Counseling Centers in the United States, Canada, Israel, and Greece. Dreikurs (1959) systematically extended Adler's basic tenets and eventually left a great legacy of literature related to the Adlerian concepts.

This type of Adlerian family counseling is the historical origin for Adlerian family therapy. It has been refined and continues today. It is best represented in the works of Dreikurs, Corsini, Lowe, and Sonstegard (1959) and Christensen and Schramski (1983). However, it is not to be considered the same as family therapy. Adlerian Family Counseling Centers have an educational emphasis. The public can attend and watch the sessions. The process is one in which the counselor first sees the parents and gets some background information, then works with the children, and finally returns to give the parents suggestions. Seldom are the parents and children seen at the same time, and there is little emphasis on the dynamic factors which we now consider essential aspects of family therapy. The comparison in Table 3.1 should clarify the differences.

Both authors of this book have not only had Adlerian training at the Alfred Adler Institutes but have also had extensive experience in family therapy. Having been trained in a variety of approaches to family therapy, we increasingly encountered evidence that Adlerian family therapy has the potential to integrate a variety of systems that we had been taught, trained students in, and had experienced. We thus began to publish articles related to Adlerian family therapy (Dinkmeyer & Dinkmeyer 1981, 1982, 1983, 1984; Sherman, 1983a, 1983b).

Practitioners of Adlerian family therapy believe in a clearly established plan and goals for each family therapy session. The therapist understands the goals and intentions, the beliefs, and the behavior of each person in the family and the family as an entity in its own right. Because all behavior has a social purpose the therapist also focuses on the transaction between the members of the family in order to understand ways to help it move toward active, constructive behavior.

One of the major tasks that the therapist works on is the process of achieving goal alignment. This means that the goals of each family member as well as the goal of the therapist fit together and move toward the same general purposes. Family therapy then becomes an opportunity for the family to become involved in cooperation, to build their self-esteem, to enable the members to see conflict in perspective, to develop a sense of humor, and to increase their social interest or their capacity to give and take.

TABLE 3.1

Adlerian Family Counseling	Adlerian Family Therapy
1. Open to the public	1. Private; one family or closed couple or family groups
2. Process involves seeing parents and family separately	2. Process involves seeing entire family at once, and then possibly alternately working with subsystems and entire family
3. Getting testimony, reactions, and suggestions from the audience	3. Identifying, discovering the meaning of, and dealing with patterns of transactions among family members, including the wide range of individual and group dynamics described in Chapters 1 and 2
4. Formulating and giving prescriptions to the parents and sometimes the children	4. Therapist as leader formulates questions and makes a wide range of inputs that reframe the problem, interpret its meaning and goal, stimulate structural moves, clarify beliefs and values, brainstorm or teach new skills and options, provide in-session and homework tasks, set up paradoxical situations, build self-esteem and family pride, negotiate conflicts and so forth
5. Emphasis is on educational techniques, new methods for existing family structure to cope with the presenting problem or situation	5. Therapeutic emphasis on changing the system and individual functioning within a new system

Therapists learn to trust all psychological movement and its meaning. What the person is doing often seems confusing. For example, it may appear confusing to hear a member of the family say one thing and do the opposite. However, it is clear that what a person does is in line with his goals, even though at the moment he may not be aware of it. Consider the following example:

Therapist to Father: "How have the family meetings been going?"
Father: "I've been too busy this week to set one up."

belief make thep when happe.

intention - our goals

We get an idea about the things that the person may be avoiding. While he says he wants to organize such meetings, the lack of commitment and participation is a better indication of his real values.

Whatever a person does reveals that person's beliefs, intentions, and feelings. Our beliefs actually make things happen. They influence how we think and certainly how we feel. Our intentions are our goals. They show our motives, values, and things we pursue. Adlerians believe that while feelings are important, they are a result of our goals and the way we think about life and our place in the world.

Thus it is important to listen and notice any movement that may reveal purpose. A family member says, "I tried to put more time into my studies" or ". . . be more understanding" and then follows with a description of the behavior. The therapist would be aware the behavior is in line with that person's goal at the moment. Family members and the system that operates between them can be understood best by systematically being aware of the factors of purpose and pattern. All of the verbal transactions as well as the nonverbal movement reveal a purpose and a pattern.

Adler and Dreikurs both emphasized the importance of word-by-word, sentence-by-sentence analysis, because it clearly reveals movement and intention.

INTERACTIONAL FORCES IN FAMILY THERAPY

There are certain forces that can be used in a group situation, including the family.

1. *Community.* Develop a feeling of community or togetherness, a climate of trust and belonging that communicates that we are here to work together for the common good. It is important to develop this feeling of acceptance, which creates self-respect and empathy among all members of the group. Frequently a family may come to family therapy attempting to scapegoat one of the members of the family or feeling it is more important to blame than to work on change. The therapist both models and notes examples of empathic listening and encourages it.

2. *Ventilation.* Family therapy provides a setting for the expression of feelings that have been internalized. Structure the family therapy session so individuals can expose their thoughts, feelings, and values. Ensure by understanding feedback that they believe they have been

heard. Ventilation provides an opportunity for both positive and negative
feelings to be shared.

3. *Change minuses to pluses.* A major objective is to convert minuses
into pluses by assigning validity to each person's point of view and
desires; by reframing negative behaviors as having a positive purpose
(the acting out child is trying to learn how to be more independent or
keeps Mom busy so she won't be too sad); and by assigning positive
intention to each person's behavior.

4. *Spectator therapy.* People can learn from the therapy session even
though they may not be speaking or appear to be involved. Don't
discount learning that comes from listening and sharing, even though
a member may be silent for a time. This is particularly true for the
adolescent or reluctant spouse who withholds his own contribution but
is truly alert to what is going on in the session.

5. *Feedback.* Encourage members to give feedback on how they are
experiencing various members of the group. Feedback is the sharing of
honest, open impressions. "You are coming across to me as. . . ." "I
am experiencing you today. . . ." The therapist models the feedback
process. It is concrete and specific: "When you pout like that it reminds
me of a young child" as opposed to "You annoy me." There is nothing
the receiver of the feedback can do with the latter statement. The
feedback process is the sharing of impressions, how the sharer is
experiencing something. It is better if it does not blame or accuse. The
sharer takes an "I am . . ." or "I feel . . ." position, rather than a
"You should . . ." position.

6. *Universalization.* It is important to help members realize that their
experiences and feelings of being discouraged, left out, not counting,
are not unique. The experience of the moment is unique to them but
actually may be a problem of other members of the group. Frequently
it is obvious that even though parents and children or a couple appear
to be very different, they may have very similar feelings. The therapist
points out that the ways in which these various feelings are being
expressed are indications of an underlying universal feeling shared by
many others, especially in similar circumstances. For example, Sally is
feeling rejected in her relationship with Fred, which is similar to how
father feels about rejection from his boss.

7. *Instill hope.* Stimulate the courage and social interest of the family

group, for these are forces that bring about change. This is done by developing positive expectations. Each week when the family comes back they can be greeted with: "Let's share what's new, good, or positive about what is happening among us." It is important to encourage any positive movement.

Understanding the System

As we define and clarify the problem in the family, it is important to do this in a nonjudgmental way with respect for the family. As the family seeks its goals, help them clarify the purpose of some of the dysfunctional behavior in the family.

- Father doesn't get the family meeting started.
- Mother does not know how to establish boundaries.
- Susie refuses to cooperate with established rules.

Those are all indications of families that are working in negative, passive, or destructive ways. The therapist helps them become aware of where their behavior is leading them. Then alternative ways to develop more active and constructive behavior are explored. The therapist learns to become aware of small behavioral exchanges or transactions which really reveal the life style of the individual speaking.

For example, father and mother are discussing a problem with their daughter Mary, age 13.

Father: "I don't know. I try to be nice but she pays no attention to me."

Mother: "You can't give up so quickly."

Father: "I have tried these approaches before, but why is it always me who has to change?"

We hear in father's comment the life style of a person who believes life is unfair.

At the same time, the therapist who is seeking to make the family more cohesive, cooperative, and energized in a positive direction will want to look at these factors:

1. What is the self-esteem of each person in the family?
2. Does each person feel lovable and capable?
3. Do they feel they are recognized as persons of worth?

4. Do they have social interest (the capacity to give and take and care about others)?

5. Are they willing to work together with people and not only for themselves?

6. Do they have a sense of humor? Are they able to see themselves in perspective, to laugh at some of their demands and counterproductive behavior, and to see some human foibles as funny rather than sinister?

As the therapist works with the family, the process of developing rapport is important to show how the system "makes sense." For example, parents will complain that the behavior of their teenager makes no sense. However, as you hear the language the teen uses to manipulate the parents to get his or her way, it is very clear how that behavior makes sense in terms of the teen's goal.

It is also important to assess the meaning of behavior. What is being communicated? What is the behavioral result? How does what the person says fit with what he is going to do? All behavior has a purpose inside the system. The family member who refuses to study, even though it means that he will be having to repeat a grade or attend summer school, finds some sense of purpose in that behavior. For example, if the child seeks revenge for felt hurts, he may act so that the family has to spend more money, is unable to take a vacation, or in some way will be inconvenienced or feel very upset.

As you analyze transactions in the family, it is helpful to understand them systemically. Is communication being given from a superior to an inferior position, for example, from a parent to a child? Is it speaking down? Is it demanding? Does it show disrespect to the person in the "inferior" position? Or is communication within the family done on more of a horizontal or equal basis in which everyone in the family is respected, listened to with a genuine attempt to understand?

In looking at the behavior revealed in the transaction, it is important to help them become aware of the meaning of the behavior and communication. Everything that occurs within the family, all the communication, affects everything else that operates within the system. Thus an understanding of the communication system of the family opens up for the therapist an awareness of the purpose, the pattern, and the movement which can be anticipated.

In looking at the material that is provided by the family through their transactions with each other, go beyond the symptoms and the surface communication to comprehending the real issue that may exist below the surface. For example, the failure to call and establish family meetings, resistance to chores, unwillingness to share in the responsibilities of family life, failure to cooperate with the homework of school, are all symptoms, but we must go beyond the symptoms to understand the underlying goal.

The Priorities

One way to assess goals is to understand the individual's number one priority. This is one aspect of the life style. Some consider the priority to be a shorthand statement about the individual's convictions which answers two questions for the individual: What is most important as I strive to belong? and What do I seek most urgently to avoid?

The priorities, in contrast to life styles, are comparatively easy to recognize. An individual, for example, can be aware of his own priorities.

The four priorities we consider are comfort, pleasing, control, and superiority. None of the priorities are necessarily better or worse than any other, or exclusive, but one is likely to be dominant. They all provide assets and exact prices to be paid. Ideally, the most effective priority would be based on being involved and concerned with social equality, cooperation, and being a contributing member of the group, while developing one's own abilities.

1. *Comfort.* The person whose priority is comfort seeks it at all costs in terms of whatever comfort means to him. As a result, he tends to be easygoing, makes few demands, and is empathic. The price he pays is reduced productivity and a tendency not to use his own talents.

2. *Pleasing.* The person concerned primarily with pleasing wants to be liked and accepted. Therefore, he bends himself to the will of others, doing favors, agreeing, serving. He does not directly assert himself so it is hard to know what he prefers, or wants, or who he really is. He becomes dependent on others to provide the acceptance he so desperately wants. The price he pays is again reduced growth and a feeling of alienation. It is as though he could never do enough or really ever truly belong.

3. *Control.* The person whose priority is control is usually very self-controlled or very concerned with controlling others. He distrusts others and/or the harm that may come from disorder. He believes firmly that he is right and he can really trust only himself. He imposes his own brand of order on relationships and situations. In the extreme, he may

become a tyrant, but his need is to be in control of situations to avoid hurt. The price he pays is a lack of spontaneity and a lessened creativity. He maintains social distance, promises more intimacy than he will deliver, and has difficulty gaining social acceptance. Any change arouses high levels of anxiety.

4. *Superiority.* The superiority priority is involved with the person who believes that it is most important to be better than others. This is different from a striving for excellence or doing the best that one can. He is concerned with being more competent, more right, more useful, or more moral. The price in this priority, of course, is that he ends up feeling overburdened, overresponsible, and overinvolved. He finds himself in frequent conflict with others who challenge his rightness or authority and therefore lives in a highly competitive world of winners and losers. The fear of losing or being beneath others arouses high anxiety.

All of the priorities represent methods for using power to attain personal significance and a place among others. As you work with families you observe how priorities influence the system. Usually two people who are concerned with control will engage in considerable conflict. At the same time, people who have the priority of superiority are always in the process of deciding who is most knowledgeable or more correct at a given moment in time.

Those whose priorities are comfort and pleasing are easygoing and frequently may be used in the family by the more overtly power-seeking individuals. However, pleasing may also be used manipulatively to gain control in social transactions. "I did you a favor, now you owe me," or "That makes me more noble than you are." The controller has an impact on the pleaser by making decisions and demands. The pleaser feels needed and significant. The superior one does for the one seeking comfort and both get something they want. They establish reciprocal roles.

Priorities are a helpful way to gain additional insight into the system. However, at any given point in time a person's position and priority make sense to the person; they form an integral part of the system. The therapist's challenge is to validate each person in his position and then help him move toward more useful active/constructive goals in the service of the priorities or change positions to alter perceptions and modify priorities. In other words, the therapist's challenge is to turn the energy that may be draining the family into more positive and more satisfying directions.

The family therapist is one who believes that people can change. Once they have identified the real issue, the therapist works to build the self-esteem of each individual family member, while also encouraging the family in more positive relationships with each other.

As you identify this functional aspect of the system, you will see that very often some of the agreements are agreements to be dysfunctional. Mother wants to get her way; the teens are interested in being independent. The agreement is clearly to fight with each other. Very often this is the only way that mother and the teens know how to relate with each other. It is important to help them recognize that this behavior (even this negative agreement) is an agreement, a way of cooperating. You can utilize this to take a step in the positive direction by indicating that you know that if they can cooperate in this way, it will be even easier to cooperate in a positive way.

THE INITIAL INTERVIEW

The initial interview is a crucial time because it establishes with the family members some ideas about the nature of the relationship and what they can expect. In the very way the therapist deals with various members of the family, they get some idea about the therapist's priorities, attitudes, and beliefs. The initial interview forecasts the four stages of the entire therapy: joining and contracting, assessment, developing awareness and reorientation, and commitment.

Joining and Contracting

It is important from the start to make some kind of contact or connection with each member of the system. This can be done by talking with them directly, asking them to tell a little bit about their perception of the problem, and staying with the meaning of behavior from their perceptions. This obviously is in contrast to waiting for the adults (father and mother) to give their interpretation of why they are there. Even though the children may not be coherent in regard to the purpose of being there, it is important from the start to join them to the system and get some idea about how they see the relationship.

Assessment

As you are listening to the various perceptions of the family members about the family system, show each person how the way in which they see things makes sense—as it does from their point of view. Very often you can break tension in this part of the contact through a sense of humor that helps them to see that you, too, are a person who makes mistakes, and you are not all powerful.

Among the things that the family therapist is seeking to determine are answers to some of the following questions, even though the questions may not be presented formally:

1. What does each person want to happen in the family relationship?

2. What does each family member see as the main challenge or issue faced by the family?

3. Are family members aware that the purpose of the sessions is to focus on change, not merely to complain?

4. What does it feel like for each person to be a member of this family and live in this family?

5. What do the family members believe and think about each other?

6. Identify the family atmosphere. Is the family atmosphere autocratic, democratic, permissive, friendly, or hostile?

7. What are the life styles, games, and patterns that are revealed in the transactions between people?

8. Identify family constellation information. As you identify father's and mother's position and you observe the position of siblings in the family, it is interesting to note whether family members often have conflict with children who are in the same position. For example, if father was an oldest child, is he having problems with the oldest child in the family?

9. Identify where the family stands in terms of some of the essential elements in developing family cohesiveness, cooperation, community, and satisfaction. This can be accomplished through questions like the following:

    (a) What is the level of self-esteem? Does each family member have a sense of worth? Does each feel valuable, capable, loved, accepted?

    (b) What is the level of social interest? Does each family member have a sense of belonging, a feeling that they are part of the group, a commitment to cooperation, involvement, and sharing?

    (c) What is the sense of humor that exists in the family? Can family members see themselves in perspective? Can they

make jokes about themselves, accept their mistakes, have
the courage to be imperfect, avoid nagging supervision and
defensiveness?

10. What roles do various members play in the family? Are they
    functioning in a variety of tasks, or does each family member
    have certain restricted roles to play in relation to each other
    in the family as a whole?

11. Identify the rules that govern family relationships. What are
    the interpersonal relationship agreements that have been es-
    tablished? How are they limiting the range of behaviors avail-
    able to members of the family? How do they reduce the options
    available?

12. What are the boundaries that have been set up? How confined
    do members feel? How restricted are they? How much inclusion
    or exclusion is felt within the family? How well are individual
    members differentiated from the others? What kinds of co-
    alitions are formed?

13. Who is for or resistant to change? As with all movement in
    a family, it is important to understand who is seeking change.
    Are they willing to change themselves? What is the type of
    change they want in the family, in individuals, and in them-
    selves? At the same time, it is equally important to analyze
    and identify who it is that is resisting change. Clarify the
    purpose of the resistance and what the person gets for that
    resistance.

14. It is traditional to become involved in the diagnosis of family
    faults, weaknesses, and psychopathology. Even more important
    is the diagnosis of the assets of the family. What are the
    general assets of the family as a unit? What are the assets of
    each family member? How do they blend into the family
    system? What resources are available to them in the extended
    family and community?

Encouraging therapists work most significantly during the diagnostic
phase of therapy. Instead of focusing only on pathology, liabilities, and
weaknesses, the therapist is equally interested in strengths, assets, and
resources. The therapist basically becomes a talent scout who identifies
assets that will enable family members to deal more effectively with
the challenges of living.

Assessment and diagnosis are closely attached to the theoretical
underpinnings of family therapy. The therapist is interested primarily

in identifying goals of the family, the transactions which are the result of the goals and beliefs, the priorities and how they interact with each other, and the characteristic patterns that the family and individuals show in their transactions with each other. The following are a few of the assessment techniques that can be used:

1. *Tentative hypotheses.* As some clues about the private logic and goals of the individual are derived, the therapist often uses a procedure called guessing or tentative hypotheses. She suggests to the person or the family as a whole some hunches she may have, raising them in a tentative way, "Could it be . . .?" or "Is it possible . . .?" and always alluding to the goal and pattern of the behavior.

2. *Tracking.* Another procedure is called tracking behavior. Each person in turn is asked to describe how the particular symptomatic behavior in the family or an individual began. Who does what in reaction to the symptom, followed by who does what next and continuing through the pattern of searching until each person's part in this purposive behavior is evident.

3. *The family constellation of the immediate family.* The family constellation and the psychological position of a person in the family are basic to an Adlerian understanding of human behavior. The primary positions that are identified in the family constellation include the only child, first child, second child, middle child, and youngest child. The patterns of behavior modally associated with these positions are described in Chapters 1 and 2.

We want to observe the position of the parents relative to the children and to each other. Is one of the parents functioning on the same level as the children? Is one of the children functioning as if he were a parent? What world view does the person develop when such a generational switch is made? The parent is likely to feel overwhelmed and believe he or she is inadequate to the tasks of life. The child is likely to feel overburdened but very powerful and significant. The two are also likely to be in conflict.

The value of understanding the family constellation is to be aware of some of the typical characteristics which are anticipated from these positions. It may be different from the foregoing profiles in Chapters 1 and 2 for many reasons. For example, a younger child who is larger and brighter than his older sibling may compete for and take over that position. If the eldest rebels, another may become the conforming, responsible one. At the same time, be aware that the meaning the child gives to the psychological position in the family is far more important than the actual ordinal position.

Developing Awareness and Reorientation

In this part of the interview the therapist begins to emphasize bringing about some change in perceptions, actions, and relationships.

1. *Exploring alternatives.* The family and family members are also given an opportunity to explore alternatives—different ways of resolving the presenting problems or changing the patterns of interacting with each other. This tests the flexibility of the system and openness to change. Often therapists can derive suggestions or ideas from members of the family. The goal is to teach them problem-solving conflict-resolution skills that can be utilized within the family setting.

2. *Identifying strengths and encouraging.* Encouragement is considered by Adlerian therapists as perhaps the most important technique available for the promotion of change. Most interpersonal problems are the result of discouragement. Thus the obvious antidote is encouragement. Discouragement comes from a variety of negative influences in the family, such as high standards, overambition, negative expectations, and pessimism. Overambition is a good example. The comment "You're doing well, but I know you can do much better" discourages. These statements, though often shared with positive intentions, are basically destructive as delivered in the communication system of the family. They lower self-esteem, feelings of worth, and desire to cooperate and work with other members of the family.

Encouragement, then, is the process of building the individual's self-esteem and self-confidence and enabling each to be more able to work with other members of the family.

The therapist needs specific encouragement skills. These skills include the ability to:

(A) Listen attentively, hearing content, feelings, and intentions.
(B) Respond empathically to the whole message.
(C) Focus on strengths and resources.
(D) Help persons see their perceptual alternatives, how something positive can come from what appears to be negative.
(E) Focus on efforts and contributions.

(F)   Identify discouraging beliefs.

(G)   Encourage commitment and movement.

Encouragement, then, is a set of specific skills: faith and belief in the clients, acceptance of them as they are, validating the goal and intention of their behavior, and reframing their behavior in a positive framework. Encouragement occurs as the therapist attends closely to each family member's communication, indicating clearly that each one, regardless of position in the family, is heard. Then, as the therapist universalizes any similarities in beliefs and feelings, the therapist encourages by helping to create a feeling of belonging and acceptance.

As the goals of each family member and of the therapist become aligned, everyone is valued for her or his full and equal participation in the process.

The therapist looks for and affirms any positive movement or involvement. The therapist must be able to see the positive side or element in anything that appears at first to be negative. For example, the trait of stubbornness can be reinterpreted as determination. The trait of anger might really indicate involvement and desire for change.

The most encouraging thing the therapist does is to help members become aware of their choices. It is basically encouraging for family members to recognize that regardless of the situation, members of the family can choose to function differently. They do not have to insist on fighting. Instead, they can learn to cooperate in more positive ways.

As members of the family increase their feelings of self-esteem and worth, they are thus more ready to cooperate and work with each other. They become encouraged by their new ability to identify each other's strengths. The therapist's personal belief that each person has the capacity to change is also encouraging.

3. *Utilizing paradox.* The paradoxical intention, sometimes called by Adlerians antisuggestion, is the strategy that encourages members of the family to practice their symptoms, that is, to consciously do that which they appear to be against or resisting. The symptom they claim they are trying to get rid of or avoid they are asked to exaggerate or do on a regular schedule. For example, a child with some nervous mannerism is asked to practice it in front of a mirror five minutes each day, attempting to perfect it. The person who is constantly worried or overconcerned needlessly is asked to sit down each day at a specific, predetermined "worry hour" and begin to list and think about all of his worries. The child who has a strong temper is encouraged to put

on a more temperamental performance. The emphasis here is on helping a member become aware of the control he has over the symptom.

The same can be done looking at the family system. Taking the case of the worrier, the therapist observes that there is a great deal of tension in this family and it is really very kind of the worrying one to assume the burden of being the chief worrier for the family. She then suggests the worry hour so he can worry very hard for the whole family. For more on paradoxical technique see forward Chapter 11 and Sherman and Fredman (1986), Chapter 6.

Adler called paradoxical intention as prescribing the symptom, whereas Dreikurs called it antisuggestion. In either case, the technique encourages the clients to emphasize and develop their symptoms even more. It is usually best to have the paradoxical recommendations for a specific period of time, and to treat them as an experiment. That is, you encourage family members to see what they are learning from the experience. The paradoxical intention makes people dramatically aware of the reality of their situation, and of the fact that they must accept the consequences of their behavior.

When the therapist confronts the client with the paradoxical refusal to engage in fighting the behavior, often the behavior becomes less attractive in the client's eyes. This procedure clearly indicates confidence that when the individual sees the problem in a magnified perspective, he will choose to change the behavior. At times, this technique may make the symptom appear so ridiculous that the counselee finally gives up the symptom.

Adler and Dreikurs taught that a symptom must be fought against if it is to be maintained. Therefore, the paradox is effective because the client comes for help and the therapist tells him to go back to what he was already doing. By not fighting the symptom, the client is now free to choose.

4. *Teaching family skills.* Adlerian family therapists will often put an emphasis on helping the family attack a particular problem by acquiring skills or methods that are more effective in resolving the problem than the method they had been utilizing.

A traditional Adlerian method is the family meeting, an opportunity for the family to make decisions together. The family meeting is a regularly scheduled meeting of all family members. The purpose is to make plans and decisions, provide encouragement, and solve problems. In contrast to an informal or emergency meeting, the regularly scheduled family meeting assures all family members that they will have a forum in which to be heard at a definite time each week. Thus plans and decisions made during the meeting stay in effect at least until the next family meeting.

The purpose of the family meeting is to find opportunities for members of the family to be heard, to express positive feelings, to give mutual encouragement, to agree on a fair distribution of the work within the family, to express their concerns, feelings, and complaints, to help settle any conflicts or recurring issues, and finally to become participants in planning family recreation. How to prescribe and structure such a meeting is described in Chapter 11.

Another process similar to the family meeting we call the encouragement meeting or the encouragement council. The encouragement meeting is designed primarily to identify things that are positive in the other person and to share them. These meetings provide a regular, systematic way to strengthen relationships within the family. The purpose of the encouragement meeting is to allow everyone to share the positive things that each sees in the others and in their relationships.

These meetings are usually scheduled in a family perhaps once a week. They should occur at a time that is quiet and free of interruptions. A family member begins by saying, "The most positive thing that happened to me today (or this week) was . . ." and continues with "Something I have appreciated about you this week was. . . ." All members of the family are given an opportunity to share. How to structure this type of meeting is also described in Chapter 11.

The encouragement meeting obviously provides an opportunity to notice the family relationships by focusing on the positive.

Once the couple has been through enough family therapy to have clarified some of the basic relationships, the family therapist may decide to teach, when appropriate, a conflict resolution process. This would be done by first presenting it, perhaps also on a sheet of paper, discussing it, and taking the family members through the process and resolution of a chosen conflict.

The steps which we suggest in the conflict resolution process include the following:

(A) Show mutual respect. Listen carefully, acknowledge the other has a point.

(B) Pinpoint the real issue, whatever priority of each member's status, prestige, or need to control is being challenged.

(C) Seek areas of agreement by concentrating on what *you* are willing to do, making no demands that other members of the family change, and agreeing to cooperate rather than bicker.

Three alternative ways of cooperating are: (1) give in fully and graciously to the other so that person gets everything he wants; (2) negotiate a compromise, make a deal; and (3) choose an acceptable alternative different from those offered (e.g., we can't agree on which movie to go to, so we visit friends instead).

(D) Mutually participate in decisions so everyone feels a part of the decision-making process, and each implements his part of the decision.

These are some of the primary educational and skill-building processes that are utilized.

Commitment

As the initial session draws to a close, the therapist asks the clients to assess what has happened, commit to continue any agreed upon changes that have occurred during the session, and carry out any tasks or agreements made to be done between sessions.

The next session is scheduled. Fees and manner of payment are arranged and permissions for tape recording or videotaping are requested if this was not previously done.

The next chapter deals with the Adlerian model for behavior change. It describes four stages of therapy and describes them as a strategy for conducting the therapy.

REFERENCES

Christensen, O., & Schramski, T. (1983). *Adlerian family counseling.* Minneapolis, MN: Educational Media Corp.

Dinkmeyer, D., & Dinkmeyer, D., Jr. (1981, Spring). Adlerian family therapy. *American Journal of Family Therapy. 9*(1), 45–52.

Dinkmeyer, D., & Dinkmeyer, J. (1982, June). Adlerian marriage therapy. *Individual Psychology, 38*(2), 115–122.

Dinkmeyer, D., & Dinkmeyer, J. (1983, June). Adlerian family therapy. *Individual Psychology, 39* (2), 116–124.

Dinkmeyer, D., & Dinkmeyer, J. (1984). Adlerian family therapy. In J. C. Hansen & B. F. Okun (Eds.), *Family therapy with school related problems* (pp. 103–113). Rockville, MD: Aspen Systems Corp.

Dreikurs, R., Corsini, R., Lowe, R., & Sonstegard, M. (1959). *Adlerian family counseling.* Eugene: University of Oregon Press.

Grunwald, B., & McAbee, H. (1985). *Guiding the family and practical counseling techniques.* Muncie, IN: Accelerated Development.

Sherman, R. (1983a). Counseling the urban economically disadvantaged family. *American Journal of Family Therapy, 11*(1), 22–30.

Sherman, R. (1983b). The power dimensions in the family: A synthesis of Adlerian perspectives. *American Journal of Family Therapy, 11*(3), 43-53.
Sherman, R., & Fredman, N. (1986). *Handbook of structured techniques in marriage and family therapy.* New York: Brunner/Mazel.

4

The Basics of Change

Consistent with a holistic theory, Adlerian psychology seeks change at several levels: (1) in perception, beliefs, values, and goals; (2) in place, structure, and organization; (3) in social interest, feelings, and participation; (4) in skills and behavior; and (5) in the direction of the behavior (the uses of power). Specific techniques to bring about change are aimed at one or more of these levels. A change in any one of these levels is likely to influence change in all of the others.

People were intelligent enough to learn to behave as they do and are therefore capable of learning new ways to behave. Some form of reorientation or reeducation is the primary process in bringing about change in both the individual and the system. However, every therapist knows that many times people do not make the changes that they say they want or they refuse to participate. Lack of behavior change is often termed "resistance." The final section of this chapter will briefly discuss the nature of resistance, which is also one of the obstacles to change.

THE PURPOSE OF CHANGE

The purpose of change is to help the individual members and the family improve themselves. This is a broader concept than remediation or cure. It involves the recognition that positive change is a lifetime occupation and that although perfection is unattainable, striving for excellence is a worthy goal. "The courage to be imperfect" is a favorite Adlerian catch phrase indicating the importance of recognizing human imperfection while constantly moving to do better. Periodic failure is a given of the process and failures provide the material for new learning. This attitude encourages a proactive stance rather than a reactive, safeguarding position and provides much greater flexibility for goal setting and problem solving.

Therapy is directed toward improving insight and understanding, correcting mistaken beliefs or goals, and generating a positive sense of optimism about meeting the challenges of life. Also, acquisition of problem-solving and conflict resolution skills is a practical need, as is a feeling of personal significance and belongingness with others. Therapy aims at a further development of social interest and social feeling along with proper regard for the self. The dictum of the ancient Hebrew scholar Hillel (Ethics of the Fathers, 1:14), is appropriate here: "If I am not for myself, who will be for me? And being only for myself, what am I?"

It is most typically a power play that brings a family in for therapy. Members are unsuccessfully attempting to overcome one another instead of solving the differences between them. "If only others would do what I want or what I know is the right thing, there would be fewer problems in the family." Therapy seeks to diffuse the power play and redirect the use of power into more constructive channels while further empowering each member and the family as a system.

Reorganizing each person's place and role in the family helps to redistribute the use of power and refocus perception and beliefs.

Thus, change in the family takes place through the development of:

1. Ways to diffuse the power play and redirect the uses of power.
2. New understanding and insight about intentions, purposes, goals, and behavior.
3. New or more refined goals.
4. New skills, knowledge, and available options, especially in improved communication, problem solving, and conflict resolution.
5. Increased courage and optimism, a sense of empowerment that I and we "can."
6. Increased social interest and positive connections with others accompanied by mutual respect for each member as an important individual.
7. New and sharpened places and roles to perform in the system under new operating rules and myths.
8. Commitment to growth and change.

No two cases are exactly alike. In this section we will describe a typical strategy for working with a family. Four stages of work are discussed: (1) defining the problem and structuring the therapeutic system; (2) assessing how the family functions and the meaning of the behavior patterns exhibited; (3) reorienting and reorganizing the family;

and (4) evaluating and reinforcing the changes, formulating next steps, and terminating. In actual practice there is much overlap in implementing the four stages.

DEFINING AND STRUCTURING

In this stage the therapist seeks to determine the presenting problem from the point of view of each member, join with the family, validate the family and each member (especially the identified client), develop rules for a cooperative therapy meeting, establish the role of the therapist in the process, formulate tentative goals and agree on a contract for the work together. Depending on the complexity of the issues and number of people involved, this may take part of a session or several sessions. The strategy for the first session has already been presented in Chapter 3. Here we present the strategy for this stage of therapy.

Defining the Problem

The family is asked a lead question such as "What brings you here?" "Who will speak for the family?" "What is happening in this family?" Ultimately, each person is asked to describe what is happening. The therapist questions until the problem is clearly defined from each person's perspective. She restates each one's wish concisely and as a simple fact. She may then try to express the problem in a more general way for the family as a whole.

For example, in the T. family, mother wants her 9-year-old son to obey her; the son wants his mother to stop yelling at him; his younger brother wants his older brother to stop picking on him; father wants mother to be more in control of the children and he wants peace in the house; and mother wishes her husband would help out more with the children and the house and give her a break. On the surface of it, if the therapist accepts any one of those as a contract she would find herself in opposition to others. However, by making a generalized statement she can avoid that trap. "It seems like the members of this family have difficulty in getting others to do what they want." Or "You seem to want more cooperation in this family."

The next step is to get the family to restate in positive terms what they think would make it better. This converts negative complaining into positive assertions. Thus "Ron never does his homework" is restated as "I would feel more at ease if Ron took responsibility for sitting down and doing his homework without being told to do it."

The therapist next inquires what will make this a better family and mediates until some generalizations are formed.

Joining and Validating

The therapist makes contact with each family member and makes some brief personal inquiries early in the session. It is important to ask if anyone is present under duress and doesn't want to be here. It is well to sympathize with that person's position and thank him for being here. As each states a position or point of view the therapist acknowledges the person and his view. She accepts and recognizes good intention for each member. She structures so that the others also pay attention and listen carefully to each member and acknowledge his needs, beliefs, feelings, and wishes as important to him. Acknowledgment does not imply agreement, only respect and willingness to pay attention, hear, and understand. It demarcates each person's individuality, place, and importance in the system. It recognizes that each person belongs to the group and affirms his personal significance in the group.

This is different from the usual communication in family conflict which disconfirms, rejects, puts down. "You didn't do that right," "It's not that way," and "You're insensitive" are common examples. Disconfirming another person leads to beliefs that one is unloved, abandoned, or victimized in the relationship resulting in hurt and bitterness and often a desire for revenge.

Validation changes both the nature of the communication and the climate in the family. This process is especially important for the identified client, who may experience himself as the family scapegoat. Even though by his behavior he cooperates to maintain this role, it is a very upsetting one. Indicating that this person too has a point and some important needs takes some of the heat off, moves him from either a one-up or a one-down to a more equal position and sets the stage for future negotiation of behavior change connected with the symptoms.

Reframing

Reframing can be another way of validating the members. The therapist assigns a new positive meaning to symptomatic behavior using the same facts but putting them in a different category that changes their meaning. A chair can be defined as an article of furniture, a wooden object, a decorative piece, something to hang clothing on or a ladder to stand on. Changing the definition does not objectively change the facts about the appearance or construction of the chair. Only the meaning is changed. Similarly, instead of a bad child, a mother who is always on my back, and a husband who is never around, the meaning of the roles can be reframed. The acting out child can be seen as trying to train himself for greater independence. The critical mother is trying to be a good parent by trying very hard to teach her child to be responsible and successful. The frequently absent father is trying very hard to be a good husband and father by striving to provide well for his family. Adlerians use reframing as a major device all through the therapy to change negatives into positives, to assign good intentions to the participants, to change the climate in the system, to help disengage the power play and to provide encouragement in place of discouragement.

The power play can be redefined as legitimate differences of opinions, styles, and roles or jobs in the family that need to be negotiated. The question now is how can these differences be resolved and how can each family member work to improve the family to become the kind of family they want it to be?

Setting and Clarifying Goals

The discussion of the problem and desire to improve the family lead to a discussion of the changes that are needed. The therapist suggests some tentative hypotheses that might explain what is going on. (See "The Initial Interview" in Chapter 3.) The intentions, effects, and consequences of current behavior are briefly discussed and linked together to reinforce the need for some new goals and means of attaining them. Each suggested goal is examined in terms of its possible consequences for each member and the family. This implies that every member belongs and is important. The examination further models that the interests of all must be considered as well as the interests of the family as a whole.

For example, the stated goal "I want my brother to stop picking on me" is reframed as "You want to be more friendly with your brother?" If this is agreeable, the children discuss what being more friendly would look like—their subjective definitions in terms of actual behaviors. The next question might be, "If you two become more friendly, what will the other members of the family do?" Another effect is that the family is being trained in social interest instead of the necessity to defeat others. They are also practicing cooperation and negotiation. The therapist is able to assess the levels of cooperation, social interest, and negotiating skills.

The Therapeutic Contract

Once the tentative goals have been defined, family and therapist commit to working toward attainment of those goals. The contract can be an open-ended number of sessions or a fixed number of sessions. The length of each session, the frequency of sessions, and who is to participate in the therapy are agreed upon. The possibility of future involvement of extended family, school, or other significant persons such as former therapists is explained. Possible future involvement in a multiple family or couples group is also indicated. Of course, the therapist uses judgment in how much to divulge at this stage. She doesn't want to scare the family away, but she may want to plant seeds for future activities.

Prescribing an In-Session Task

The therapist seeks agreement from the family to perform a task immediately in-session toward one of the agreed upon goals. Some examples are: (a) "I know that you have come to solve some unpleasant difficulties, but for now could we observe some of the strengths of this family? Could each of you face each member of the family in turn and tell him three things about him that you really like or are proud of?" (b) "Could you negotiate an agreement with your son on what time he is to be home on school nights?" (c) "Could you all talk together and arrange for a family outing this weekend?" (d) "Could the parents decide together what their expectations are for Mary's school achievement?" (e) "Would the family please draw a communal family picture for me?"

The task chosen is to reflect not a difficult part of the family problem, but rather a fairly simple one. It allows the therapist to observe the family in action. It provides a measure of their willingness to cooperate or the degree of resistance in the system. The therapist can identify who is likely to be the most resistant. Family roles and coping styles are also revealed. If the task is successfully completed the family is encouraged to think that they can resolve their difficulties; this lets them go home with at least some accomplishment in the session. If the task involves a decision they are to implement at home, they are asked to report on the results during the next session.

The Rules of the Game

To perform its task every group has to have structure, purpose, and a set of rules by which to operate. As the therapist works during this

initial stage she establishes rules as each comes up. Some examples are:
(a) Speak for yourself rather than for another person. (b) We speak
one at a time and listen carefully to whoever is speaking now. (c) Can
you acknowledge what the other person is experiencing and that it is
true for him? Instead of complaining can you state what you want in
positive terms: "It would really make me feel good if you would . . ."
(d) If you make an agreement you are expected to keep it. Unilaterally
changing or ignoring it discounts those with whom you made the
agreement. That is a hostile act. Don't agree if you intend not to keep
the agreement. (e) The therapist differentiates the parents from the
children indicating that neither is superior to the other but they have
different jobs to perform in the family. She may spell out the differences
in function in a general way. To draw the distinction she may talk
with the parents and tell the children not to interrupt and vice versa.
For example, the children may be asked to work out without parental
interference how children's television time together will be used and
how programs will be chosen. (f) Each person must take responsibility
for his or her own behavior.

Role of the Therapist

The therapist generally assumes the role of democratic leader and
expert in the therapy group. She works for agreements between herself
and the family and among the family members for actions to be taken.
However, she also suggests, questions, reflects, interprets, reacts, provides
information, mediates, allies with subsystems to adjust the uses of
power, encourages, reinforces, confronts, teaches, and prescribes with
permission. If the family does not agree to accept a prescription, it is
unlikely to be implemented.

The therapist seeks first to join with the family's present line of
movement and then through her interactions to turn with them toward
a more constructive and effective direction of organization and action,
and finally to leave them.

The Truce

In order to defuse the power struggle even further, the therapist
declares a truce and seeks the agreement of the family to accept and
observe it. "No one is allowed to fight this week, no matter what the
provocation. You will not initiate a fight even though you are not
getting what you want or don't like what another member is doing,
and you will not fall for the bait being set out for you by anyone else.

You have lived this long with your dissatisfaction about the situation, you can handle it for another week."

Usually, the fighting has been going on for a considerable period of time prior to therapy. The therapist shares her observation that clearly no one is winning this struggle. There is a balance of power among the opponents. Whatever they are doing to overcome one another is not working. She suggests, "Since you cannot control the others and get what you want, is it possible that you can control your own behavior? You all have a lot of experience cooperating in the conflict. Can you now use that skill in cooperation to stop the fighting?"

The truce does not solve the conflict, but it does help the family members to take personal responsibility for their own actions and to exercise control over the symptom. It reduces the level of tension and anxiety in the family and underlines that fighting also requires cooperation. If the truce is generally kept, it is very encouraging to the family that they can bring their situation under control. It indicates that there is some flexibility in the system and that their resistance to change is manageable.

Occasionally, when the fighting is totally out of control and includes the presence or the danger of physical violence, the therapist may take an extreme authoritarian position. "This is (name of therapist)'s law. There will be absolutely no violence in this family! It is not to be tolerated. I will call the police if necessary. Each of you is a good person and you deserve to live in a family that does not threaten you. There will be no violence, no matter what the provocation." Though often resented, such a declaration from the therapist is often a big relief for the family and provides the external control needed to make up for the lack of internal controls currently available to stop abuse.

ASSESSMENT

The Function of Assessment

The second stage of therapy emphasizes the function of assessment. We would like to know exactly what is happening in terms of the symptom, the family life style, the life style of each member, multigenerational themes and patterns, how the family and its members relate to one another and to other systems, and the directions of the movement. We examine multigenerational place in system, the nine family dynamics discussed in Chapter 2, and the underlying perceptions and beliefs upon which the structure and movement are based. Pressures are exerted by changes taking place in the life of the family such as births, deaths, and unemployment, which require new behavior patterns and sometimes reorganization and a revised identity for the system. Our purpose is to carefully describe the symptomatic behavior, to discover its meaning, its purpose, and the goals being served. This process goes on all through the therapy. Further, everything done to assess what is going on will affect the system and perhaps influence change.

Since behavior is purposive and relational behavior contains some measure of complementarity and reciprocity in role relationships, we can infer that the symptom is also somehow useful to its participants and not merely a consequence of their interaction. The same reciprocity involves cooperation in maintaining the symptom. Therefore, knowledge of how the symptom is useful is helpful in working for change and avoiding unnecessary resistance. The implicit assumption is that if the behavior is dysfunctional, it is related to faulty perceptions and ideas, which may or may not have been functional at another time. As instrumental behavior, the symptom is in fact an intended solution to some important problem of life such as belongingness and achieving significance and superiority (in the Adlerian sense of that term; see Chapters 1 and 2), or safeguarding from perceived danger or harm. We need to get beyond the symptom to the underlying goal and the beliefs that sustain it.

We believe that individual motivation contributes to both the creation and maintenance of the existing system and cannot be ignored. Therefore, individual life styles and goals will influence the system as well as be influenced by the system. The interaction of individual and system needs to be assessed.

Case Example: The Family That Needs Recognition and Attention

An example is the case of John (32) and Mary (32) and their two children, Peggy (12) and Alan (10). The presenting problem is that Alan is doing poorly academically. Mother is a nurse-educator and supervisor impatient with her position under the control of physicians, most of whom are males. She would like more recognition and independence in her work. To get it she wants to go to medical school but believes her husband would not approve and holds her back. Mary complains that her husband does not understand her and her parents never appreciated her for herself. She is the oldest of three children and has been superresponsible in her family of origin. She is perfectionistic and very demanding of herself. Although responsible and a high achiever, she believes she could never please her parents; it was never enough. She could never really attain independence and be her own person. She is always subject to the demands of others. Mary further believes the children should have no tasks at home and should be treated permissively. She believes that John is neither sufficiently ambitious nor intellectually interested. She wants more space from John, feels depressed, and threatens divorce.

John is the elder of two brothers. He experienced his father as cold and unloving. He could not gain his father's approval even though he is very responsible and a high achiever in school. After graduation from college he entered his mother's business and managed a store for her in a loose partnership arrangement. He hopes to improve and expand this business. His brother also works in the business in another store with mother. Brother is seen as not as creative or responsible as John. Father died a year ago. John feels terrible that his father never expressed his love or approval before his death. He believes that everyone in the family should share tasks and be responsible. For him closeness as expressed by physical presence is very important and he wants Mary to spend more time at home with him and to expect more of the children.

The couple married at age 19 and both families approved of the marriage. They are friendly with both extended families, who rarely interfere with the internal affairs of this family. The couple are of similar religious and cultural background. Mary sees herself as more intellectually interested and ambitious than John. John sees himself as successful and more social in relation to friendships outside the family and wants Mary to be more social.

Alan began to do poorly in school several months ago, about the time his mother became more irritable and depressed. His teachers report that he does little or no homework or work in school, but otherwise causes little trouble. He always promises to improve. When made to stay after school and work he merely dawdles and daydreams unless an adult works directly with him. He does the same at home where father began to sit with him to do his homework. He does do family chores when told by his father to do so and is immediately supervised. Mary instructs John to leave the boy alone and then lectures the boy on the importance of achievement. Father than complains to Mary that she is cold to him and Alan and unhelpful and that she is not home with them enough. Mary then withdraws. This pattern occurs regularly.

Peggy is the good child who does everything she is told. She achieves well in school and does the tasks assigned by father at home. She tattles on Alan when he fails to do his task. Mother and father frequently praise her. She often tries to boss Alan and tell him what to do.

Each member of this family is seeking recognition and significance through some attention-getting device, but each has chosen a different way to achieve it based on the experiences in the families of origin and individual life style.

Peggy seeks and gets much praise for being a good girl. Mary works very hard professionally and ambitiously wants to obtain the most prestigious title in the medical field—physician—and the power and recognition that come with it. She demands that others appreciate and understand her for who she is, but doesn't really share herself. Alan obtains a great deal of attention through nonperformance. Others sit with him and are close to him. John too wants attention by having his wife sit with him. Instead he sits with Alan and they keep each other company. As long as Alan is there occupying their attention, Mary and John don't have to work out the difficult agreements connected with medical school, handle the death of John's father, or reconcile their different needs for distance and closeness. Both parents are eldest children, responsible and wanting to be the boss. Alan, as the youngest child, wants to be pampered and babied somewhat. And Peggy chooses to be the responsible, oldest child.

The power play is exerted to get others to give one the added recognition and attention that each believes is missing and that he or she needs to be significant. This is the personal sense of vulnerability that they communally share. No one gets enough and the power play continues. The parents undercut each other in their discipline of Alan and have difficulty in making decisions together. No one wins. When John demands more attention from Mary she feels suffocated, misunderstood, and not good enough—as she had in her family of origin. When Mary withdraws John feels abandoned and rejected as he did with his father. Mary wants to teach John through her behavior that it is OK to be separate and independent. He doesn't need to depend on his father's approval. John seeks to teach Mary through his behavior that it is OK to be close without losing her personhood. Neither really knows how to develop intimacy. The children serve as a bridge between them, Peggy by being the model of a good child who elicits their pride, and Alan by uniting them around a problem. In addition, father and son have an overt alliance as victims and mother and daughter have an overt alliance of superiority and achievement. Mother and son collude to provide father with company so mother can have more space.

The family myth is that "No one truly recognizes me or pays attention to me for who I am," and "I can never be good enough or do enough." Educational achievement and responsibility are the major family values. Thus underachieving is an excellent symptom for Alan to gain attention, even if it is negative attention. It brings him more closeness, since father and teachers sit with him, and supposed independence from control, since no one can make him. The symptom thus reflects the major issues in the family as each strives to get what is missing in order to achieve a goal of greater superiority through more attention and recognition.

Assessment Techniques

The data available are almost unlimited and can be overwhelming and confusing. The objective is to get at the essential information to understand the meaning of the behavior and to formulate a change process. We want to get to the essence. That means getting beyond the symptom to the critical underlying goals.

Assessment can be based on direct observation of behavior in session, family self-reports about what goes on outside of session, results of tests and inventories (see Fredman & Sherman, 1987), reports by others about the family and its members, family reactions to therapist behaviors, and the therapist's feelings and reactions to family behaviors.

The data may be analyzed in many ways. The data about the family may be compared with Adlerian theory to determine their meaning in theoretical terms. The data can be used to create a descriptive profile of the status of the family. They can be compared with social norms in similar circumstances, social norms representing current common sense and cultural expectations. They can be compared with social norms historically. The norms of the moment may be transitory. The data may be handled intuitively and empathically by the therapist who synthesizes the meanings through analogical thinking and feeling. Most powerfully, the data need to viewed within the internal logic of the system and its individual members. It is their meanings and goals which direct the behavior.

Following are some of the most common Adlerian diagnostic techniques.

1. *Tracking.* Tracking has somewhat different meanings when used in different theories. Here it is used as a probing technique. The therapist asks each person to describe how the symptomatic behavior, or any behavior pattern, begins. Then who does what in reaction to it, followed by who does what next, and continuing the questioning until each person's role in creating and maintaining the pattern is evident. Similarly, if the therapist wants to get at the core belief system she can probe: If this is so then what does it mean and then what does that mean and so on until the underlying philosophy is revealed. Tracking

also helps the therapist and family remain focused on a particular issue. Through the process of association or as a form of resistance it is easy to keep moving from one thing to another without seeing anything through. The therapist keeps the family focused on one thing by constantly following a single line of inquiry or behavioral tasks until it is completed.

2. *Examination of a typical day.* One member, or the family together, outlines an ordinary day in the life of the family from the first person to rise until the last one is asleep. Pressure or conflict points are identified in daily living and the way the family copes with these pressures and conflicts are seen in context, which may help us better understand how and for what purpose they occur. A great deal is revealed about the structure and relationships in the family as they discuss daily routines. Is the family orderly or chaotic? Are boundaries observed? Are roles clear? Are parents effective leaders? Do the members cooperate or compete? What are the operating rules of the family?

3. *The family constellation and genogram.* It is useful to solicit and chart a multigenerational family history. The chart of this history is commonly called a genogram. The information helps us to better understand the context in which families operate and to identify important family themes and rules, nodal events in the family life cycle, each person's place in the extended families, current and historical patterns of relationship, the availability of relationship options, family values, and the directions of behavior currently and over time. Birth order, major illnesses, deaths, divorces, lovers, major successes, levels of education and occupation, ethnic and religious affiliations, geographic locations and migrations, special ties and emotional cutoffs, perceived personality characteristics, and roles and behavior around the symptom are elicited from the family. The data are recorded as a chart on a sheet of drawing paper where they can be seen in an aggregate context.

It is useful to begin the genogram by inquiring who is living in the household and who else is considered a member of the family. Next the behavior connected with the symptom is plotted. The history of the symptomatic nuclear family is recorded, including the courtship of the parents. Then the families and family history of each spouse are added to the diagram. Following is a very abbreviated genogram of the S. family of John, Mary, Peggy, and Alan just reported.

Any therapist can make up her own symbols to construct the genogram, but those that follow on pages 70 and 71 are common in the

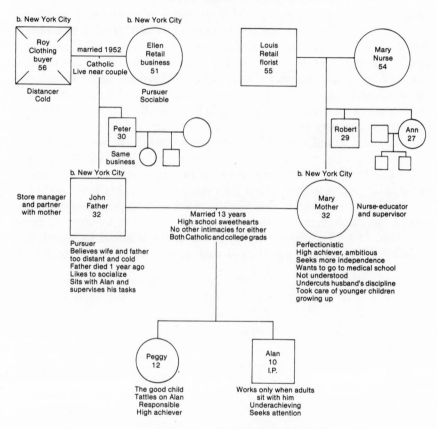

Family values: education, responsibility, procreation,
Eutholocism, recognition
Family myths: No one recognizes me for who I am.
I can never be good enough or do enough.
We are achievers.

Figure 4.1. Genogram of the S. Family

field.* The genogram reveals virtually all of the factors discussed in the diagnosis of the case in the case example section above. For further information on the genogram see Carter and McGoldrick (1981), Guerin and Pendagast (1976) and Sherman and Fredman (1986).

4. *Early recollections.* The early recollection is a powerful projective

---

* Genogram symbols were reprinted from the *Handbook of Structural Techniques in Marriage and Family Therapy,* Copyright© 1986 by Robert Sherman and Norman Fredman. New York: Brunner/Mazel.

technique. Since a person is remembering at this moment, the memory is organized according to present perceptions and needs. That a specific memory out of the multitudes available comes to mind at this moment indicates that it has some special significance now, however incidental it may appear. By structuring the question the therapist can obtain information about the life styles and motivations of individual members, family guiding lines or issues in the family of origin, or the original unstated marriage contract. Some sample questions are: "Would you please think back to when you were a very young child and recall the earliest event that comes to your mind, a specific incident." "What is the earliest memory you have of a specific event involving your mother (father, child, grandparent)?" "Does the situation we are experiencing or discussing now remind you of an event earlier in your life (or the life of this family)?" "Can you recall the first time you met your spouse? What most impressed you about your spouse during that first meeting?"

The clients are asked to describe the event as though it were occurring now in as much detail as they can recall. It is best to write it down verbatim. After describing the event, the client is asked to report how it makes him feel now recalling it and what part of the event stands

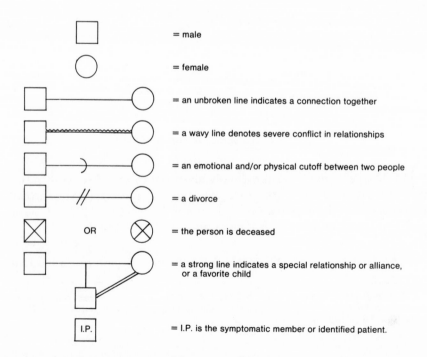

= male

= female

= an unbroken line indicates a connection together

= a wavy line denotes severe conflict in relationships

= an emotional and/or physical cutoff between two people

= a divorce

= the person is deceased

= a strong line indicates a special relationship or alliance, or a favorite child

= I.P. is the symptomatic member or identified patient.

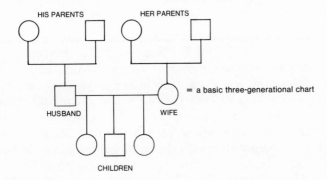

HIS PARENTS   HER PARENTS

HUSBAND   WIFE

CHILDREN

= a basic three-generational chart

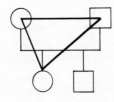

= a triangle identifies a relationship in
which a third person is brought into a
dysfunctional relationship between a pair
in order to reduce the anxiety or to
stabilize that dyadic relationship

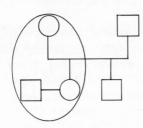

= a line around a combination of members
points out that these members are in
alliance or collusion

= child in utero

A

= abortion or stillbirth

d. 1972   = died in 1972

out as most vivid. If there is no ending described, he can be asked how it ends.

The data will yield important themes, beliefs, values, and goals of the life style, view of self, world view, optimistic or pessimistic attitude toward life, expectations, and even the favored sense modality (visual, kinesthetic, aural) for learning and coping. The context and direction of the power play that this person will pursue are also likely to emerge.

Adlerians have experimented with many variations of the early recollection and most Adlerian sources contain something on it. See Dinkmeyer, Pew, and Dinkmeyer (1979), Manaster and Corsini (1982), Mosak (1977). Sherman and Fredman (1986) also provide examples of its use.

5. *Metaphors, imagery, and fantasy.* This really includes an entire body of techniques that emphasize the use of analogy and utilize so-called right hemisphere of the brain functions. Examples are sculpting, dream interpretation and enactment, role playing, imagining an inner adviser within the self, imagining the family engaged in a scene or activity, pretending to have the symptom, composing or selecting a story, song, picture, or family photographs. See Sherman and Fredman (1986) for descriptions of such techniques and sources of further information about them.

In their language and behavior clients produce many metaphors that the therapist can observe. "This child drives me up the wall." "My parents are always on my back." "I see my mother as all mouth." "This family is like an exploding atom." "I can't hear myself think." "He has a rotten attitude." Those are all common metaphors. But each represents a different sense modality and a different direction of behavior. The first metaphor, for example, is kinesthetic and means that the speaker is being pushed too far and doesn't know what to do. He wants to escape. The last metaphor clearly indicates that the speaker is right and the other is both wrong and bad and the other must change. The speaker wants to be the judge, which is of course superior to being the criminal.

The symptomatic behavior is itself a metaphor for the issues in the family. Phobic behavior indicates a problem around issues of control and perfectionism. Running away pictures the need for separation and recognition of individuality. Depression signals discouragement and the need to be pursued, helped, and appreciated. A chronic physical illness such as asthma may portray the difficulty to breathe in this family because of fear, tension, rage, secrets, or a rule prohibiting the normal expression of anger. The physical illness can be intensified as a family symptom.

REORIENTING AND REORGANIZING THE FAMILY

Efforts toward producing change begin with the first telephone call or request for a meeting. The processes of structuring the therapy and diagnosing the behavior already put the family in a new place—the therapeutic system—and they provide the family with a good deal of information and possibly important insights about themselves, change some of the rules and goals of behavior, and model new ways of interacting. In this stage the emphasis is on those procedures that will enable the family to find and implement more effective, appropriate, constructive, and satisfying solutions to the problems and relationships of its members; to reorganize itself; and to integrate a new identity. This stage often is referred to as the middle phase or working-through phase of therapy.

In this section we outline the sequential steps for working through a case. Some of the specific techniques that can be employed to bring about change are described in Chapters 3 and 12. Among those described are encouragement techniques, sculpting, the family and couple meetings, assignment of behavioral tasks, and paradoxical methods. Many more techniques frequently used by Adlerians can be found in Grunwald and McAbee (1985).

Interpretation and Confrontation of Existing Perceptions, Roles, and Goals

Having made a more thorough assessment of the organization and behavior of the family, the therapist interprets her findings back to the family by describing what she observes about the way they think, organize, and act and the possible purposes of what they are doing. Among the interpretations presented is a description of the existing power play and its negative consequences. Typically, behavior is framed in positive ways that confirm and validate each member and the family as a system. The therapist points out that in spite of this the family seems not to be satisfied with the outcome, which leads logically to an examination of existing goals and means and encourages the search for better options.

With a more resistant, rigid family the therapist might dramatize the members' behavior. "Everyone in this family seems to want to be the boss. You must do what I want or else." "This is a family that needs a lot of drama and makes a lot of noise. Everything is a big deal. There are no little deals." "This is an amazing family. It is in competition with the Lord. Everyone in it must be perfect all the time and no mistakes are possible." "When did you decide to be the scapegoat for this family? . . . the family inspector general? . . . the alarm clock?"

Goal Setting

Based on the assessment and the family's reaction to the description and interpretation of their behavior, more refined goals are formulated by the family than were defined in the first stage. Each member is made responsible for his own behavior and his own behavior change. Attempts to change someone else as a goal are not considered acceptable. They are likely to be as ineffective as past attempts. The family members discuss what kind of family they would like to be and what kinds of conditions and behaviors will bring that about. We want to be happy or just like every other family or like it used to be are too vague. Each must spell out what he or she wants in positive, concrete, operational terms: "I want to tell my son how much I love him and how proud I am of him"; "I want to be more responsible for my own schoolwork and get better grades"; "I want to spend more time with my husband." Since the goals are directed at the self they tend to engender less conflict with others. The problem is usually a lack of trust that the other will do what he is "supposed" to do.

The second order of goal setting is to have each member select things that he will do for another member and for the family as a group. At this point all negotiations are between each member and the therapist in defining personal goals.

Some goals may be quite large and involve numbers of steps. The therapist assists the family to divide both the group goals and the personal goals into a reasonable sequence according to practicality. Which one will be pursued first, second, and third in order. Then each goals is divided into smaller subgoals that can be addressed in order. The large goal may be too discouraging to given members. The family needs first to learn that they can make some change. Then they can become more confident of ultimately achieving what they want.

Negotiating Differences

The essence of the power play is to overcome the others to get what you want. The therapist points out that each person in the family is different, has different needs and perspectives, and most particularly may have different opinions: "Isn't it lucky that you have these differences, which add so many additional possibilities to your lives?" The complementarity of their differences is also stressed as a strength of the family system: "It is fortunate, Mrs. James, that you are so socially adept and can serve as the social leader of this family while your husband is so handy around the house and loves to stay home and improve the house." The therapist points out that a difference of style or opinion does not mean that there is a lack of love, merely a difference of opinion or style. If everyone was the same, they would be bored with one another.

Since differences are inevitable among different people, they now need to learn how to negotiate their differences rather than accuse one another of evil intent. The therapist engages the members as a democratic group leader in the identification of differences that are interfering with the accomplishment of their goals and helps them to arrive at agreements. Although there are many conflict resolution techniques, modeling democratic process and teaching three specific techniques usually works well. The three techniques are:

(A) Give in completely and graciously to the others and see to it that they get the full gratification of getting what they want. If all the members practice this, it will not be 50-50, but each should get all of what they want a reasonable amount of the time.

(B) Make a deal. Negotiate a compromise so each gets part of what he wants.

(C) Accept the fact that no agreement is possible and agree to do something else that can be agreed upon. An alternative is to move to a higher level of goal and choose an activity that is agreeable toward that goal. For example, if we can't agree on a uniform time to have dinner, but we want to find family times together, can we find another way for the family to be together?

Reorganizing Places and Roles in the System

Birth order, guiding lines from families of origin, physical endowment, life cycle issues and circumstances will affect place and role in the system. A superadequate parent and an inadequate child are frequent pairings in family therapy. A younger child who outstrips an older one, a child who mediates between the parents, a grandparent who undercuts the parent in child rearing are other familiar examples. Playing victim (the one who always loses or feels aggressed against), charmer (the con artist or seducer), pursuer (initiates ideas and chases others), distancer (withdraws and withholds), and the peacemaker (the middleman who tries to make everything nice) are additional typical roles.

The therapeutic task is to help clients give up their dysfunctional roles and encourage them to assume more appropriate or functional roles.

Some of the techniques available are dramatizing the existing role, sculpting, interpreting the mistaken purpose and goal of the role, prescribing a role reversal, changing the meaning assigned to a role, getting others to behave differently in relation to that role so that it fails, raising the cost of performing the role, and negotiating a new role.

Overcoming Obstacles

Many different kinds of obstacles may arise or be thrown up in the way of the changes planned. Lack of information, lack of skill, lack of trust, and lack of confidence; fear of failure, fear of success, fear of loss of control, status, or power; a sense of disloyalty to family and extended family members, family myths and values, and existing personal and family identity; longstanding habit patterns that continue to be cued into service; and lip service to agreed upon goals while continuing to disagree with them are among the more common obstacles encountered.

The therapist either provides necessary information to perform the agreed upon tasks or make the necessary decisions or she helps the family obtain the information needed from other sources. The family is usually more empowered if they get the information for themselves. Similarly, new skills are either taught and practiced in session or members are encouraged to seek out the means for acquiring the needed skills. Thus we would teach democratic process and negotiation, conflict resolution, and communication skills. The family may need help in developing daily routines and structures for the children, reasonable forms of privacy, and customs and traditions which promote family cohesiveness. Parents may need coaching in child rearing and discipline. Boundaries may have to be set and maintained and new roles acquired.

Lack of trust inhibits performance of new behaviors. Clients are encouraged to operate under the idea that this is the first day of the rest of their lives. They don't have to forgive past indiscretions or misbehaviors but rather accept them and move on and experiment starting now. What will make it different now is that they are part of a new therapeutic organization in which new agreements have been arranged in which each will take direct responsiblity for his own behavior. However, the therapist avoids giving any kind of guarantees. It is possible that people will fall back, but knowing better will perhaps reestablish the new behaviors to which they committed themselves. Falling back is predicted and normalized as part of the process for growth. It cannot, however, be used as an excuse for not doing. There are no excuses in the process.

Lack of confidence is based on a pessimistic attitude which may be part of a pessimistic world view or result from lack of trust or low self-esteem. The techniques of encouragement described in Chapters 3 and 12 may be utilized to help the members move forward. Reframing the behavior and attitude in a positive connotation is often helpful: "Of course you worry about this. You are a very sensitive and caring person. That's why you will carry out this new behavior." The opposite may also work: "How long will you need to be a victim (chaser, undeserving, depressed)?"

The fear of loss is based on feelings of discouragement. When discouraged, people tend to behave in avoidant and protective ways that are very rigid and extremist in their approach. Again the encouragement techniques described in Chapters 3 and 12 can be very helpful. Once the fear is acknowledged and validated, it may be useful to introduce small behavioral tasks which are easily performed to build encouragement. Another strategy is to change the situation by changing the modality in which the therapist engages the family. The use of dreams, role playing, imagery, games, fantasy, sculpting, art and music techniques, and expanding the system by bringing in extended family or creating a multiple family group are among the many methods available. Paradoxical interactions are also often effective.

Issues of loyalty are less obvious. The genogram and life style data are the best sources for identifying problems of loyalty to persons, values, and myths. Helpful in acquiring insights about and confrontation of loyalty issues are such questions as: "Who taught you this?" "When and how did you learn this?" "Who would be displeased if you did this?" "What would be the risk or danger if you did this?" Prescribing a ritual that uses a family myth in a new way and blocking its old application is another useful technique. For example, a family in which many secrets are kept may be asked to lock the doors every Tuesday night from seven to eight, gather around the kitchen table, permit no interruptions, and talk about anything that bothers them. But no one is to tell anyone else about these meetings or reveal what takes place in them. Another set of questions to help differentiate personal values from prior family values and expectations are: "How are you like your mother (father, mother-in-law, father-in-law, grandparent, son, daughter)? How are you different from each of them?"

Identity is very much tied up with myths and rules and expected solutions. "If only mom would stop yelling irrationally, this family would be fine." "No one should do or say anything that will upset dad." "We are a very close family." "No one in this family can do anything right." "We are just plagued by bad luck." "Everyone in this family must be supersuccessful." First the myth or rule is validated as a positive force. "This family is very protective of dad, who is a very passionate man. If we help him do you think he can handle upsets? Is it possible that he is not as weak (or as monstrous) as you think?" Then we can put father in a new place. "Father, can you talk to your family and help them to know you better? They don't know what a complex person you are." Father thus retains his power position but his use of power is shifted to join with his family by taking a positive initiative.

Habits are simply the customary patterns of behavior in the family. When one does something the other automatically responds in a usual way which confirms the first person's behavior. The entire change process is designed to alter such patterns. New behaviors already introduced are further reinforced and additional techniques are used to implement change. The prediction is made that falling back is normal and they can notice what they did and get back on target. A technique that is often effective in getting them back on target is to have the members invent cue words or signs from their vocabulary which when given will signal that the person needs to stop what he is doing and get back to the agreed upon behaviors without discussion or criticism. An example is a member who typically judges and criticizes others who has agreed to stop that and use a different approach to get what he wants. When this person becomes critical and judgmental in the old way, the others simply hold up a finger and point to it without discussion or criticism, thereby alerting the offending one to get back on target. In doing so the family refuses to cooperate in the old power play.

Someone pretending agreement who sabotages it is rejecting of the change process, hostile toward the therapist, in competition with the therapist, or a pleaser who cannot admit to disagreement but who handles disagreement in a passive-aggressive way. In response the therapist has a number of alternatives. She can take a one-down position: "OK, you win. What do we do now?" Or, "I was mistaken last week in helping to arrange this agreement. What do you think would be better?" Since pretending agreement is one form of resistance, the therapist can use any of the many techniques for dealing with resistance. They are described later in the section called "resistance." Among them are renegotiating the agreement, confronting the hostility or competition, describing the behavior to the person, questioning intentionality, and the use of paradox.

Follow-through and Follow-up

Once agreements are made or tasks or prescriptions are accepted, the therapist asks for a firm commitment from each member to carry out his part of the agreement. It is emphasized that each person is fully responsible for his part no matter what the others do or don't do. *I'll try* and *maybe* are not acceptable as an agreement or as a commitment. They are told to report their progress and results at the next meeting. If the therapist believes that one member or the family needs more structure, they may be asked to call the therapist at a specified time prior to the next meeting to report that the task has been done. The therapist inquires carefully about the performance of the agreement at the next meeting. She evaluates the results and either reinforces the improvement or, if using paradox, restates the paradox and cautions about the risks of change.

If the changes are proceeding well, the therapist may choose to stretch out the time between sessions to once a month, once every three months, and a final session.

EVALUATION AND TERMINATION

In this stage the therapist reviews with the family what issues came up, what has been done, and what the next steps are.

Criteria for Termination

At a surface level, whether the presenting problem has been resolved as a source of conflict and is now being handled in a more functional way and whether the subsequent goals formulated by the family have been achieved or are well along in the process of being achieved are determined.

The therapist wishes to observe if the family is functioning with greater feelings of *satisfaction*. Are they behaving more *effectively* in getting what they want? And are their goals and behavior patterns *appropriate* to their situation as a family and within the community? Has the family as a system and its individual members developed an adequate level of social interest and social feeling? Are they more open and optimistic or more structured and organized as needed? Do they feel good about who they are, where they are, and where they are going? Do they have a practical plan to get to where they are going?

Measuring Outcomes

The therapist can discuss all the foregoing questions with the family and obtain their self-report on what has been accomplished. She can also utilize her own observations of the family's behavior in the sessions. There are many tests and inventories available that the therapist can administer, some of them even computer ready, if she wishes another view of the family's progress. The therapist can use projective techniques such as changes in the early recollections, dreams, images and fantasies, and sentence completions. Sculptures and sociograms can be utilized to observe changes that have occurred in status and roles. The therapist can obtain data about changes in specific behaviors. Is the child getting better grades and reports in school? Does the child perform agreed upon tasks at home? How often do parents consult on child-rearing policies and practices? Does the family engage in a weekly family council? Did mother obtain the job she said she wanted or join in the activity desired? Does father spend the agreed upon one hour per night with the children after dinner? Is the young child sleeping in his own bed? Finally, has the symptom disappeared?

Refinement, Reinforcement, and Projection

Based upon the evaluation process, the therapist helps the family refine the chages that are being made. Agreements and goals are sharpened. Misunderstandings are corrected. Efforts to find loopholes to circumvent agreements are stopped while the need that underlies such efforts is recognized. The family is encouraged to attend to that need. The situation is used as a means of instructing the family to remain open and flexible to new needs and inevitable changes in the life cycle.

The constructive changes made are reinforced and their willingness and ability to care for each other and to make necessary changes are validated once more. Their strengths are reviewed both as a family and as individuals. Newly acquired roles, rules, and myths are confirmed. However, if paradoxical techniques were the major tactics for change, the therapist would review these changes with the family and continue to caution about the risks of changing too fast and enjoin them to be wary, unless she is confident that the new behavior is firmly in place. Then she might say that perhaps she was wrong in her predictions and it is fortunate that the family did not take her advice.

The last step is to project ahead and ascertain that the family and each member have appropriate plans for the immediate future and longer term and a reasonable notion of how to appropriately and effectively attain them. They are now ready for continued growth and to say goodbye.

Termination

Ideally termination occurs with the successful completion of the work as described above. Of course, pressure for termination can come from other sources such as resistance, geographic moves, financial adversity, illness, therapist departure from the agency, or the inappropriateness of the case for the worker or agency. We cannot discuss all of those eventualities here.

Typically, we do not encourage and utilize transferential relationships. Family members have each other. We may engage in creating temporary alliances with one or more members, but because these are shifting patterns we do not engender the deep feelings and attachments endemic to classical psychoanalysis with individuals. Therefore, termination is a less emotional process with fewer problems of separation from the therapist. Nevertheless, the family may come up with a new problem to avoid losing the shelter of the therapist's leadership. The therapist acknowledges the problem and reiterates the family's success in dealing with problems and expresses her strong confidence that they now know how to handle it. She also stresses that she remains available if there is a future need and there are also many other fine therapists available should something happen to her.

Follow-up

A follow-up is planned as part of the termination process. The follow-up may be a scheduled session after six months or scheduled phone interviews after three months or six months. The objective is to repeat the Stage 4 process, reinforce the changes, and ascertain whether the family needs additional help. It is also part of the therapist's assessment of the outcome of her work. From such follow-up sessions she can learn much about the effectiveness of her work.

The above model also must take into account that some people refuse to participate and others consciously or unconsciously choose not to make changes in their behavior or in their place and role in the system. The therapist needs to understand the purpose of not changing and that the existing behavior is somehow more valued, even if uncomfortable and dissatisfying.

RESISTANCE

Definition

Clients do not always do what they say they want to do and they do not always do what the therapist expects them to do. This phenomenon is often defined as resistance. Some authors such as De Shazer (1984) assert there is no such thing as resistance, whereas others such as Anderson and Stewart write an entire book about it (1983). Papp (1983) states that all of therapy is designed to overcome client resistance. The therapist is seen as being in a double bind. The family gears their efforts toward the maintenance of the existing system and against change, thereby trying to defeat the very therapist whom they ask to help them change. Most theorists who write about it and most workers describe resistance only in negative terms. However, in the Adlerian view it has both positive and negative purposes.

Adlerian View of Resistance

Every organism needs to maintain its own integrity. There has to be a boundary that separates the organism from every other thing in the world. That boundary creates resistance to the flow of energy. To create such a boundary and to have the freedom of choice within that boundary a person must have the power to say both yes and no. The young child practicing saying no is separating himself from his parents and other objects in the world to become a distinctive entity in his own right. External forces are constantly impinging upon us. We must exercise some measure of control or we lose ourselves. The same is true for a family system. Those who experience difficulty in controlling those forces feel powerless and oppressed and for survival either succumb as noble victims or rebel by whatever means are available and suited to their life styles.

We notice as therapists that existing behavior serves some useful purpose and giving it up will indeed cost something of value. We also notice that as therapists we are not all-wise or omnipotent and clients sometimes turn out to be the wiser for not making particular changes.

It is not our intention to overcome personal or family integrity. That is why we emphasize validation, encouragement, choice, and agreement as major elements of change. That is also why we cannot ignore the individual within the system. We recognize that there are legitimate obstacles to change. Many of the obstacles described in the section on overcoming obstacles are forms of resistance. These obstacles are interpreted and validated for the clients, who are offered assistance to overcome them. This is also a major element of paradox which interprets and confronts the family with its own truth. Following are four categories of techniques for dealing with resistance.

Techniques to Cope with Resistance.

1. *Renegotiate the goals and agreements.* Accept that for the moment the clients' behavioral goals are different from their stated ones or the ones held by the therapist. Find out what the clients are willing to do rather than what they are not willing to do and arrange a new agreement.

2. *Make the clients aware of what they are doing.*

   (A) Describe to the clients what they are doing so that they can now observe their behavior and then ask them what their intentions are and what they want to do about it.

   (B) Confront clients with their behavior and the consequences of it. They are challenged to have the courage to change or the courage to be imperfect and take the risks of change.

   (C) Describe the effect the behavior has on you and what you feel you would need to do in response to such behavior.

3. *Assign positive connotation to the behavior by reframing its meaning.* Turn the fear or hostility aside. The therapist does not fall for the bait of getting into a power play. After acknowledging the client's position, the therapist reframes its meaning, assigning it a positive connotation: She may then choose to continue with the original agenda.

4. *Join the resistance.* We can join the resistance by agreeing with the clients, even exaggerating or dramatizing the point for paradoxical effect. This results in the therapist coopting the negative, oppositional stance of the clients. To remain oppositional they must switch to the positive or yes position. No matter what the client says, within reason, the therapist finds good reasons to strongly support that position. It is helpful sometimes to add a sentence about what a shame it is that the clients should have to sacrifice so much to maintain that position.

One kind of resistance is the desire to terminate prematurely, as interpreted by the therapist's assessment. In addition to the above categories a few alternative suggestions to maintain the family in therapy are: acknowledge the power of that person in the family and in the therapy and his ability to leave; in the case of a child sympathize with his distress but assert his presence is vital even if he chooses not to participate; suggest that you have been thinking that it would probably be fruitful at this time to meet less frequently and spread out the sessions; have an evaluation session to identify progress already made and what remains to be done.

Another problem of resistance is getting an unwilling client to come in. Often the person present who says the other doesn't want to come really doesn't want him there. A few suggestions are: The therapist calls the person and issues a straightforward invitation indicating the person's presence and help are needed. In our experience the therapist's call is often sufficient. With more determined resisters letters can be sent describing the sessions and stating that the missing person is talked about. Perhaps he would like to come in and present his side of it. A confrontation can be made in severe cases charging the missing person with doing great harm to his family by his absence and placing the responsibility for it squarely on his shoulders.

The next chapter deals with the construct of a family system in Adlerian psychology and points out how Adlerian family therapy can serve as an integrative theory of family therapy encompassing many of the ideas and techniques common to other popular theories.

REFERENCES

Anderson, C., & Stewart, S. (1983). *Mastering resistance: A practical guide to family therapy.* New York: Guilford Press.

Carter, E. A., & McGoldrick, M. (Eds.) (1981). *Family through the life cycle.* New York: Gardner Press.

De Shazer, S. (1984). The death of resistance. *Family Process 23*(1), 11–17.

Dinkmeyer, D. C., Pew, W., & Dinkmeyer, D. C., Jr. (1979). *Adlerian counseling and psychotherapy.* Monterey, CA: Brooks/Cole.

Fredman, N., Sherman, R. (1987). *Handbook of inventories for marriage and family therapy.* New York: Brunner/Mazel.

Grunwald, B. B., & McAbee, H. V. (1985). *Guiding the family: Practical counseling techniques.* Muncie, IN: Accelerated Development.

Guerin, P. J., & Pendagast, E. G. (1976). Evaluation of family systems and genogram in P. J. Guerin (Ed.), *Family therapy theory and practice.* New York: Gardner Press.

Manaster, G., & Corsini, R. J. (1982). *Individual psychology.* Itasca, IL: Peacock.

Mosak, H. H. (1977). *On purpose.* Chicago: Alfred Adler Institute.

Mosak, H. H., Schneider, S., & Mosak, L. E. (1980). *Life style: A workbook.* Chicago: Alfred Adler Institute.

Papp, P. (1983). *The process of change.* New York: Guilford Press.

Sherman, R., & Fredman, N. (1986). *Handbook of structured techniques in marriage and family therapy.* New York: Brunner/Mazel.

5

Adlerian Family Therapy as an Integrative Theory

THE NEED FOR INTEGRATION

The number of theories and versions of theories in family therapy are multiplying rapidly. They are based on several different world views, epistemologies, or paradigms. Because of this, theories cannot be combined into one unified integrative theory which includes all the others. Nevertheless, clinicians who read the literature and observe representative masters in action find many good ideas and techniques in different theories that they would like to adapt and use.

There are several vehicles for doing this. One can choose bits and pieces from everywhere as needed without formulating any kind of systematic theory. One can learn several different theories well and choose the one to apply in a given case or situation. One can search out those premises, principles, and techniques in each theory that have been empirically tested and demonstrated to be effective and seek ways to combine them in a new integrative theory, thus inventing a new theory.

The bits and pieces method is atheoretical and depends on the subjective, pragmatic intuition of the clinician to choose well and not cancel out one good idea with another. It has no power to make generalizations or form testable hypotheses. The alternating theories method implies that there are serious deficiencies in the theory of first choice which necessitate moving to another theory. Theory is viewed as relativistic and interchangeable. Learning one theory really well takes a long time. Learning several theories well takes even longer. Knowing a theory well is different from having *familiarity* with multiple theories, which is a part of most academic training programs.

Inventing a new integrative theory is an ongoing activity of many theory builders. However, as Patterson (1985) points out, most practitioners are not skilled theory builders. More typically their task is to choose among theories available. They will be influenced by their teachers and by their own world view. The proponents of each theory claim that their model is closest to the truth, truth being defined within the paradigm of the same model and world view.

Zukav (1979) presents the following illustration:

> Reality is what we take to be true. What we take to be true is what we believe. What we believe is based upon our perceptions. What we perceive depends upon what we look for. What we look for depends upon what we think. What we think depends upon what we perceive. What we perceive determines what we believe. What we believe determines what we take to be true. What we take to be true is our reality. (Zukav, 1979, p. 328)

Once the ideas of a theory become reified, the theory is in danger of becoming a closed system, stuck like the dysfunctional families with whom we work. The line between total relativism in our theories and the rigidity of having "the truth" is where most of the practical action in the field actually takes place. We need some principles to guide us and an openness to reconsideration and change, a willingness to see what the other fellow is doing and to try on new ideas.

Barclay (1983, p. 2) offers a suggestion: "To gain perspective, it is often necessary to view the topic from alternative positions. Creative solutions are often found in examining interfaces between unlikely systems." Toward this end we have asked five contributing authors who trained in Adlerian psychology and studied more than one theory extremely well to compare and contrast Adlerian theory with some perhaps unlikely other systems. Sperry (in press) also compares Adlerian family therapy with 9 other approaches.

As a result of their work and our own observations, we believe that those clinicians who can accept the world view described in the preceding chapters will find Adlerian psychology an excellent vehicle for incorporating and integrating many of the important ideas and techniques generated and described in other theories. Adlerians find much that is familiar in other theories, a factor confirmed by the analyses presented by our five contributing authors.

We recognize that similar concepts are not identical ones and that differences are not merely a question of semantics. If there were no important differences, there would be few separate theories. Differences are valued by Adlerians as the source for growth as efforts are made to create new syntheses.

We propose Adlerian family therapy as a model that attends to most of the concerns expressed in most of the other popular theories. Therefore, much of what is contained in other theories can be comfortably accounted for or synthesized within Adlerian theory. The theory meets the criteria suggested by Brabeck and Welfel (1985, p. 355) of "demonstrable utility, logical correctness, empirical validity, and superior explanatory power."

Adlerian theory has been used for three generations in many countries with widely diverse populations with considerable success and client satisfaction. It is more inclusive and flexible than exclusive and limiting. It treats both itself and human systems as capable of change rather than as mechanistically determined. The premises of the Adlerian model and derivative principles are carefully spelled out. The model is internally consistent. Each part supports, reinforces, and derives from the others. Many research studies are reported during the last 70 years in Adlerian and other books and journals such as the *Individual Psychologist, Individual Psychology,* and *Individual Psychology: The Journal of Adlerian Theory, Research and Practice.* However, the general quality of the research is no better than that done to test most other theories. We hope for more effective studies in the future.

Because the theory is broad in scope, internally consistent, based on the principle of unity and wholeness, and very practical and down to earth in its observations of the instrumentality of human behavior, the theory does indeed have superior power to explain.

Adlerian theory possesses several critical properties of inclusiveness that give it enormous capability to integrate a great deal from other theories. These properties provide it with the unique opportunity of meeting the needs of clinicians who want to be able to utilize the good things they find in the field in a unified, systematic way rather than working with bits and pieces or inventing their own unified theory.

The same properties of inclusiveness contain premises, principles, and techniques that allow us to classify Adlerian theory in important ways as a systems theory, a developmental theory, a social interaction theory, a behavioristic theory, a communications theory, a cognitive theory, an experiential/existential/gestalt theory, a multigenerational approach, a structural theory, a strategic theory, an object relations/ego psychology/analytic theory, and a metacommunications approach. The brief descriptions that follow only suggest the possibilities involved to illustrate the point. The next five chapters deal with the issue in more detail.

SPECIAL PROPERTIES OF ADLERIAN THEORY FOR INTEGRATION

Adlerian theory emphasizes the internal unity of all organisms and their unified functioning as integral parts of larger systems and the entire cosmos. All parts of the whole are therefore to be included. It is a systems theory that examines the patterns of interactional relationships within the systems and among the systems. The context of the family, both historically and in interaction with its culture and community, is carefully considered. Functioning in love, friendship, work, relationship to the cosmos, and the self-esteem of person and family are all critical factors in human behavior. One's place in the system, the relationships among the places, the boundaries between places, and how each place fits into and reinforces the whole are investigated. Behavior and symptoms are regarded as purposive and organized within the system. These and many other elements of general systems theories and of structural and strategic theories are relevant in Adlerian psychology.

Since family therapy as a separate discipline seems largely to predicate its existence on the idea of a systemic approach to human behavior, it behooves us to first examine Adlerian family therapy as a systemic approach.

The System in Adlerian Psychology

System, from the Greek word *sustema,* is a "composite whole." It is an organized "group of interacting, interrelated or interdependent elements forming or regarded as forming a collective entity" (*American Heritage Dictionary of the English Language,* 1970, p. 1306).

The Adlerian concept of the family as a system is consistent with the world view and epistemology expounded in the previous four chapters. It is an open-ended human system rather than a predetermined mechanistic one. It is subject to the enormous complexities and vagueries of the human condition and supported by the power of the human mind and spirit. Each system is regarded as a highly individualized creation of its members living in a particular context. Therefore, human systems are neither universal nor subject to some basic general laws of the universe such as those conceptualized in the realm of Newtonian physics. Einstein long ago rejected Newton's world view as did many ancients before him. There are, however, many common things that occur in human systems that make the construct of human systems very useful for therapists.

Carich and Willingham (in press) supported by Allen (1971) describe the roots of family systems theory in Adlerian psychology. They report and document that many systems concepts found in other theories are readily available in the early works of Adler and his followers. In fact Adler and Dreikurs are viewed as the originators of family group systems therapy according to Broderick and Schrader (1981) and Nichols (1984).

The most important principles of general systems theory are holism, purpose and order, the functional subordination of parts to the whole, subjective perception, the balance between stasis and change, the homeostatic balance, and circularity based on complementarity and reciprocity rather than causality of behavior. The symptom serves the purpose of maintaining the homeostatic balance and is usually triggered by pressures for change. Within the context of Adlerian theory there are many similarities to general systems theory and some differences in point of view or of emphasis. Following is a description of the Adlerian view of a human system.

1. *The system is a unified whole.* Holism is a critical principle in general systems theory. When Adler invented the name Individual Psychology to describe his theory he was referring to the essential unity within any structure and its unity as a part of still larger wholes. The whole and its parts can be understood only in relation to one another. All systems theories agree with that. Adlerians add that you cannot understand a family without paying attention to its members and you cannot fully understand a person without paying attention to his family, culture, and community and their combined history, goals, and anticipations of the future, very human factors not found everywhere in nature.

2. *The system is founded and modified by human choices.* In concert with other cognitive and humanistic theories Adlerians propose that human behavior is influenced by the subjective meanings assigned to experience and the concluding beliefs derived from those experiences. What we think and how we feel influence the choices we make and the kind and direction of behavior pursued. We cannot determine or control all the things that occur in our environment, in our bodies, and in our lives, but we can decide what to do about them. These choices acted out create the organization and patterns of relationship that constitute the system. Choices are not randomly selected. They are in the service of established or emerging values and priorities leading to hoped-for outcomes.

Choices are very much influenced by what goes on in the system, but they are not predetermined by it. One member can refuse to cooperate. He can move in another direction even if pressure for conformity is brought to bear against him. Individual choices become a force for exerting pressure to change the system. We have all seen how a single serial rapist or murderer on the loose can force an entire community to reorganize its way of life. When the therapist joins with one family member to assume a new and different role in the family, the family reorganizes to accommodate the change.

Ellen and Ralph were respectively pursuer and distancer in their family with Ellen trying to get Ralph to spend more time with her and the children. When Ellen agreed to become apologetically "unavailable" to her husband and to give him all the space he wanted, Ralph, not wanting so much distance, began to chase her, thus changing the system. As Ellen demanded less closeness, Ralph demanded less distance.

General systems theory needs to pay more attention to this element of choice and the motivation that underlies it.

3. *The system is organized with purpose and order.* Adlerian psychology, like general systems theory, is a teleological model. The system by definition is an organized whole. Its existence is purposeful and its behavior is purposeful. Therefore, organization and behavior are instrumental to the purpose. But once a system exists, one of its major purposes becomes to maintain its own existence. Adlerians further propose that a healthy system is proactive and strives to improve itself, not just maintain itself. The human system will also recognize its interdependency with other systems and express feeling and interest in them and a desire to participate with them.

Adlerians stress that there is an underlying private logic idiosyncratic to each system which provides it with order and leads it to organize and function in a particular way. If this logic is understood, then the organization and its behavior make logical sense even if they appear bizarre to outsiders. The private logic is defined by the subjective perceptions of the family and its individual members. The idea of subjective perception is consistent with general systems theory.

4. *The parts of the system are functionally subordinated and complementary to the whole.* As prescribed in general systems theory, for the system to work it is necessary that the elements be organized together in a functionally subordinated way. Each person contributes to the whole in order to maintain and enhance the family. Some measure of individual independence is subordinated to the system for mutual benefit. Thus the system is neither the sum of its parts nor greater than the sum of its parts. The parts contribute what is needed for the system

to function in its unique way. In a well-functioning family this is an aspect of social interest and is primarily done through the process of reciprocal role taking so that the divergent needs of the system are met.

Whenever people have anything to do with others they must cooperate, even if it is to fight, hate, or ignore one another. The cooperation between the needy and the needed ones is a good example. Someone who needs to be needed in order to achieve his goal of superiority cannot fulfill his goal unless he finds another who agrees to be in need and to be helped in a dependent way. If the dependent one finally decides that he no longer wants the help, it puts the system in jeopardy unless the members agree to cooperate in a new way. The human system thus requires a good measure of complementarity among the members to make up the integrated whole and change requires a reintegration of the whole.

Cooperation and communication within the system can be either positive and constructive or negative and destructive and still operate in a functionally subordinated way to maintain the existence of the system. We may assume that the quality of life in a family that relies mostly on positive and constructive communication may be much more satisfying than its opposite. Similarly, the goals of a system may bind its members together whether they are socially acceptable or destructive. Somehow the behaviors within the system complement each other.

5. *The system provides for continuity and change.* As all theories would agree, the family is subject to the forces of stasis and change. How can it continue to maintain its internal integrity while constantly evolving and adapting to meet the challenges of life? General systems theory views change as something that upsets the existing homeostatic balance necessitating a systemic reaction to restore that balance. The need to maintain a homeostatic balance is regarded as the major motivating force in the system. Consequently, man is placed in the position of being primarily a reactive creature.

Adlerians regard man as both reactive and proactive. There is a need for some measure of equilibrium within a system and among systems. If man is proactive, then he is a problem seeker as well as problem solver. He strives to improve himself through positive changes. In a drive toward self-completion and self-improvement, a homeostatic balance can only be a temporary condition in a healthy system. The action directed toward maintaining stasis may be thought of by Adlerians as a homeostatic tendency, although this is not Adlerian vocabulary. We think of it rather as used to maintain integrity, customs, and traditions.

Resistance encountered in therapy also often is used to maintain internal integrity and continuity of the system. However, some of the behavior directed toward conserving things as they are is regarded as avoidant, largely neurotic, and for the purpose of safeguarding from anticipated harm rather than improving the situation.

When safeguarding behavior is used neurotically it is usually reactive and defensive. It leads to rigidity and is based on antithetic thinking— all or nothing, always or never. A person or family thinking that way is usually frightened, discouraged, and pessimistic. Such people are the ones who seek to solve life's problems and face the tensions of change by doing more of the same. In general systems theory terms this is the stuck family or family at impasse. The typical direction of behavior is to avoid or to attack or to manipulate, perhaps by becoming helpless or excessively pleasing. A family that defines itself as victims is a typical reactive family.

The Lowens are such a family. This is a single-parent family with four children. Father, who left, has little to do with them and contributes no money; mother feels overwhelmed and is unable to support the family or discipline the children. She believes that employers never give her a "break" and the work is too hard. She frequently is out with assorted illnesses. She doesn't know what to do with the children. She seeks help from the agency to get the children straightened out.

The children do poorly in school. They believe the teachers are unfair, other children pick on them, and schoolwork is uninteresting. They take solace and find fun in drugs and alcohol. The more they are punished in school or at home the less they do. Mother and teachers periodically give up on them. The children always blame others for their difficulties. The second-born child and eldest daughter allies with mother in trying to parent the others, but she too is barely getting by. A common belief in the family is that "No one appreciates who I am or respects me and *they* are always picking on me." What they want is for others to stop picking on them and to give them or do for them what they want. They use others rather than grow themselves.

This family believes that they are somehow always at the mercy of the behavior of others. They feel oppressed, are pessimistic in their view of life, anticipate further bad things will continue to happen to them, and act to avoid future harm as the principal goal. Risks to one's sense of selfhood such as failure or criticism are to be avoided. Behavior becomes increasingly rigid and is limited to a narrow range at either extreme of aggressing against the oppressors or seeing themselves as powerless and seeking rescuers to save them. Power is directed toward conserving and escaping rather than solving problems or growing.

A proactive family defines itself as competent, successful, significant, belonging, and responsible for its own behavior. The members have an optimistic attitude toward life and are curious about it. They seek change and new options and adaptations. They see life as an interesting—if sometimes difficult—challenge, and even occasionally tragic. They expect to succeed in their endeavors and are not overwhelmed by periodic failures. They are most particularly problem seekers as well as problem solvers. They look for new horizons and new challenges and are bored without them. They do not tolerate boredom well. They make and implement long-term plans that they expect will add to their success and development. They expect to contribute and do something of significance in the world.

Proactivity is stimulated by the drive to move from an inferior position to a more favorable one. The purpose of human life, of person, and of family is not merely to survive, but to actualize and improve itself, to become what it can become. This belief, stated in different terms, is supported by epistemologies as different as theology, idealistic and existential philosophies, and social Darwinism.

The Adlerian contribution is the importance of beliefs and subjective perceptions in how a family will organize itself for both continuity and change.

It is important here to distinguish between changing behavior and changing a system. Watzlawick and others (1974, strategic systems theorists) differentiate between what they call first-order and second-order change. In first-order change the system remains intact, but members may exchange positions or adjust some of their behavior such as learning to be more courteous to one another. For example, the "bad" child corrects his behavior and the "good" child now begins to act out. The purpose of the acting out is to get father involved with the family. The first-order change of correcting the behavior of the first child does not alter the family's need or purpose, so the second child steps into that role, thus maintaining the system as it was. Second-order change involves a reorganization of the structure, function, and relationships—the system is reorganized and changed. To continue our example, father and mother are brought closer together as husband and wife, mother becomes less demanding, and the children no longer need to act out. Each member has to take a new place and learn a new role. Adlerians see the need for both first- and second-order changes in the system.

6. *The human system is dynamic and ever moving toward goals.* The elements in the human system are in constant motion over time and

at a given time forming many evolving patterns of relationship. As a child grows older he demands more independence and may move closer to one parent and create more distance from the other. He may stay away from home for longer periods of time and be capable of and expected to perform more complicated tasks. The kind and direction of the movement is influenced by the goals and priorities of the system, life cycle and environmental changes, cooperation and competition among the members, and the consequences of the behavior. The movement is always forward toward the goals. There is some difference here with the general systems theory concept of circularity of behavior. We firmly agree with general systems theorists that there are repeating patterns of behavior and that cause-effect relationships are not of central importance.

(a) Goals and priorities

Some patterns tend to be more essential to survival and actualization. A person cannot do everything. He assigns greater value to some things than others. These are priority lines of movement that are followed most frequently in competition with other possible lines of movement. They tend to be embodied in continuing reciprocal role behaviors and can be identified as repeating patterns of behavior. These patterns are directed toward particular individual and family goals. A given goal may be proactive or reactive. The value of the goal determines which lines of movement will be given the higher priority and followed. Movement is therefore in a forward direction toward the goal even if the goal is created to safeguard or avoid rather than to achieve. Since not all goals are consciously formulated, the person or family may not be fully aware of the purpose of their behavior. Even repeated patterns of reciprocal behavior, then, are forward moving rather than circular. Forward movement, as used here, does not imply a straight line, but rather a continuing general direction toward the goal. It may well include some weaving up and down and back and forth along the way as specific situations and changes come up.

Since the line of movement is continuous and toward a hoped-for more favorable condition, the goal is always some form of change in the current status. The idea advanced by some general systems theorists such as Papp (1983) of a no-change model is thus inconsistent with our view of a system. Yet, in another vein, Adler did believe that a life style pattern, once developed early in life, is likely to persist with some modification throughout life unless something special, such as a course of therapy, intervenes to produce a significant change in its pattern.

(b) Life cycle and environmental changes

Changes brought about by development or by changes in larger systems of which the family is a part will encourage the flexible family to reorganize to meet the challenge of those changes and to modify some of its goals and priorities. The pressure of such developments may threaten the pessimistic family leading it to become more rigid and dysfunctional in its existing patterns. This is in agreement with general systems theory.

(c) Cooperation and competition

Movement in a human system involves cooperation and competition. Competition is really another form of cooperation because there is no competition without an agreement to compete. I cannot overcome you unless you try to match me. And I cannot dominate over you without competition unless you cooperate and agree to be under me. This paradox is what allows paradoxical interactions to be so effective. The therapist invites the clients to cooperate by competing with the therapist's suggestions.

(d) Feedback and consequences

Behavior of course elicits results, outcomes, or feedback. The Adlerian term is consequences. Positive consequences (or a positive feedback loop) provide the members with encouragement to continue to perform the same series of acts in similar situations. Positive means that it is successful in terms of the goal being pursued, not necessarily good or satisfying in a more objective sense.

Strategic therapists interpret a negative feedback loop as a way of restoring the homeostatic balance, thus inhibiting change. When the husband is too abusive to his wife, she becomes severely depressed and he in turn behaves more kindly toward her again, restoring a better balance. The symptom of depression acts to maintain the system by controlling the husband's abusive behavior. However, it is also evident that whether a consequence is perceived as positive or negative depends on the subjective meanings assigned by the participants.

(e) Case example

The following familiar situation illustrates the concepts of goals and priorities, repeating patterns, forward movement, and consequences or feedback from an Adlerian perspective.

A family comes in complaining of a child's misbehavior. He refuses to do his homework or chores and keeps asking others to buy him things and do things for him. He asks many questions and engages in long discussions when asked to do anything. He claims that others do not want to do things for him. The direction of this child's behavior appears to be to make many people pay a great deal of attention to him. He seems to believe that he is neglected. Operating under the principle of love me or hate me but don't ignore me, he constantly makes his presence felt. Parents and teachers spend a great deal of time with him trying to persuade him to behave differently, often scolding and punishing. The consequence of their scolding and punishing is the reinforcement of his belief that he is not liked and that others will not pay any attention to him unless he makes them. His behavior is successful in drawing attention to him and making him count in the eyes of others. So he continues to repeat the actions that engage others with him and they continue to oblige.

The parents and teachers want to be good parents and teachers and want to teach him to behave properly, so they have incentive to spend time and energy with him and mete out punishments to pursuade him to be a good boy. Thus the pattern daily is repeated over and over again. The child wants to be a good child respected and liked by others and watch television rather than to lose the privilege and be yelled at. However, his priority is to be noticed and to count at any cost, so he continues his successful attention-getting behavior. His line of movement is forward to gain attention. The parents and teachers are also moving forward to correct his behavior in order to be competent parents and teachers. Their reciprocal goals and methods maintain the repeating pattern of behavior. In this sense Adlerians agree that system behavior is frequently circular in movement.

(f) Movement in the system is future oriented

The human system does not function primarily on the basis of predetermined cause and effect relationships. It is based on choices made in each situation in relation to short- and long-term goals and anticipation of consequences. However, we all learn styles and methods of relating and of getting what we want or avoiding what we don't want. Much of the behavior within the system is guided by habitual ways of doing. Although we always have some degree of choice, we frequently act out of habit rather than think through a familiar situation each time it seems to us to be occurring again. In such a mode we stop evaluating the situations and the consequences of our acts until the negative consequences are strong enough to suggest a change or until we perceive ourselves or the situation differently. The task of therapy is to identify with the clients the mistaken goals or methods being employed and to help formulate and implement new ones in their place.

Given the foregoing description of a human system, the task of the therapist is to examine the interactions within the system, observe the directions of the priority lines of movement and their consequences, and understand the movement in terms of the subjective purpose of the movements, the subjective goals.

It is evident from the comparison of Adlerian and general systems theory concepts of the nature of a human system that there is a great deal of similarity between them, and Adlerian psychology definitely contains the properties of a systems theory.

Temporal Time Inclusiveness

Although oriented primarily in the present, the theory posits the importance of themes and patterns that extend from the past within the life style of the individual, family, and culture. It stresses the importance of future-oriented goal striving and the influence of anticipation of the future on present behavior. The therapist examines themes and patterns of behavior over time and stresses the direction of the line of movement expressed by the behavior. Thus, except for the notion of predeterminism, which is rejected, factors in psychoanalytic, ego, and multigenerational theories that are concerned with the past are all relevant. The concern of gestalt, structural, and systems theories with the present or here and now as the only place and time in which action can take place is similarly emphasized by Adlerians. The attention devoted by existentialists and social learning theorists to the process of becoming and anticipation of the future are also attended to by Adlerians.

Development

This a developmental model of human behavior. Person and system are dynamic entities that change and evolve over time in a changing, evolving universe. The notion of themes and patterns in meeting the evolving challenges of life is preferred to the idea of fixed life cycle or psychosexual stages as providing greater flexibility to explain. For example, the need to cope with separation and connecting at new levels occurs in every stage of life from birth to death. By adapting the elements inherent in life stages theories to the notions of themes and patterns, many of the ideas included in analytic and multigenerational theories can be incorporated. Similarly, themes and patterns are involved in dealing with the concept of transitions in strategic approaches. However, Adlerian family therapy, by emphasizing ongoing themes and patterns, further concentrates on the *direction* of development and change. We assess where it is coming from, where it is, and where it is going.

Social Interaction and Exchange

Since all persons are regarded as socially embedded, the interactions among people are seen as the central focus of learning and changing behavior and the major factor in social organizations. The exchanges with others through which we identify personal and collective goals, get what we want and need, resolve differences among us, and attain our goals are deemed crucial factors. There are therefore important similarities with social psychologically based theories. However, the idea of social interest rejects the thesis in social exchange theories that *all* behavior is essentially selfish and based on some immediate kind of quid pro quo. Certainly some behavior is and needs to be selfish. However, for Adlerians, altruistic behavior is seen as part of the human repertoire among those who learn to develop social feeling. Adlerian psychology thus provides an additional major criterion for family therapy: The family and each member need to develop social interest and the capacity to participate, receive, give, and take as a measure of growth and functional ability in the family.

Behaving, Thinking, and Feeling

Different theories emphasize behavior, cognition, or emotion as the most important element. Adlerians recognize that all three have a role to play. Along with structural and strategic therapists, Adlerians focus more on what a person does than on what he says or feels. Adlerians add that what he does represents the priority value in solving a problem and attaining a goal. Consistent with cognitive theorists we also see that the behavior serves a system of beliefs which stimulate the feelings and attitudes held. The beliefs in turn are based on the subjective perceptions of the persons involved. Systems and cognitive theorists agree on this. The beliefs then trigger feelings appropriate to their meaning. Of course, once intense feelings are aroused, as proposed by existentialist and self theorists, they continue to influence subjective perceptions, beliefs, and actions.

Adlerian theory is very much a cognitive model. Reality is represented and organized by the way a person thinks and the subjective meanings attached to life experience. Behavior is seen as purposive and orderly and directed toward subjective goals. This is consistent with general systems theory. The Adlerian contribution is to stress that all three elements interact and make up the whole.

Problem Solving

Meeting the challenges of life requires a continuing attention to identifying and solving problems large and small. The process of stating the problem, clarifying its meaning and consequences, setting goals that would encompass a solution, formulating a plan to attain the goals, learning the information and skills necessary to carry out the plan, evaluating and refining the plan, and reinforcing the new behaviors are part of the Adlerian system of reorientation or reeducation in therapy. Teaching specific skills, such as how to negotiate differences, and giving specific behavioral assignments as part of a plan for change, such as conducting a weekly couple conference to increase intimacy and understanding, are an integral aspect of the therapy.

The Adlerian process is closely related to learning theories and the work of behavioral and problem-solving therapists, such as integrative problem-solving family therapy (Henderson and Duray-Pabst, in press). It is also similar to the work of rational emotive therapists like Ellis (1962, 1977) who urge clients to take a more scientific approach to assessing their situations and beliefs and solving their problems. And it is similar to the approach of multimodal therapists such as Lazarus (1981).

Communication

Interactions are all some form of communication among the participants. Correcting and improving the communication is an essential ingredient of the Adlerian model. Pointing out the consequences of particular patterns of communication and their probable goals are other factors attended to. The sometimes hidden meanings of the communication are revealed. This includes many thoughts and feelings that are unexpressed or are indirectly displaced and expressed inappropriately. Such skills as psychoactive listening (client-centered and behavioral theories), affirming rather than disqualifying (strategic theory), learning how to conduct family meetings and conflict resolution techniques (behavioral and social learning theories) are taught. Magical thinking, hinting, withholding information, lies and distortions, misunderstandings, double messages, and double binds are all dealt with (stragetic/

communications/interactive theories). In this sense the Adlerian model is very much a communications theory and incorporates the work usually done by such theorists.

Adlerians add their concern with the private logic underlying the communication, the purpose and goal of the communication, and the direction of the communicative behavior.

Experiential/Existential Factors

Adlerian psychology encompasses many of the major ideas of gestalt and existential psychologies. Like them, it is a teleological, subjective, phenomenological approach. The private world of subjective meanings organized by the individual and family based on their subjective perceptions is the central focus of the theory. Life is dynamic and open-ended in an ever-changing universe. The drive to become—to complete—to actualize oneself or family is the major motivating force in both psychologies. Behavior is largely based on the process of making choices for which one is responsible. The action is in the here and now. The therapist uses herself actively as a leader in the process of change describing observations back to the clients, being empathic and genuine, giving authentic and accurate feedback. The therapist invents behavioral experiments to help clients explore both current and new ways of being in the world to help them more accurately perceive themselves, acquire new insights and understandings, reorganize their perceptions, and change their behavior. Adlerians focus on all of these.

General systems theory also embraces many of the foregoing principles and tactics such as teleology, subjective perception, action in the here and now, behavioral experiments, and the therapist as an active leader. However, Adlerians also urge that subjective data are to be checked against common sense, the meanings assigned by most people to the same or similar phenomena. They make empathic hunches and describe them back to the clients as tentative hypotheses and help clients observe the consequences of their acts and goals. They go beyond the present to deal with themes and patterns of behavior over time and anticipations of the future.

Ego and Object Relations Factors

Adlerian psychology began as an analytic theory. However, it differed from Freudian thinking in many ways; for example, its emphasis on social interaction and rejection of predeterminism. It is more consistent with the modern analytic emphases of ego psychology such as the importance of cognition and conscious behavior, individual motivation and dynamics as an influence on the family, the influence of old business from the family of origin on behavior in the present procreative family and choice of a mate. Individual dynamics and insight are regarded as critical to understanding of the family and helpful in producing change. Family legacies, loyalties, and introjects so important in the work of Boszormenyi-Nagy and Spark (1973), contextual and multigenerational therapists, are very much part of Adlerian thinking about family guiding lines and assumptive values. This leads inevitably to thinking in multigenerational terms.

Multigenerational Factors

There are, of course, several multigenerational theories, each of which approaches the work somewhat differently. Adlerians will meet with any part of the whole (system) available. However, ideally, we will investigate the entire multigenerational family system to discover guiding lines, assumptive values, and unfinished business, to repair cutoffs, and to identify place in the larger system and boundaries within the system. Parents and children are seen together and separately. We seek out life style patterns and how they mesh together in the family organization. We also recognize that cultures evolve over generations and may produce intergenerational conflict and misunderstanding. This is particularly true in a nation such as the United States with its continuing influx of immigrants from nations with other cultural backgrounds.

We also observe that children are often unaware of the pressures and situations faced by the parents or grandparents and vice versa. Therefore, there is little sympathy and appreciation for the behaviors being manifested. One aspect of obtaining the family constellation is to generate a better understanding of the worlds and challenges faced by different generations of this family. What was the experience of the parents in their relationship to their parents?

Such concepts as contagion of anxiety, fusion and differentiation, and thinking about triangles (Bowen, 1978) are not inconsistent with Adlerian principles such as fear of inferiority, the need to respect individuality and connect through social interest, and the concept of coalitions among family members. Sending adult children to work out issues with their parents or bringing parents and siblings into session with an adult child (Framo, 1982) are also modalities compatible with Adlerian thinking to work out guiding lines, assumptive values, strengths, individuality, and rootedness, and to resolve old conflicts. How much multigenerational work is required depends on the complexity of the problem.

Metacommunication Approaches

Metacommunication approaches may be used with many different theories. Adlerians are advocates of the use of humor, fantasy, imagery, metaphors, art, music, drama, dreams, poetry, stories, sculpting, and choreography as ways of understanding and changing behavior. Experience that has an impact analogically through what is referred to as right brain hemisphere functioning and which circumvents the defenses that clients have already built up in highly structured digital thinking are powerful resources. Adlerians have long used psychodrama, art, dance, and music therapies and hypnosis as an adjunctive part of their work.

Individual and System

Some of the early proponents of modern family therapy in their efforts to find a completely new way to work rejected any emphasis on the individual or individual motivation. They insisted that only the family system and systems laws be considered as family therapy. Adlerians never accepted this error, which was perhaps exaggerated by the desire to differentiate family therapy as a separate discipline rather than as an adjunctive modality within existing disciplines. Both individual and system need to be included. The system is created by and changed by individuals in interaction. The system exerts great influence on the behavior of each of its members and each person exerts great influence on what kind of system is organized. It's a dual pathway. Since 1984 many articles and American Association of Family Therapy convention presentations have sounded a theme that seems to reflect the "rediscovery" of the individual. Framo (1982) and others have insisted all along that both individual and interactive system must be attended to.

Complexity

The effort in science is to search for the simple building blocks and to formulate some general laws that will explain all occurrences. But human behavior is exceedingly complex and exists within very complex social and physical circumstances. It requires a complex theory that is able to include the vast range of the human condition rather than focusing on one narrow part of it.

By this point the reader may have a strong notion that we are proposing that Adlerian theory can be all things to all people. We are not. But as demonstrated by the 12 preceding characteristics described in this chapter, it is a complex theory that overlaps the narrower foci characteristic of most other theories. It is this comprehensiveness and complexity which make it an ideal candidate to serve as an integrative theory that can keep growing and incorporating much that is created and refined in other theories. In turn, this complexity stems from Adler's idea of the unity and wholeness of all things.

Five contributing Adlerian authors who are well trained in another major theory were invited to compare and contrast that theory with Adlerian psychology in order to examine the possibility that many important ideas and techniques could be accommodated within the Adlerian framework and to identify critical differences. The five theories are the communications/human validation process model of Virginia Satir; the cognitive rational emotive model of Albert Ellis; structural family therapy; interactive strategic family therapy as represented in the MRI model; and strategic family therapy.

Each contributor was asked to assess the following areas: definition; historical development; basic concepts; conceptions of the well-functioning and dysfunctional family; role of the therapist; concepts and techniques for assessing the system; concepts about how behavior change takes place; techniques most frequently used; a summary of the findings; and supporting references.

Given the nature of the task to compare and contrast another theory with Adlerian psychology, there is an inevitable amount of interrelationship of ideas among these chapters and the other chapters in the book that describe Adlerian family therapy per se. It may also be noted by the reader that just as there are differences of opinion among strategic theorists or those of any other school of thought, there are differences among Adlerians. In fact unanimity would be inimical to the theory and its future growth and development.

To obtain comparisons among the theories' 66 concepts, change methods and techniques considered important in different family therapy theories were listed. Experts in six different theories were asked to rate the degree of emphasis or acceptability of each item within the framework of their own theories. The ratings on the table report their opinions. There was no communication among the raters. Each acted independently.

The ratings on the Adlerian psychology position represent a consensus among five experts in the field who rated the items independently. The ratings on each of the other theories were provided by only one representative of that particular theory, the person who authored the chapter on that theory in this book. We cannot claim that a sample of adherents of any of those theories would rate the items the same way. However, there was a very high level of agreement among Adlerians as to whether a given item was to be accepted or rejected and on the degree of emphasis for most items. One might assume that the same would be true for additional raters representing the other theories.

There was a general acceptance of 74.3% on the items among the six theories compared. There was a high level of agreement on how much emphasis to place on a given concept or technique on almost half the items. This indicates that our proposition is correct—there is a great deal of overlap among the theories.

Further, our proposition that Adlerian theory in particular overlaps to a high degree with most other theories is well borne out by the fact that on over 92% of the items, the Adlerians were in agreement with the majority of the other theorists on the degree to which these items were accepted or rejected. Table 5.1 (see pp. 106-107) illustrates how Adlerian theory compares with other family therapy theories described in the next five chapters.

TABLE 5.1
Comparative Emphases Among Family Therapies Reported

Abbreviations of ratings of theoretical emphasis, importance, or acceptability: H= High, M= Moderate, L= Low, and O= None. Circled ratings indicate the level of probable acceptance of an item not specifically described or accounted for in a given theory. **MAJOR CONCEPTS**	Adlerian (consensus)	Satir (Bitter)	MRI (McKelvie)	Strategic (Kelly)	Structural (Hirschorn)	RET (Croake)	Agreement among the six theories[a]	Adlerian agreement with majority of six theories[b] (Yes = +, No = —)
1 Holism	H	H	H	H	H	O	H	+
2 Teleology, purpose, goal directedness	H	M	M	M	H	H	H	+
3 Subjective perception	H	H	O	M	O	H	L	+
4 Insight	H	M	O	O	O	H	L	—
5 Belief systems, myths	H	H	H	L	L	H	M	+
6 Personal responsibility and freedom	H	H	O	L	O	H	L	+
7 Self-esteem	H	H	L	(L)	O	O	L	+
8 Interpersonal congruence	M	H	O	L	(L)	O	L	+
9 Differentiation	M	H	L	(L)	H	O	M	+
10 Family history and guiding lines	H	H	L	L	O	O	L	+
11 Here and now	M	H	H	H	H	H	H	+
12 Anticipation of the future	H	M	L	(L)	O	M	M	+
13 Individual	H	H	L	L	O	H	M	+
14 Family system	H	H	H	H	H	O	H	+
15 Suprasystems	H	H	L	(M)	H	O	M	+
16 Social context and situation	H	H	H	H	H	L	H	+
17 Family life stages or evolution	L	H	L	(L)	H	O	M	+
18 Homeostatic balance/equilibrium	M	H	H	H	O	O	L	+
19 Circular causality	M	H	H	H	H	H	H	+
20 Power	H	L	M	H	H	H	H	+
21 Boundaries	M	H	M	M	H	O	H	+
22 Alignment	M	L	L	M	H	L	M	+
23 Contact-withdrawal cycles, intimacy	M	H	L	M	H	L	M	+
24 Joining	H	H	L	L	H	O	M	+
25 Open, direct, authentic communication	H	H	L	(M)	(H)	H	H	+
26 Coping stances, priorities	H	H	M	(L)	(M)	M	H	+
27 Feedback, consequences	H	H	L	H	(H)	H	H	+
28 Resistance	M	O	H	H	(H)	L	M	+
29 Growth as the primary objective	H	H	O	L	O	L	L	—
30 Remediation as the primary objective	M	M	H	H	H	H	H	+
CHANGE								
31 Insight	H	M	O	O	O	H	L	—
32 Encouragement	H	H	L	(L)	(H)	L	L	+
33 Cooperation	H	H	L	M	H	(H)	H	+
34 Goal-setting	H	H	M	M	(H)	M	H	+
35 Social interest	H	H	L	O	H	O	L	+
36 Congruent communication	H	H	L	L	(H)	O	L	+
37 Reframing, positive connotation	H	H	H	H	H	O	H	+
38 Therapist modeling	H	H	L	(M)	H	H	H	+
39 Problem-solving techniques and other skills	H	H	L	H	H	H	H	+
40 Unbalancing the system	(M)	H	H	M	H	O	H	+
41 Realigning the structure	M	M	M	M	H	O	H	+

	CHANGE (continued)	Adlerian (consensus)	Satir (Bitter)	MRI (McKelvie)	Strategic (Kelly)	Structural (Hirschorn)	RET (Croake)	Agreement among the six theories[a]	Adlerian agreement with majority of six theories[b] (Yes = + No = —)
42	Realigning roles and relationships	H	H	H	H	H	O	H	+
43	Prescriptions	H	O	H	H	H	H	H	+
	TECHNIQUES								
44	Genogram, family constellation	H	H	L	Ⓛ	O	O	L	+
45	Encouragement	H	H	L	Ⓛ	Ⓗ	L	M	+
46	In-session tasks, enactments	H	H	M	H	H	M	H	+
47	Validating, confirming	H	H	L	Ⓛ	Ⓗ	O	M	+
48	Interpreting, confronting	H	O	L	O	O	H	L	—
49	Coaching, educating, skills training	H	H	M	M	H	H	H	+
50	Prescribing	H	O	H	H	H	H	H	+
51	Tests and inventories	L	O	L	O	O	L	H	+
52	Contracting	M	L	H	M	Ⓗ	H	H	+
53	Negotiating agreements	H	M	H	M	Ⓗ	H	H	+
54	Behavior rehearsal	M	H	M	Ⓜ	Ⓗ	H	H	+
55	Reassociation of reference groups	Ⓜ	Ⓗ	M	Ⓛ	O	O	L	+
56	Introducing new roles, rules, myths	M	H	M	M	Ⓗ	L	H	+
57	Touching	L	H	L	O	O	O	M	—
58	Experiments	M	H	L	H	M	H	H	+
59	Circular questioning	Ⓜ	O	M	Ⓛ	H	O	L	+
60	Paradoxical interactions	H	L	H	H	H	O	M	+
61	Pretending, acting "as if"	H	M	H	H	Ⓗ	L	H	+
62	Humor	H	H	H	Ⓜ	Ⓗ	H	H	+
63	Metaphorical stories	M	H	H	O	Ⓗ	L	M	+
64	Art, poetry, dreams, dance	M	M	L	O	Ⓗ	L	M	+
65	Role playing, drama	M	H	L	M	Ⓗ	L	M	+
66	Imagery	M	M	M	O	O	H	L	+

PERCENTAGE OF AGREEMENT AMONG THE THEORIES	N = 66 No. Items	% Items
[a] High level of agreement among six theories — (H) (Ratings for each theory on an item are within one level of each other with a maximum of one theory differing by two levels)	32	48.5
Moderate level of agreement among six theories — (M) (General acceptance of the item among the six theories with no more than one theory rejecting the item with a zero rating)	17	25.8
Total level of general agreement	49	74.3*
Low level of agreement among the six theories — (L) (Ratings given for each theory on an item range widely from (H) to two or more zeros)	17	25.8
[b] Adlerian theory in general agreement with the majority of the five other theories (Adlerians agree with three or more other theories in accepting or rejecting an item)	61	92.4

---

* Extra 0.1% due to rounding off of fractions.

REFERENCES

Allen, T. W. (1971). Major contributions: The individual psychology of Alfred Adler: An item of history and a promise of a revolution. *The Counseling Psychologist, 3*(1), 3–24.

Barclay, J. R. (1983). Searching for a new paradigm in counseling. *Personnel and Guidance Journal, 62,* 2.

Boszormenyi-Nagy, I., & Spark, G. (1973). *Invisible loyalties: Reciprocity in intergenerational family therapy.* New York: Harper & Row.

Bowen, M. (1978). *Family therapy in clinical practice.* New York: Jason Aronson.

Brabeck, M. M., & Welfel, E. R. (1985). Truth in counseling theory: A rejoinder to Patterson and Rychlak. *Journal of Counseling and Development, 63*(6), 355.

Broderick, C. B., & Schrader, S. S. (1981). The history of professional marriage and family therapy. In A. S. Gurman & D. P. Kniskern (Eds.), *Handbook of family therapy.* New York: Brunner/Mazel.

Carich, M. S. & Willingham, W. (In press). The roots of family systems theory in the Individual Psychology of Alfred Adler. *Individual Psychology: The Journal of Adlerian Theory, Research and Practice.*

Ellis, A. (1962). *Reason and emotion in psychotherapy.* New York: Lyle Stuart.

Ellis, A. (1978). A rational-emotive approach to family therapy. *Rational Living, 13,* 15–20.

Framo, J. L. (1982). *Explorations in marital and family therapy.* New York: Springer.

Henderson, T., & Duray-Pabst, M. (In press). An integrative problem-solving approach. *Individual Psychology: The Journal of Adlerian Theory, Research and Practice.*

Lazarus, A. A. (1981). *The practice of multimodal therapy.* New York: McGraw-Hill.

Nichols, M. P. (1984). *Family therapy concepts and methods.* New York: Gardner Press.

Papp, P. (1983). *The process of change.* New York: Guilford Press.

Patterson, C. H. (1985). New light for counseling theory. *Journal of Counseling and Development, 63*(6), 349.

Sperry, L. (In press). Contemporary approaches to family therapy: A comparative and meta-analysis. *Individual Psychology: The Journal of Adlerian Theory, Research and Practice.*

Watzlawick, P., Weakland, J., & Fisch, J. (1974). *Change: Principles of problem formation and problem resolution.* New York: Norton.

Zukav, G. (1979). *The dancing wu li masters.* New York: Morrow.

6

Communication and Meaning: Satir in Adlerian Context

James Robert Bitter

A PERSONAL INTRODUCTION

In 1980 I reached one of those times in my life when I felt stale. Whatever I knew about me, about living, or about my work I had known for a long time. I was a male in my mid-thirties. I was a son, a brother, a cousin, a friend, and a neighbor. I was an educator in a graduate counseling program and a counselor for individuals and families experiencing a multitude of difficulties. I was an Adlerian: the possibilities for a meaningful life suggested in Adler's writings were a standard for most of my efforts. Each day was filled with a variety of interests and activities, but I seemed to have very little energy.

In July of that same year, I went to Montreal, Quebec, to be part of a month-long training program conducted by Virginia Satir and two members of her AVANTA NETWORK.* The first part of my journey was filled with anticipation and self-protection. I had heard that Satir was magic and wonderful. I had read *People-making* (Satir, 1972) and *Conjoint Family Therapy* (Satir, 1983). I had been moved and challenged by both books. Still, I was an Adlerian, and I was not about to give up this precious connection in my life.

Within a matter of hours, Satir won my heart as well as my mind.

James Robert Bitter, Ed.D., is a Professor of Counseling at the West Virginia College of Graduate Studies.

* In 1981, the month long growth experiences became known as Process Communities. Satir began to use nine AVANTA members to facilitate group learning during the month. The AVANTA NETWORK is composed of human service professionals from an assortment of disciplines who receive regular training from Satir. Through communication enrichment, Parts Parties, and Family Reconstruction, Process Communities become learning centers for becoming more fully human. For additional information, write to: AVANTA NETWORK, 139 Forest Ave., Palo Alto, California 94301-0162.

She asked each of us to taste what she had prepared, but to swallow only that which tasted good (that which fit what we felt and what we thought). With each day, there was something new to add to my understanding of self and others. I discovered new ways to understand old and cherished beliefs, new ways to approach my teaching and my work, and even new ways to conceptualize Adlerian psychology. I had given up nothing, and I had added so much that was useful to me. My energy was back, and I felt the same excitement I had experienced the first time I watched Manford Sonstegard conduct Adlerian family counseling.

My excitement endures, and my understanding continues to grow. The pieces I have learned from Satir enrich my Adlerian foundation. New possibilities emerge. With this chapter, I want to share my own picture of family therapy, a synthesis of two therapy systems. I also hope that my excitement about new meanings, growth possibilities for families, and enriched communication in therapy is manifest: such excitement is the art of Virginia Satir.

DEFINITION

Virginia Satir has called her therapeutic approach by a number of different names. Each one has reflected a revised emphasis in her work. In 1964, Satir's work with families was called *Conjoint Family Therapy* (Satir, 1983). Her emphasis on making connections within the family and between herself and the family was the foundation for therapeutic change. She saw the core of human experience being expressed in each individual's feelings. She used her understanding of communication and metacommunication to gain access to those feelings that could make connections with others and free the individual for growth and new possibilities. She also wanted to help each person within the family to reconnect with disowned, ignored, or distorted parts of himself or herself. Each connection was for the purpose of making what was splintered whole: helping people to feel more fully connected to their personal resources and helping family members to feel more fully functional in their living. The word "conjoint," meaning joined or connected, still reflects a significant emphasis in her work.

As Satir continued to observe communication processes within families, she began to notice that people seemed to have four dysfunctional ways of relating when their stress level was high. These communication patterns were called blaming, placating, being super-reasonable, and irrelevent (Satir, Stachowiak, & Taschman, 1975). Each communication approach had a coping function and as such it involved the whole person. Satir could see people adopting virtually universal stances or postures any time they began to communicate dysfunctionally. These postures gave her the means to sculpt each family. Each sculpture was a human tableau: a picture of the relationships among family members (the family system and the communication style of each member). Since all families are understood to be dynamic in nature, movement, and change, each sculpture was a drama: a picture in process.

In recent years Satir's emphasis on meeting families in process and promoting a change in experience as well as communication has been reflected in the renaming of her therapy. She has referred to it as a "Process Model" (Satir, 1982) and later "The Human Validation Process Model" (Satir & Baldwin, 1983). Both titles reflect the activity and human movement that are involved in her current practice of family therapy.

This (Process) model is one in which the therapist and the family join forces to promote wellness. The heart of the model consists of all those interactions and transactions translated into methods and procedures which move the individuals in the family and the family system from a symptomatic base toward one of wellness. (Satir, 1982, p. 12)

Satir is a communications/systems therapist whose focus is on promoting growth and health and releasing energy in individuals and families (Satir & Baldwin, 1983). She uses a family's communication patterns to gain access to the family system. Dysfunctional communication both contributes to and is an expression of a dysfunctional system. A system is only as good as the relationship of its parts. When any of the parts stop working effectively, energy is blocked and the whole system is affected. Satir works to make the parts (the people) in each family whole and differentiated. She creates a context in which "differentness" can be valued, meaning can be clarified, and relationships can be revitalized. Energy in the system is then released. The family process is back in flow. The system and its members are open and growing.

Functional family systems are manifest in congruent communications. Congruence necessitates the freedom to experience fully with our senses, to feel and to think what we will, and to express directly and accurately the results of that freedom. It is precisely what we sense, feel, and think that makes us unique and individual. When each person's uniqueness can be clearly expressed in the family, when each person's differentness can be valued as an important part in negotiations and functioning, and when each person's individuality is treated as an important part in the growth of the family, then therapy can be terminated. The system as well as each individual has all the energy and resources needed to be functional in the world.

Satir's conception of therapy is very much in harmony with Adlerian thinking. Adlerians, too, see human behavior as creative movement, and the interaction among family members is essentially a choreography of life style connections. These connections are expressed in the patterns of communication as well as the goals toward which the family members strive. Health is the energy and movement toward self-fulfillment, community involvement, and ultimately community improvement. In this context, a mutual respect for each person's differentness is a potent force for growth.

HISTORICAL DEVELOPMENT AND PERSPECTIVE

The historical developments of Adler and Satir are as unique as the people who emerged. Each faced a different set of challenges in distinctly different times. In many ways, the therapies they developed reflect the particulars of their lives, their special places in history, and the opportunities of their individual generations. Still, the similarities are most remarkable. Both were pioneers and creators in psychology and psychotherapy. Both wanted to give their knowledge to the world. Both were detectives and explorers on a quest for an understanding of the human soul. Both discovered the importance of the family system as a means of helping people grow in a functional and useful manner. There is a presence associated with each of them that in part has inspired people to live better, more fully human lives. It often seems to me that Adler and Satir were two pathfinders whose roads never crossed even though they traveled the same route.

Satir reports that she started her detective work at the age of five, becoming a "children's detective on parents" (Satir, 1982). Her early memory suggests the significance she gives to communication processes and the messages involved. It also set the stage for a lifetime of observing and being involved with family relationships. "I was curious about everything, including those things I was 'too young for,' or that 'weren't for girls' " (Satir, 1982, p. 13).

Satir started her career as a teacher. For six years she taught in five different schools in a variety of socioeconomic and geographic locations. Like Adler, she used schools to gain access to families. During her tenure, she met with over 200 of her students' families, seeking and gaining parental support for helping children with physical and psychological difficulties.

What I learned at this early stage was that:
1. Parents can be assets to their children if we know how to enlist their help;
2. If children have problems, something is going on in the family or has happened in the past which affects the child;
3. Difficult problems can be solved if we trust that we can and if we create a trusting atmosphere and work at gaining access to the necessary human resources. (Satir, 1982, p. 15)

Because of her experience with families, Satir enrolled in a college of social work, hoping to learn about "people's insides." This was at a time when the divisions between psychology, counseling, and social work were not so delineated: each school was seeking to understand the dynamics of human living. Her work with delinquent girls gave her another chance to meet with and learn about families. Furtmuller (1964, p. 335) suggests that Adler used his own family (in addition to his child guidance clinics) as a source of stimulation for theory and practice with families and individuals. Similarly, Satir used every opportunity with families to learn and develop methods of intervention.

In 1951 Satir entered private practice. That practice served mostly high-risk clients for whom traditional psychotherapy had not worked. Just as Adler was drawn toward family interviews in the child guidance movement* he created in Vienna, Satir quickly moved toward family therapy as a means of promoting change.

In March 1959, Satir joined Don Jackson and Jules Riskin in creating the Mental Research Institute in Palo Alto, California. The Institute grew out of the work of these people and their associates Gregory Bateson, William Fry, Jay Haley, Paul Watzlawick, and John Weakland:—the creators of the contemporary systems approach to family therapy (Jackson, 1968). The Institute was an association whose primary endeavor was research, but for Satir the association represented a first collaboration with people who validated her own discoveries about human interaction. This group provided the same initial excitement for

---

* The Child Guidance Movement in Vienna was quite different from the ones established in the United States. Adler saw the parents, the children, and the children's teachers in his public clinics. In the United States, most child guidance centers were established for mother and child. Satir's inclusion of all family members was a marked change in typical family intervention in the United States.

her that the original Psychological Wednesday Society* must have provided for Adler. Both groups included people who sensed that they were on the cutting edge of new discoveries.

Satir soon became bored with research. She felt that her area of contribution would be in the training of therapists. In the fall of 1959 she opened the first formal training program for family therapy using a communications/systems approach (Satir, 1982). Unlike Adler in Freud's circle, Satir felt important and valued. The new direction she chose did not require the kind of split that Adler and his associates found necessary in 1911. During the early 1960s the atmosphere in California was highly supportive of diversity, new discoveries, and change.

In 1964 Satir went to Esalen, a center in the Big Sur for most of the developing and nontraditional therapies of that time. By 1967 she was the director of training. Her training at Esalen provided people with a model for growth that enabled individuals to be more fully human. The growth model allowed a focus on movement just as Adler's teleological model had over thirty years earlier.

Both Adler and Satir in their respective times had learned a pathological orientation for understanding human difficulty. Both rejected that model in favor of a holistic, interpersonal, educational and humanistic approach. Both rejected the notion that the absence of a symptom was the same as the presence of health. For Adler, a symptom had a purpose that was expressed in a social setting. For Satir, the presence of a symptom is simply the first clue presented about an individual's blockage of energy and growth: movement is constricted. For both, the answer was an educative process for living better. "I saw that growth was an ongoing process of sorting, adding on, and letting go of that which no longer fit. . . . (And) I now see therapy as an educational process for becoming more fully human" (Satir, 1982, p. 22).

BASIC CONCEPTS

Both Adler and Satir maintained a constant focus on what people could become. This is the essence of a growth model of psychology, and it partly accounts for the tremendous number of parallel concepts in the two approaches. Their concepts are remarkably free of dubious

---

* The Psychological Wednesday Society started in 1902. In 1908, the name was changed to Vienna Psychoanalytic Society. It is often called, today, the Freudian circle (Ansbacher & Ansbacher, 1964, p. 338).

psychological terminology. Some of the more significant conceptual comparisons follow as a foundation for theoretical synthesis.

Holism* is the first concept that seems to be accepted by both Adler and Satir as a basis for understanding human beings. In Individual Psychology, holism is equated with the unity of the personality (Ansbacher & Ansbacher, 1956, p. 189), which occurs after a person's self-selected life goal has been established. A person's thoughts, feelings, beliefs, convictions, attitudes, and actions are all expressions of one unique individual. Due to the dynamic relationship of the parts as well as the creative uses to which people apply personal characteristics, each individual is always more than the mere sum of his or her parts.

Satir's concept of holism specifies the ways in which the "self" is constructed. "Virginia sees the core of every person, the 'self,' as being in the center of a mandala" (Satir & Baldwin, 1983, p. 176). The mandala contains eight separate aspects of human organisms. These aspects are connected in a constant interplay that is the major influence on the health and development of the individual.

The first four aspects are treated as structural components of human beings. They include the physical body, the intellect or left brain, the emotions or right brain, and the five senses. Just as Adler suggested, Satir sees these parts as interrelated functions. In a statement that parallels Adlerian theory, Satir discusses the relationship of feelings and thoughts. "Thought and feeling are inextricably bound together; the individual need not be a prisoner of his feelings but can use the cognitive component of his feeling to free himself" (Satir, 1983, p. 125).

The last four aspects are needs that individuals must satisfy for continued growth and development. In a sense these parts of the mandala are similar to certain demands Adlerians characterize within the tasks of life: the tasks of friendship, work, intimacy, self-esteem and one's relationship to the cosmos. Satir's are the interactional or social needs, nutritional needs, contextual needs, and spiritual needs. ". . . each of us is a system. While we can study and talk about each part separately, they function together, just like any system. Just like a family" (Satir & Baldwin, 1983, p. 180).

The process of human development in Satir and Adler provides another set of similar concepts. The motivation for early development, according to Satir, is the desire for continued existence. All children come into the world in a helpless state (Satir, 1983, p. 57). They literally

---

* Both Satir and Adler adopted the concept of holism from the same person. The term was coined by General Jan Smuts, former prime minister of South Africa, and was used in his book *Holism and evolution* (Smuts, 1961).

depend on their parents for survival. Every child, therefore, assigns a special significance to the words, gestures, tone, feeling, moods, attitudes, and actions of these adults. It is the parental posture toward and communication with children that make the difference in the development of their self-esteem. When parents fail to validate a child's ability—when they ignore it (emotional neglect) or punish it—the result is one more step toward low self-esteem.

While Adler recognizes the tremendous influence of parents on the development of children, he also notes the extent to which children create their own meaning and interpretations. From the very beginning, a child's recognition of helplessness is characterized by inferiority feelings: these are not abnormal (Ansbacher & Ansbacher, 1956, p. 117). They act as a motivational force for growth and development, a stimulus to overcome perceived obstacles. When inferiority feelings, however, become so exaggerated that they constrict the child's movement and worth, then these feelings have become an inferiority complex. Such a complex may be assumed either as a reaction to perceived negative influence or as a result of mistaken notions and faulty interpretations.

Although Satir and Adler may differ slightly on the origin and development of discouragement, the concepts (and results) of low self-esteem and the inferiority complex are essentially the same. They are also in substantial agreement about the needs for a productive and useful life. They are personal validation and encouragement, independent growth, and a closeness with and contribution to others. " . . . every individual is geared to survival, growth, and getting close to others and . . . all behavior expresses these aims, no matter how distorted it may look" (Satir, 1983, p. 24).

Satir's emphasis on the importance of survival needs and people with survival significance is her foundation for considering the social embeddedness of human beings. "Every human being came from two other people and was thus essentially born into a group" (Satir & Baldwin, 1983, p. 179). Social contact appears to be an innate need and the basis for continued validation and growth.

In addition to the social group, every child is born into a social setting: a context in which the person comes to understand the world as well as his or her value and place in that world. Throughout life, every human interaction is composed of at least three elements: the person (or self), others, and the nature and requirements of the social context. All three elements are involved in congruent communication and must be considered when people want to make meaning clear. To deny any element is to distort meaning and suffer the consequent confusion and dysfunction.

Adler also understood these elements to be present and the foundation for human life. He suggested that all human beings are born into a community which places on them demands that cannot be escaped. There is an "iron logic of communal life" (Ansbacher & Ansbacher, 1956, p. 127): each individual will live better insofar as he or she promotes the welfare of the whole. This is the basis for a "common sense." What we say and do make common sense if they fall within the parameters of the general welfare (Ansbacher & Ansbacher, 1956, p. 149).

Communication reflects this process. In an attempt to make meaning, each individual must constantly shift from self to other and back again— at one moment sending a message of personal interest or conviction and then receiving a response. The process of speaking and listening involves a balance and cooperation, a give and take. For messages to be clear and meaning to be created, mutual responsibility is also required. Accurate message sending means saying what I think or feel so that the other can hear me in our specific social context. Accurate listening involves full attention to the message and the message giver, clarifications, and careful consideration (Satir, 1983, p. 88). A breakdown in either is a breakdown in meaning and understanding. In perhaps a small sense, each breakdown puts a little more distance between people attempting to make contact in the community.

When any individual takes responsibility for self, acts cooperatively with others, and attempts to meet the needs of a given situation, Adlerians (Ansbacher & Ansbacher, 1956; Dreikurs, 1950) say the person acts with social interest. The parallel concept in Satir's system is called *maturation*. Both Adler and Satir use these concepts as a "touchstone" for assessing the growth and well-being of people and families.

> A mature person is one who, having attained his majority, is able to make choices and decisions based on accurate perceptions about himself, others, and the context in which he finds himself; who acknowledges these choices and decisions as being his; and who accepts responsibility for their outcomes. (Satir, 1983, p. 118)

Family Constellation is Adler's term for what Satir calls the family system. Both of them would agree that the family system includes "parents, siblings, and others living in the family of origin" (Griffith & Powers, 1984, p. 41). There is a marked difference, however, in their assessments of that system.

Adler often uses the term "family constellation," giving only a passing consideration to parents before he fully develops the influence of psychological birth position on children (Adler, 1930, 1931, 1938). His emphasis on children creating their own unique position in the family is evident even in his discussion of parents in an unhappy marriage. Adler (1931, pp. 132–133) acknowledges the dangers for children raised in a disruptive marriage, but he also suggests that children are skilled at reading dissension and playing one parent against the other.

It is likely that Adler developed his early emphasis on children within the family system because much of his child guidance work started as a support system for public education (Terner & Pew, 1978, pp. 60–62). He wanted to help parents and teachers understand children's faulty concepts and mistaken ideas so that useful corrective procedures might be employed. This emphasis on the impact of children on the family was organized teleologically when Dreikurs (1940) first presented the mistaken goals of children's misbehavior. Dreikurs' skill at presenting these goals to children often led to what he called a "recognition reflex" (Terner & Pew, 1978, p. 157), making goal disclosure a significant focus in his therapy.

In contrast, Satir (Satir, 1983) places most of her emphasis on the relationship of the parents and the self-esteem exhibited in that relationship. Children are presented as much more reactive to parental influence, and childhood disturbance is most frequently treated as a symptom of marital difficulties. When a couple's relationship is characterized by disappointment, that experience involves incongruent communication and defensive posturing. Their communication betrays low self-worth, and their defensiveness suggests their inequality: the difficulty each has in being a separate individual in an interdependent relationship. The child, having his or her own needs, is forced to adapt to what the parents are willing and able to give. The child's survival depends on that adaptation. As the dissension between parents increases, a child's deviant behavior is viewed as a functional response to a dysfunctional system (Satir, 1983, p. 48).

When parents can handle themselves with each other, then Satir believes they have the resources to be leaders for the family. They will be able to incorporate the new child as a member of the family triad without being driven apart or consumed by the helplessness of the infant. As the child grows, he or she will gain an identity (a place in the world) and a belief about the trustworthiness of relationships. The child will also gain a sense of personal power (Satir & Baldwin, 1983, p. 172).

Within the basic family triad—mother, father, and child—the forces for cooperation can be quite strong, providing that both parents have high self-esteem. Families develop rules in the hope of fostering family cooperation. In healthy families, the number of rules is small, and they are consistently applied. The rules are humanly possible, relevent, and flexible with changing situations. Satir (Satir & Baldwin, 1983, p. 203) believes that the most important family rules are the ones that govern differentness (uniqueness) and the sharing of information (communication). These are the rules that affect a family's ability to function and to be open to and optimistic about change.

A complete picture of the family constellation (the family system) is really drawn with the help of Satir's process for family maps (Satir, 1972) and her family-life chronology (Satir, 1983). These descriptions reveal aspects of the family atmosphere, family values, and family rules within an intergenerational family constellation. Adlerians will find that the addition of psychological birth position information gives further depth and meaning to the process. It adds a balance to the focus on adult relationships and adult impact. It adds a richness to our understanding of the family as a system.

FUNCTIONAL AND DYSFUNCTIONAL FAMILIES

In functional families, parents with high self-esteem are the foundation of the system. Each of the mates has a sense of value and worth as an individual as well as a trust and confidence in the relationship. In addition, it is possible for people in the family to be different. When differentness leads to disagreements, the difficulty is treated as an opportunity for growth rather than an attack on the system. In functional families, each person is allowed a separate life as well as the shared life of the family group. In addition, different relationships are also given room to grow.

(a) Mother is able to allow the child a father–child relationship.
(b) Father is able to allow the child a mother–child relationship.
(c) Yet both mates make it clear to the child that he can never be included in their relationship as mates. (Satir, 1983, p. 73)

Dreikurs and Soltz (1964, p. 224) expressed this principle in one line: "Individual relationships between two people belong to the two involved." Adlerians, therefore, accept Satir's list and would add that parents must allow their children room to form relationships with each other; with grandparents, aunts, uncles, cousins; and with members of the larger community (e.g., teachers, ministers, friends, and neighbors).

Both Adler and Satir posit a healthy family system to be an open system. The open system is characterized by choices, flexibility, and freedom within the family order. "It even has the freedom to be [a] closed [system] for a while if that fits" (Satir & Baldwin, 1983, p. 192). In an open system, change is at least expected if not welcomed. Growth is change, and change is a part of every living organism and situation. Change is seldom easy and often poses a new set of problems. In an open system, problems are met as a challenge and an opportunity. Because difference in family members is encouraged, the range of possible problem-solving strategies is even wider than the sum of individual resources. "In open systems, managed by love and understanding, resources are seen as ever-present possibilities" (Satir & Baldwin, 1983, p. 193).

The acid test for a functional family is open communication. In healthy families, people are able to speak for themselves. They are able to say what they see, hear, and feel instead of what they think they should have experienced. The ability to comment freely on family life and family events is encouraged. There is an exchange of appreciation and validation statements within the family. Complaints are addressed as hopes for a better situation. Questions can be asked, and clear/direct answers will be given. Concerns and worries can be voiced. Information is shared and made available to those who want it. In this atmosphere, people feel the support for taking risks and for learning new ways of living.

Both theories note that dysfunctional families start with the low self-esteem of one or both of the marriage partners. People with low self-esteem or an inferiority complex invite confirmation of their inadequacy and expect their lives to turn out badly. The feeling is easily caught by others and can permeate the whole family (Satir & Baldwin, 1983, p. 195). When people with low self-esteem marry, they hope that the other will make up what they feel is missing in themselves. In essence, each puts the other in charge of his or her own self-esteem with an implied demand: "Help me feel good about myself!" When the exchange is made, they resent the loss of control over their own happiness as well as the responsibility for the other's happiness. The marriage is characterized by low self-worth, high hopes (expectations), and low trust (Satir, 1983, p. 21).

Since children depend on adults to meet their needs, they are forced to take what life hands them. When parents cannot adequately meet their own needs, very little of themselves is available for the child(ren). Adult disagreements turn into battles filled with accusations and moralizing (Satir, 1983, p. 18). These battles most often go underground around the children. The children, sensing the danger of the battle, become confused and worried about their place in the family, their survival. When a child becomes an identified patient in the family, that child is a reflection of the pain that the parents are experiencing.

Adlerians note that children both reflect parental pain and create their own way of interpreting and relating to parental conflict. Their self-determined response often acts as a further stimulus to parental helplessness and pain. The cycle and the system continue to support an unending discouragement.

In dysfunctional families, the system is closed. Rules are invented to mask the fear of differences and bolster low self-esteem: in effect, family members are expected to act, think, feel, and be the same. Some rules are fixed and rigidly applied even if they don't fit the situation. Others are administered inconsistently with the ebb and flow of daily life. Parents manage largely through the use of fear, punishment, guilt, or dominance. The closed system eventually has to break down as it reaches the end of its ability to cope (Satir & Baldwin, 1983, p. 192).

When rules can no longer keep a dysfunctional family system intact, stress is augmented in the family and its members. The members handle their stress by adopting a defensive position. Satir (Satir, 1972, 1983; Satir & Baldwin, 1983; Satir, Stachowiak, & Taschman, 1975) has delineated four universal communication patterns which express an organized defensive posture that she calls stress positions. Specifically, they are the postures of "blaming," "placating," being "super reasonable," or "irrelevent." Satir's descriptions make use of her understanding of communication, her skill with sculpting, and her focus on the present, the here and now. These stress positions expand and balance the "personality priorities" developed by the Adlerian, Israeli psychologist Nera Kefir (1971, 1981). She originally designated four priorities which she named "superiority," "pleasing," "control," and "comfort." Each personality priority is presented as a dominant behavior pattern with supporting convictions that a person uses to cope. In essence, each priority represents an approach to problems and a desired position that the person hopes will produce safety. I believe that Satir and Kefir have discovered the same universal responses to stress; they just describe them from different perspectives.

By using these perspectives as if they were two points on a line, it is possible to create a highly detailed stress flow chart. At one end of the chart, Virginia's description of dysfunctional communication patterns represents the person's immediate attempt to cope with a stressful situation. At the other end, Kefir's priorities represent an idea or a goal the person hopes will produce safety in a threatening situation. In between, it is possible to describe the words and feelings, body tensions and physical symptoms, fears and sacrifices that are involved with each approach. Table 6.1 provides a summary of each position in a behavioral description.

The following descriptions are a portrait of each position as they are expressed when people experience stress and distress.

Placating-Pleasing

People who placate are willing to sacrifice themselves in an effort to please others. A stance is adopted which suggests a willingness to accept anything: a person is pictured as being down on one knee with one hand over the heart to demonstrate sincerity and one hand raised in supplication. No matter what is said or asked by others, people seeking to placate will always agree and attempt to be sincerely ingratiating. They feel helpless without others, because inside they sense that they are worth nothing. Placating people say "Yes" to any request, no matter what they think or feel. There is always a little nervousness behind their actions, because they have little ability to evaluate effectiveness for themselves, and they are in a complementary stance for a person who is blaming. Those who agree to anything have a lot dumped on them. They carry the weight of others' satisfaction on their shoulders. It does not take long for placating to cause nausea and other difficulties in the stomach and digestive tract.

More than anything else, people who placate fear rejection. They both expect it and want to avoid it at all costs. In the end, however, there are too many people to please. They feel pulled in too many directions. Their energy is fragmented and they are never able to establish their own wants, their own convictions, their own identity. They have tried to be too many different people to too many significant others.

Blaming-Superiority

The other side of placating is a stance Satir calls blaming. Blaming people will sacrifice others and even the context to maintain and preserve themselves. Their significance depends on being one-up and having power. When problems occur, it's anybody's fault but theirs. Blaming people are pictured with their pointing finger out. The person has one foot forward, one pointing arm extended, and the other hand on his hip. The eyes narrow, and the jaw becomes tight and fixed as the person leans into an accusing posture. The words express disagreement and criticism. There is irritation just below the surface that becomes

TABLE 6.1
Dysfunctional Movements in Response to Stress

Satir's Stress Positions	Words	Feeling (Extreme)	Body Tension	Physical Distress (Symptoms)	Self, Others, and the Social Context	Thing I Most Want to Avoid	Price I Will Pay	Kefir's Personality Priorities
Placating	Agreement	Anxiety → (Neurosis)	Shoulders	Stomach + Digestive Tract	(diagram S/C/O)	Rejection	Loss of identity/Fragmented energy Too many people to please	Pleasing
Blaming	Disagreement + Criticism	Irritation/Anger (Acting Out)	Back Pain	Constriction/Muscle tissue/High blood pressure	(diagram S/C/O)	Worthlessness + Meaningless	Overworked + Overburdened	Superiority
Super Reasonable (Computer)	Rational	Fear to come out (Psychosomatic)	Neck/Back	Secretion blockage/Peculiar complaints that defy diagnosis	(diagram S/C/O)	Humiliation + Embarrassment	Social distance	Control
Irrelevant (Distracter)	Distraction/Changes the subject/Takes no stand	Confusion (Psychosis)	Headaches	Dizziness + Nervous System	(diagram S/C/O)	Pain or stress	Low productivity	Comfort

anger when challenged. The constriction felt in the back puts pressure on every part of the body from muscle tissue to blood.

Worthlessness and meaninglessness must be avoided. Because self-worth is defined as being on top, in charge, and blameless when difficulties arise, people seeking superiority are constantly engaged in outdoing and overdoing. They will often complain about being over-worked or overburdened even when things are going well. When stress increases, the blaming person either overwhelms the problem or finds and assigns fault to others. "If it weren't for you, everything would be alright" (Satir, 1972, p. 66).

Superreasonable-Control

The superreasonable person acts as if he or she were a computer: the head is able to work well with information, but everything below the neck is turned off. Superreasonable people sacrifice themselves and others in favor of the more manageable context. This computerlike stance is pictured with rigidity and stiffness. With both feet together, the body upright, the arms and hands held tightly against the person's sides (the military stance for being at attention), information can flow in and out without a single feeling being associated or acknowledged. The words are rational, abstract, and often long, even if inappropriate. Sounding bright is as important as being intelligent. Principles (especially for what is right) are revered: "It," the right way, is more important than the people involved. Self and others are not considered.

Superreasonable people want to keep everything under control—especially their feelings. They live in fear of coming out in the open. Their stress is often experienced in psychosomatic difficulties or peculiar complaints that defy diagnosis. Their stiffness affects the back and neck. Their insides begin to dry up, and normal secretions are often blocked. Under stress, they seek to control situations and people so that they can avoid any humiliation or embarrassment. The price they pay is a sense of social distance or isolation: a disconnection from themselves and the support of others.

Irrelevant-Comfort

Comfort has a special meaning in this context. Rather than the maintenance of pleasure and ease, it is any situation lacking pain or stress. Stress is created by people in a given setting. The distracting person is attempting to eliminate self, others, and the context with irrelevance in the mistaken hope that the stress or pain will go away.

Irrelevant people are pictured in motion: everything is going in different directions, but going nowhere. The feet may be turned in, the body floppy, and the head moving back and forth. This posture is the counterpart to the superreasonable stance and quickly leads to dizziness. Irrelevant statements never fit the context. They are a change of subject; a question answered with a question; loosely bound statements with missing links, connections, or transitions. The voice is often singsong, disconnected from the meaning of the words; it may go up or down in tone without apparent reason. No stand is taken by distracting people, because any disagreement may lead to stress. Irrelevance temporarily shifts the focus of others away from an actually or potentially painful situation.

Distraction turns mild stress into confusion. Too much confusion and dizziness can lead to headaches, affect the central nervous system, and at its most extreme become psychosis. The constant motion and lack of focus make it next to impossible to accomplish anything. In the name of maintaining this narrowly defined sense of comfort, a person often gives up a feeling of productivity and with it a little of his or her self-worth.

Several clinicians (Brown, 1977; Kefir, 1971; Pew, 1974) have suggested that each person has a number one priority. I believe it is more likely that people tend to rely on one approach more than the others when stress is encountered. They have a lead system that is their initial safeguard, their first line of defense. Any or all of the dysfunctional communication patterns may be used, however, depending on the people involved and the given situation. In addition, some people face stress in a functional manner with congruence (Satir, Stachowiak, & Taschman, 1975) and social interest (Adler, 1938). Using the same dimensions contained in Table 6.1, a functional approach can be described as in Table 6.2.

Congruence—Social Interest

Congruent people sacrifice nothing to stress: not themselves, others, or the context. Stress is not turned into distress; it is treated as a challenge that can be met in a useful manner. People in this position are grounded (in reality), flexible, and flow with the situation. Their eyes are bright and clear, and it is as if their whole body is paying attention. They are alert. They are balanced. They are able to make full use of their senses as well as their other available resources.

The words of congruent people match their feelings and their experience. There is an integrity to what they say: an emotional honesty.

TABLE 6.2
Functional Movements in Response to Stress

Satir's Functional Position	Words	Feeling	Physical Condition	Self, Others, and the Social Context	How I Face Stress	Resources	Adler's Number One Priority
Congruence	Match feeling experience Match Direct/Clear "I" statements	Centered	Full of breath Balanced	(circle: S, C, O)	Courage/Confidence	My senses My talents My connection with others Choices/Options	Social interest

There are no double-level or double-bind communications. The situation is approached as a task to be solved. "Anything can be talked about; anything can be commented on; any question can be raised; there is nothing to hold you back" (Satir, Stachowiak, & Taschman, 1975, p. 49). The result is directness and clarity, options and real choices.

It is social interest which supports the courage and confidence necessary to handle stress. Because of a sense of belonging and connectedness, people in this stance can ask for help in clear voices with no sense of being diminished. Indeed, many of life's problems can be handled as group problems, using the multiple resources of a number of people.

Through congruence and social interest, those qualities which are blocked in dysfunctional positions can be liberated and "renovated." Renovated pleasing produces tenderness, compassion, and considerateness as well as a certain intuition about the feelings of others. Superiority liberated of its one-up quality is assertiveness, the ability to stand up for yourself. Persistence and competence follow. The superreasonable position can be transformed into a creative use of intelligence, skill at organization, and an eye for detail and preciseness. Finally, when focus and tension-reduction are attained, irrelevance becomes spontaneity, playfulness, and even a gift for peacemaking and real comfort.

ROLE OF THE THERAPIST

As in Adlerian psychology, the overall role of the therapist is to introduce a more fully functional humanness into the family system. This role of the therapist (and goal of therapy) requires a personal conviction that change is possible and desirable; that all human beings are oriented toward growth; and that every system and every person have the resources within them to produce growth. In essence, the therapist views the family as being in the process of living and becoming—no matter how stuck the family may appear. Given the circumstances, their difficulties and struggles are the system's best attempt at survival. In that attempt are the seeds for success. This optimism is the antedote to the feelings of defeat with which a family often enters therapy. It is expressed in a nonjudgmental attitude, an appreciation for the multiple influences affecting the family and its members (Satir & Baldwin, 1983, pp. 226-7). Optimism and encouragement are also central to Adlerian family therapy.

By entering the family system as a health agent, the therapist agrees to be a nurturing partner in the process of change and development. The "person" of the therapist—all the senses, beliefs, roles, attitudes, and convictions that he or she has—is the most important part of any therapeutic intervention. To be as fully human and open to others as possible is therefore more important than expertise and technique (Satir & Baldwin, 1983, p. 209). It is the combination of congruence and social interest that makes a therapist effective.

A congruent therapist makes full use of his or her senses in the service of understanding others. To define the social feeling that Adler thought was necessary, he quoted a phrase from an unidentified English author: "To see with the eyes of another, to hear with the ears of another, to feel with the heart of another" (Ansbacher & Ansbacher, 1956, p. 135). Satir (Satir, 1983, p. 257) echoes this imperative:

> . . . when I am listening to somebody, I am also looking at him or her and am aware of all his or her moving parts. I am aware of all the changes that may be going on. I am listening with my full self, with all of my senses.

It is the full use of one's senses which allows a person to observe, ask about, and comment on those parts of the family system that are ignored, denied, or distorted. Full use of senses also includes an awareness of self in relation to others. A therapist learns to trust his or her reactions and feelings and to manifest these internal responses as part of the feedback system in therapy. Such personal interventions require both flexibility and vulnerability: a willingness to go with the flow and make mistakes. To use Dreikurs' (1970) term, the source of a therapist's flexible vulnerability is the "courage to be imperfect."

With courage, a therapist is not afraid to ask unasked questions (nothing is assumed), to look at pain and difficulties in the family, and to face the tasks which have hitherto been avoided. With the feeling of being "centered," which is part of feeling in charge of oneself, the therapist can be nurturing, give confidence, reduce fears, and provide hope. Mosak (1984) uses the words *faith, hope,* and *love.*

Satir's style of nurturing involves her whole self, her whole presence. Her emphasis on touch distinguishes her therapeutic process from most of Adlerian psychotherapy, which primarily relies on cognitive interventions. Satir's hands both give and receive information. A touch of each family member's hands can tell her how people are feeling; a touch of a child has been known to quiet, comfort, or provide encouragement.

> The little five year old was on my right. . . . she was moving back a little bit. By this time I had the feeling that she was regarded as the troublemaker in the family and was rather on the outside. I slipped my hand around her back—she had a nice, round back—and I found myself feeling the enjoyment of touching her.

I think she felt this as a message of encouragement to be a part of the group. (Satir, 1983, p. 249)

It is the therapist's responsibility to provide structure in family therapy. The therapist has a sense about where people are in the process and where to go. Having a therapist who seems to be in charge inspires confidence in families who have no idea about where they are going.

While Satir's structure shares a few similarities with the Adlerian approach, her stages of therapy are essentially different from the process proposed by Dreikurs. Dreikurs (1967) suggested four stages which emphasized the goals and interventions of the therapist: forming a relationship, psychological investigation, psychological disclosure, and reorientation. Satir (Satir & Baldwin, 1983, p. 221) sees the therapist as a leader of the process, and her stages of therapy parallel phases of human learning: making contact with what is new and with others; experiencing the chaos of change, of going beyond what is known; and an integration of what was unknown into what is known and is now usable.

Adler suggested that human dysfunction was largely the result of mistaken interpretations. "In practice we attempt to undo the great errors, to substitute smaller errors, and to reduce these further until they are no longer harmful" (Ansbacher & Ansbacher, 1956, p. 187). Similarly, Satir views most human dysfunction as the result of faulty learning. Based on these views, both rejected the medical model in favor of an educational model. Both saw a fundamental relationship between the roles of teacher and therapist: they were two role/functions on the same continuum (Satir & Baldwin, 1983, p. 223).

In her role as a therapeutic teacher, Satir—like Adler—has a fondness for questions. Questions help her to understand the dynamics of individuals and families. Questions allow her to help clients find their own answers. She suggests that her process is similar to the Socratic method, similar to "a midwife [who helps] in birthing an idea which was inside" (Satir & Baldwin, 1983, p. 183). Families often have the experience of excitement at discovering something new that was always inside their own members. Learning has occurred.

Adler (1929, p. 73) declared that psychologists must never worry about success in therapy: to be concerned about success is to forfeit it. In an almost identical statement, Satir suggests that a lack of self-concern is the key to feeling energized and effective at the end of an interview.

I would get drained if I kept asking myself all kinds of questions like "Am I doing it right? Will people love me? Am I going to come out with a cure?" If I started to do that, I would lose track of the system and process that are going on and I would be on *my* story rather than the story of the family. (Satir, 1983, p. 251)

ASSESSING THE SYSTEM

Assessments and interventions in Conjoint Family Therapy are made at three different levels. Satir seeks an understanding of individuals, paired interactions (dyads), and the family system (which she sees as a triad or set of triads). An individual's ability to function is based on a personal evaluation of self-worth. That evaluation provides either an enrichment for or a retardation of the system as a whole. Through an assessment of communication patterns, the therapist obtains a microscopic focus on relationships and the ability of family members to connect and cooperate. Self-esteem and communication contribute to and are reflected in either an open or a closed system. Family rules support and maintain the overall system. Presenting problems are important only insofar as they help the therapist gain access to these three levels in the family structure.

Assessing Self-worth

Both theories state that all human problems are inevitably social problems, because they take place in a social context. Problems affect both our feelings about ourselves and our relationship with others. To understand a problem, the therapist must ask about the meaning that people associate with the difficulty. "A problem in itself has no meaning independent of how the concerned individuals feel about it" (Satir & Baldwin, 1983, p. 195). Some understanding can be gained from statements that are made when a person is trying to cope: " 'I can't do it.' (I am little, insignificant.) 'They won't let me do it.' (Others are bigger than I am. I am a victim.)" (Satir, 1983, p. 221).

In a similar vein, Adler (Ansbacher & Ansbacher, 1964, p. 194) suggested that even descriptions of family members reveal a statement about self. "He was loving" means "he was loving to me." "She was strict" can be translated "she was strict with me, and I had to struggle to be me and be free." Indeed, since people can use any adjectives to describe family members, some aspect of self-worth is usually projected in the selection of traits. Qualities to which a person assigns a negative connotation were usually involved in the person's diminished sense of self-worth. Conversely, qualities to which a person assigns a positive connotation usually enhanced self-worth, contributed to a feeling of belonging, and were treated as necessary to the person's survival.

Assessing Communication

Communication is the means by which people connect, make meaning with one another, and therefore make a life together. Communication is functional when family members are able to clearly and directly state or request anything; when clarification is possible for all parties; and when feedback is possible and allowed. Such communication demands cooperation, a willingness to participate and contribute. It is in itself a measure of social interest.

When communication becomes dysfunctional, people have a hard time making meaning together. Their feelings of being valued and connected are affected. Speech patterns are marked by incompleteness, deletions, incongruence, and over-generalizations. When members of the family cannot comment on or clarify distorted communications, they live in confusion.

Sometimes communication is distorted by a process that Satir (Satir & Baldwin, 1983, p. 197) calls *nominalization* in which "active portions of an experience are represented by static words." Instead of saying "I am angry," the person states that "anger seems to be happening everywhere, all the time." Nominalization puts distance between the person and the experience and disowns responsibility for personal feelings. *Denominalization* is the process of reconnecting a person to that person's experiences by helping him or her to say what he or she is feeling.

Miscommunication can also occur when people extrapolate a total communication from one segment of behavior. This process, called *complex-equivalence,* is frequently present in a family that uses a lot of unclarified gestures and other nonverbal cues. First a meaning is invented for the behavior; then the meaning is personalized. A person in the family yawns, and another member assumes the person is bored, especially "bored with me." Again, the therapist must make it possible for people to ask questions and clarify meaning.

As noted before, the way in which a person uses communication as a defense or safeguard suggests something about his or her low self-esteem as well as the disharmony in the family. A person who blames a lot wants desperately to be valued and connected with others. A person who is constantly placating wants to have a real identity and feel wanted and included by others. When someone presents a super-reasonable front, he or she wants the fear to go away. If feelings and connections with others were not so scary, there would be much less need for constant controls. And if life were not perceived as dangerous, the person using irrelevance would love to regain focus—to see, hear, and experience life as it really is. Interventions which decrease the threat anticipated by family members increase the possibilities for change and growth.

Sculpting is one such intervention. What Satir hears in the communication of family members she also sees in the postures of the stress positions. An arrangement of family members in positions that fit creates a sculpture that is immediately recognized by the participants. In this sense, sculpting acts as a check for the assessment Satir has made (or family members have made) about coping strategies. By setting the sculpture in motion (allowing the positions to change and adjust), a first assessment of the family as system can also be obtained.

Assessing Rules

An assessment of the rules which govern the behavior of the family is another means of understanding the system. The therapist pays special attention to the rules that govern communication—especially expressions of affection and anger. Adlerians understand feelings to have a purpose. In this sense, the expression of affection suggests something about the way in which family members connect. Conversely, the expression of anger has the effect of distancing one person from another: they can only connect by colliding. Rules about expressing affection and anger have to do with how family members come together and get apart.

Family rules also address how people will function with one another. The system will be dysfunctional if the rules are unclear and misunderstood. Clarification is the antedote. The system will also breakdown if rules are outdated, unfair, or inappropriate to present situations. In these situations reconsideration and transformation are needed. The rules that protect the self-esteem of one or more members of the family must be handled with the most care. "These rules usually operate without people's awareness and can be touched on only when family members feel very secure with the therapist" (Satir & Baldwin, 1983, p. 206).

Assessing the Family Life Chronology

Satir (Satir, 1983, pp. 145-177) uses a formal assessment procedure that she calls "The Family Life Chronology." Her carefully outlined approach develops a picture of three generations: the present family, the family of each of the parents, and the family of the future that will be based on the current experiences of the children. The chronology really consists of three assessment sub-procedures which can be identified as (a) family maps, (b) a list of all family events—all comings and goings—from the birth of the grandparents to the present, and (c) a tracking of everyday family life. This assessment tool is the counterpart to an Adlerian assessment of family constellation, family atmosphere, family values, and a typical day (Christensen & Schramski, 1983), but it requires much greater detail.

Starting with the present family, the therapist gathers a full cast of characters and arranges them in a map. The map includes the parents, children, and any other people who have been significantly associated with the family or family members. The original map is enlarged to include the family of origin for each of the parents in the present family. The three maps provide the basis for a chronological history of the family. By noting descriptions of family members, comings–goings and changes, and coping processes, a pattern of family learning begins to emerge. That learning and its expression are grounded in present time and space when the therapist seeks descriptions of a typical day and the arrangement of the home. When the Family Life Chronology is complete, it is basically what Adlerians would call a life style assessment of the family system.

The form of the Family Life Chronology produces a history of the family. The experience often fills gaps in the information that each mate has about the other. It frequently provides children with their first real in-depth picture of their parents and their background. It can produce some understanding of why people act, think, and feel the way they do: private interpretations are acknowledged and shared. Most important, the procedure allows the therapist multiple opportunities to assess self-worth, communication, and rules; to ask questions that have not been asked; to seek comments from family members that reflect what they really see, hear, and feel. The result is assessment and intervention in a nonthreatening atmosphere.

Adler's unique contribution to assessment and intervention was his teleological approach (Ansbacher & Ansbacher, 1956, pp. 92-94). In an effort to escape the limitations of drive psychology, Adler discovered the influence of the future, the purposeful striving of human beings. An understanding of goals and purposes is the foundation for psychological intervention in all Adlerian therapy. Dreikurs' (1940, 1948, 1957) conceptualization of the mistaken goals of children's misbehavior firmly embedded the teleological approach in Adlerian family counseling.

Satir created a therapy which could heal people in the present, the here and now, emphasizing growth and movement towards the future. Many of her interventions reflect an awareness of purpose which she calls "hopes" or "good intentions" (Satir, 1983, p. 213). Her primary orientation, however, is in the present. The influence of fictional goals on present levels of self-esteem and communication patterns has not been developed in her work.

Satir is constantly looking for the ways in which energy is blocked in the family system. Energy is often blocked when old learnings do not fit the situaton as it is now. Old learnings can be reexamined, however, and updated to meet present needs. Changes in behavior and the system are more the result of adopting new views—learning a new process—in the present than a correction of faulty goals.

THE BEHAVIOR CHANGE MODEL

In a process model, problems are never the problem. As Adlerians note, it is the way in which people cope with problems that makes them either functional or dysfunctional. The experience of being stuck is characterized by the sense of having limited options for understanding difficulties, for acting, and for working with others. Whatever the method of coping, it is the person's best attempt so far at handling problems. The coping strategy, how the person acts, can be traced directly to the experiences he or she has had and the interpretation associated with those experiences. "Changing how and what one looks at, seeing new possibilities and interpretations, and discovering various options will automatically lead one to a new coping" (Satir, 1983, p. 147).

The feeling of being stuck is usually self-inflicted and supported through the acceptance of restrictive rules incorporated as if they were literal taboos. "There is only one right way to do things" is the most common form of being stuck. This approach is always linked to a sense of safety or survival and stifles the thrust in people to be creative. Like Adler, Satir (Satir, 1983, p. 250) constantly encourages people to push beyond the taboos within themselves and within the system: to look at life in a new way, to consider different options, to clarify meaning and process with each other, and to check possibilities against reality.

Toward this end, Satir becomes a model for congruent communication. She is a human in the family system who risks asking direct questions, who clarifies, and who helps others to do the same. She spells out non-verbal and double-level messages. She points out discrepancies and asks people what they make of them. She completes gaps in statements and information and challenges inappropriate expectations (Satir, 1983, pp. 224-227). She will also challenge any purely negative interpretations—

usually by giving voice to the hopes and good intentions behind dysfunctional behavior. Each intervention makes meaning clearer and more manifest in the family process. It allows people to feel better about themselves and each other.

Satir (Satir, 1983, p. 258) suggests that the transformation of stress positions starts when the therapist tunes in to both the hopes and fears associated with the various postures. As in every other aspect of change, it is not a matter of stopping the dysfunctional aspects but rather a matter of adding what is missing. When someone is placating, Satir tunes in to what the person wants just for one's self and the loneliness that is felt. She will bypass words of blame, anger, and hate to touch the need to be valued, the hurt, or the longing to be connected to others. A person who approaches life in a superreasonable way receives the experience of being really heard and seen: a person-to-person contact. A person who uses irrelevance to distract is like a crack in a vase. Any additional pressure will cause it to break. Satir adds support and reassurance in an effort to strengthen. The support makes it possible to focus and face difficulties without becoming overwhelmed by the pain or stress.

Satir treats children as capable of handling the same interventions as adults. She helps children hear what is present but has been hidden from them. She helps children express what they see and feel, comment on the happenings in the family. She also expects children to contribute and act in a responsible manner. An example of how closely Satir attends to language is presented in a gentle confrontation with a child who is attempting to duck responsibility for her behavior.

> *Daughter:* I didn't *mean* to kick him.
> *Therapist:* Well, let's see now, Patty. It was your leg that somehow landed against his leg. How can a leg do that all by itself? That's very curious. (Satir, 1983, pp. 201–202)

Just as Adler and Dreikurs wanted to make a difference in every session, Satir works with a family until a new possibility is created. There is no guarantee that she or the family will be available tomorrow. Her time with families is therefore flexible and varied. Her use of techniques and tools as leader of the process is also varied. The end in view is always the same: the opening of a new window through which to see ourselves and others differently; an enhancing of self-esteem; a releasing of the ability to live more creatively with other members of the family.

STRATEGIES AND TECHNIQUES

Any description of strategies and techniques must be presented within the context of the therapeutic process. The process is the life of therapy; strategies and techniques are useful only insofar as they facilitate that process. Most of Satir's tools for therapy have been developed as a spontaneous response to the therapeutic or educational needs of a special family or group. No matter how effective the interventions prove to be, they can never be divorced from or be a substitute for the human presence and contact of the therapist.

The use of techniques depends to a great extent on the therapist's intuitive sense about what is needed by a specific family in a given context. That determination may be modified as the process unfolds, but the answers to some basic questions often provide a starting point.

What is going on right now [with this person or family]?
What is present but not manifest?
What needs to be changed?
What would I like to accomplish?
What would be a good way to accomplish the immediate goal I
see right at this moment?
What resources do I have at my disposal in terms of time, people,
and context?
Are individual family members ready for the experience that is
developing in my mind?
Will this experience achieve the expected outcome, or would an-
other one fit better? (Satir & Baldwin, pp. 242-243)

Three of Satir's techniques have already been mentioned: touch, sculpturing, and reframing.

1. *Touch.* Through the use of her hands, Satir gives and receives information. She also provides nurturance, comfort, reassurance, and encouragement.

2. *Sculpture.* The use of sculpture often is paired with stress positions to illustrate family interactions and the ballet of the family system.

3. *Reframing.* A shift in the perceptions of an inappropriate behavior can be accomplished by reframing for constructive consideration, movement, and growth. The therapist gives voice to the positive results the person hoped to achieve. "The therapist decreases threat of blame by

accentuating the idea of puzzlement and the idea of good intentions" (Satir, 1983, p. 142).

In addition to these techniques, Satir often makes use of metaphor, drama, humor, ropes, and encouragement.

4. *Metaphor.* Adler, Dreikurs, and Mosak had a gift for and often used metaphors to communicate a difficult interpretation or meaning, to educate, or to conceptualize a person's life style in an image or "handle" that represented the person's movement (Bitter, 1985). In much the same manner, Satir uses metaphor to convey an idea or feeling, to teach, or to suggest options that are not readily apparent. A metaphor creates some distance between the family and a threatening situation, making it easier to hear the needed information or possible learning (Satir & Baldwin, 1983, p. 245). Satir delivers metaphors with a voice, tone, and rhythm that absolutely engage the listener—a talent similar to that of the late Milton Erickson (Rosen, 1982).

5. *Drama.* Drama puts family metaphors, stories, and situations into action. The therapist asks family members to enact events that are reported so that the situation can be re-experienced and fully examined. The process makes the past come alive, which is frequently useful in helping children understand events that happened before they were born (e.g., their parents' meeting or life in their parents' family). "This allows them to look at the situation with new eyes and enables them to achieve new insights and develop new connections with the people they relate to" (Satir & Baldwin, 1983, p. 246).

6. *Humor.* Satir's use of humor is similar to that suggested by Adlerians such as Walter O'Connell (1969). Satir uses it to add friendliness and relaxation while making contact with people. She uses it to modify the intensity of a difficult situation and thereby reduce the need for defensive reactions. She uses it to clarify by deliberately understating or overstating a perception; and she uses it to nudge, to encourage a little movement or change. She also recognizes and highlights the natural humor that emerges from everyday family interactions. It is this latter humor which serves as a strengthening agent for families, giving them a new way to experience their joint difficulties.

7. *Ropes.* One of Satir's most dramatic interventions involves her use of ropes (Satir & Baldwin, 1983, p. 251). Satir keeps many yards in ready supply. They help her to dramatize connections and communi-

cation patterns as well as family movement and entanglements. In family therapy, each member will be given a piece of rope and asked to tie it around the waist. This rope represents a starting with self. As people interact, the end of each rope is handed to different family members. It does not take long for the tugs and pulls, the restrictions of family movement, to become self-evident. The feelings that are produced in family members tend to replicate those they experience in daily life.

8. *Encouragement.* "Altogether, in every step of the treatment, we must not deviate from the path of encouragement" (Ansbacher & Ansbacher, 1956, p. 342). Adler's therapeutic imperative is woven through every thread of conjoint family therapy: it is a tapestry of encouragement. There is the optimism that people can handle themselves well with each other; a faith in the life-force of the family; the belief that parents can be cooperative leaders of the family and that children can find their proper place and grow to have mastery over their lives. The therapist uses every opportunity to convey "I value you" statements (Satir, 1983, p. 212), encouragement and validation that builds a person's self-esteem.

Two therapeutic experiences are Satir's special creations: family reconstruction and parts parties, which are described in some detail by Satir and Baldwin (1983, pp. 253–263).

9. *Family reconstruction.* Family reconstruction is a psychodrama, a historical reenactment of significant parts in an individual's family life chronology. The experience is designed to make the source of old learnings clear and to add humanness to a person's view of parents and self.

10. *Parts party.* A parts party is a personification drama of characteristics an individual has projected into a party setting. The experience develops into a picture of the inner conflicts that shackle and constrict our best efforts. The goal of the parts party is to transform the conflicting parts into a harmonious balance. This experience constitutes a psychodramatic approach to what Dreikurs and Mosak (1967) called the fourth life task, "getting along with yourself." Among Adlerians, Adeline Starr (1977) has also used psychodrama to address this life task.

SUMMARY AND SYNTHESIS

Throughout this chapter, I have presented Virginia Satir's Human Validation Process Model in relation to the principles and form of Individual Psychology. Similarities in the two therapies abound. Both Adler and Satir created a systemic approach oriented toward growth. Both theories embraced the concepts of holism and social embeddedness. Both theorists saw children start life in a stage of helplessness and delineated the importance of the family on human development. Both theorists posited an open system as a goal as well as a description for functional families. There are also marked and significant differences between the two therapeutic systems—especially in the area of process for change. Using the similarities, however, as a foundation for integration, the differences can be approached as complements that enhance each other.

Perhaps the greatest difference in their conceptualization of the family system lies in the emphasis that Adler and Satir place on the subsystems of the family group. Adler provided detailed descriptions of psychological birth positions, sibling relationships, and childhood interpretations. These descriptions along with Dreikurs' presentation of children's mistaken goals defined the creative life and the impact of children upon the family. Satir pictures children as much more reactive to the subsystem of the parents. She suggests that the relationship and self-esteem level of the marriage partners accounts for the development of family pain and dysfunction—and the creation of Identified Patients in family systems. The combined foci of the two theorists enlarge and enhance our understanding of the human dynamics of the family.

Satir's focus on communication and process makes it possible to define both functional and dysfunctional interactions in family life. The pairing of her stress positions with Kefir's personality priorities allows a full description of defensive postures that block the energy and creativity of individuals in the system. The addition of "congruence-social interest" as a functional approach to stress provides a means for involvement and re-orientation—a new process for growth. In this sense, communication and teleology can share an equal significance in assessment and intervention, motivation and change.

For almost five years I have been developing an integration of Adlerian counseling and Satir's process therapy. I have been greatly influenced by my friends in AVANTA; by the marriage and family therapy of Gerald Mozdzierz (Mozdzierz and Friedman, 1978; Mozdzierz and Lottman, 1973); and the action therapy of Kirsten Sonstegard. Satir's description of the therapist as a leader of the process distinguishes all of these professional influences in my life. It is an understanding of purposefulness, private logic, and life style which introduces a personality profile to the family system, but process makes change possible and allows social interest to develop in the here and now.

An example of this integration in action is a two day workshop which can be held as a special session in many family education centers. The process is especially effective with families of teenagers who want to improve understanding and relationships within the system. The process is experiential and involves both family members and observer-participants from the community.

The first day is devoted to family reconstructions for each of the parents. This process allows the history of the Family Life Chronology to come alive and develops a fuller understanding of the humanness of mom and dad. The day ends with a sharing of what has been learned— especially by each mate about the other and by the children about the parents. In addition, the observer-participants of the community will have learned something about their own lives that will deserve attention. On the second day, each of the teenagers is the focus of a parts party. When the parents are asked to share what they have learned about their children, they will often respond as if they have met them for the first time. A picture of a family with tremendous strengths and resources is developing. A family meeting at the end of the workshop brings that picture to life. By maintaining a focus on only one family issue, the energy of the family is able to generate multiple options and possibilities that fit for each member as well as the whole family.

ANNOTATED REFERENCES

Jackson, Don. D. (Ed.). (1968). *Communication, family and marriage.* Palo Alto: Science and Behavior.
  A composite of the papers and research generated by the Mental Research Institute group in the 1960's, including papers by Satir, Jackson, and Haley, to name a few.

Satir, V. (1972). *Peoplemaking.* Palo Alto: Science and Behavior.
  This is Satir's vision of how people become and grow. It is filled with both information about and exercises in family process.

Satir, V. (1982). The therapist and family therapy: Process model. In A. M. Horne & M. M. Ohlsen (Eds.). *Family counseling and therapy* (pp. 12–42). Itasca, Ill.: F. E. Peacock.
  An overview of Satir's process model with a typescript example. Also included is a biographical sketch which describes her personal learnings in relation to her life experience.

Satir, V. (1983). *Conjoint family therapy* (3rd ed.). Palo Alto: Science and
   Behavior. (Originally published, 1964; 2nd ed., 1967).
   The primary source for Satir's approach to family therapy: the third edition
includes a marvelous chapter on how Satir meets people and another on how
she works with larger systems.

Satir, V. & Baldwin, M. (1983). *Satir: Step by step.* Palo Alto: Science and
   Behavior.
   Satir's latest guide to the Human Validation Process Model. The first part
of the book is a transcript with commentary. The second part of the book,
written by Satir's friend Michele Baldwin, is a thorough presentation of theory.

Satir, V., Bandler, R., & Grinder, J. (1976). *Changing with families.* Palo Alto:
   Science and Behavior.
   A collaboration by the three authors on patterns of communication and the
process of therapy. Bandler and Grinder continued to develop their concepts
under the title of Neuro-Linguistic Programming.

Satir, V., Stachowiak, J., & Taschman, H. A. (1975). *Helping families to change.*
   New York: Jason Aronson.
   Based on materials presented by the three authors at a set of workshops and
seminars, the book contains two chapters by Satir plus an interview with her
and a presentation of a simulated family.

ADDITIONAL REFERENCES

Adler, A. (1929). *Problems of neurosis: A book of case histories.* London: Kegan
   Paul, Trench, Truebner & Co.
Adler, A. (1930). *The education of children.* New York: Greenberg.
Adler, A. (1931). *What life should mean to you.* Boston: Little, Brown, & Co.
Adler, A. (1938). *Social interest: A challenge to mankind.* London: Faber &
   Faber.
Ansbacher, H. L. & Ansbacher, R. R. (Eds.). (1956). *The Individual Psychology
   of Alfred Adler.* New York, Basic Books.
Ansbacher, H. L. & Ansbacher, R. R. (Eds.). (1964). *Superiority and social
   interest: A collection of later writings.* New York: Viking Press.
Bitter, J. (1985). An interview with Harold Mosak. *Individual Psychology,*
   41(3),386-420.
Brown, J. (1977). *Comparison of two methods of identifying personality priorities:
   A research study on the personality priorities.* Clinton, Md.: B. & F. Associates.
Christensen, O. C. and Schramski, T. G. (Eds.). (1983). *Adlerian family coun-
   seling.* Minneapolis, MN: Educational Media Corp.
Dreikurs, R. (1940). The child in the group. *Camping magazine,* December, 7-9.
Dreikurs, R. (1948). *The challenge of parenthood.* New York: Duell, Sloan &
   Pearce.
Dreikurs, R. (1950). *Fundamentals of Adlerian Psychology.* New York: Greenberg.
Dreikurs, R. (1957). *Psychology in the classroom.* New York: Harper & Row.
Dreikurs, R. (1967). *Psychodynamics, psychotherapy, and counseling: Collected
   papers.* Chicago: Alfred Adler Institute.

Dreikurs. R. (1970). The courage to be imperfect. *Articles of supplementary reading for parents.* Chicago: Alfred Adler Institute.

Dreikurs, R. & Mosak, H. H. (1967). The tasks of life II. The fourth life task. *The Individual Psychologist, 4*(2), 51-56.

Dreikurs, R. & Soltz, V. (1964). *Children: The challenge.* New York: Hawthorn.

Furtmuller, C. (1964). Alfred Adler: A biographical essay. In H. L. Ansbacher & R. R. Ansbacher (Eds.). *Superiority and social interest: A collection of later writings* (pp. 309-394). New York: Viking Press.

Griffith, J. & Powers, R. L. (1984). *An Adlerian lexicon: Fifty-nine terms associated with the Individual Psychology of Alfred Adler.* Chicago: AIAS, Ltd.

Kefir, N. (1971). Priorities: A different approach to life style and neurosis. Tel-Aviv, Israel: Paper presented at ICASSI.

Kefir, N. (1981). Impasse/Priority Therapy. In R. J. Corsini (Ed.). *Handbook of innovative psychotherapies* (pp. 401-415). New York: Wiley.

Mosak, H. H. (1984). Adlerian psychotherapy. In R. J. Corsini (Ed.). *Current psychotherapies* (3rd ed.) (pp. 56-107). Itasca, Ill: F. E. Peacock.

Mozdzierz, G. J. & Friedman, K. (1978). The superiority-inferiority spouses syndrome: Diagnostic and therapeutic considerations. *Journal of Individual Psychology, 34*(2), 232-243.

Mozdzierz, G. J. & Lottman, T. J. (1973). Games married couples play. *Journal of Individual Psychology, 29,* 182-194.

O'Connell, W. E. (1969). Humor: The therapeutic impasse. *Voices, 5*(2), 25-27.

Pew, W. (1974). The number one priority. Chicago: Paper presented at the 22nd annual meeting of the North American Society of Adlerian Psychology.

Rosen, S. (Ed.). (1982). *My voice will go with you: The teaching tales of Milton H. Erickson.* New York: W. W. Norton & Co.

Smuts, J. C. (1961). *Holism and evolution.* New York: Viking Press. (Original work published, 1926).

Starr, A. (1977). *Psychodrama: A rehearsal for living.* Chicago: Nelson-Hall.

Terner, J. & Pew, W. L. (1968). *The courage to be imperfect: The life and work of Rudolf Dreikurs.* New York: Hawthorn.

7

The MRI Interactional View and Adlerian Psychology: A Comparison

William H. McKelvie

The MRI Interactional View (IV) is based on a systemic circular epistemology derived from cybernetic theory. IV focuses on the processes of communication within human systems. In a family, stability (homeostasis) is maintained by rules which can be learned by observing how the behavior of the members falls into a pattern. In psychotherapy, the therapist intervenes to disrupt family rules that maintain troublesome behavior. Therapeutic goals are clearly defined and interventions strategically designed to fit each situation.

In 1979, Carol Wilder sent Gregory Bateson a copy of her article "The Palo Alto Group: Difficulties and Directions of the Interactional View for Human Communication Research" for his comments. In a return letter (Wilder-Mott, 1981, p. 37) Bateson wrote that her effort to clarify and assess the work of the Palo Alto Group (Mental Research Institute) was analogous to Hercules' attempt to clean the Augean stables: The more he shoveled, the more the horses produced. In this chapter I am confronted with both Mental Research Institute (MRI) and Adlerian theoretical horses and so it is to be anticipated that the final product will not be totally "clean." However, it is hoped that readers with a systemic background will be stimulated to explore the rich contribution that Individual Psychology (IP) has for marital/family therapists, and likewise that IP therapists will become aware of what the strategic systemic models have to offer them.

William H. McKelvie, Ed.D., is an Associate Professor at the Adler Dreikurs Institute, Bowie State College, a founding member of The Alfred Adler Institute of Washington, D.C., and a psychologist in private practice specializing in marital and family therapy. On sabbatical leave in 1982, he was a Monthly Resident at MRI attending numerous workshops, observing therapy sessions, and interacting with the staff.

Several articles by Individual Psychologists (Adlerians) have explored the possible contributions of the MRI Interactional View (IV) to IP. In developing their Adlerian approach to marriage counseling, Pew and Pew acknowledged borrowing "from communication theory family therapy approaches (especially the Palo Alto group), psychodrama, social work, and probably many other sources of which we are not consciously aware" (1972, p. 192). Kern and Wheeler applied the MRI concept of second-order change to child-rearing practices taught in Adlerian parent study groups and concluded that "the principles of second order change are similar to democratic (Adlerian) techniques as they are applied to such problems as dealing with attention getting, power struggles, and feelings of discouragement" (1977, p. 231). Coeguyt (1979) analyzed the paradoxical strategies employed in Oscar Christensen's Adlerian Family Counseling Center from the perspective of the double-bind hypothesis and suggested that there was a basis for an exciting dialogue between Adlerians and those holding the Interactional View. Similarly, Schramski (1981), in a brief article highlighting the parallels between IP and IV, urged that there be more interaction between the two approaches.

A perusal of contemporary literature on family therapy reveals few references to the extensive work of Adlerians in the field, and based on my conversations with the MRI staff, only Watzlawick was more than superficially familiar with IP and in fact has cited Adler in several of his publications (cf. Watzlawick, 1978, pp. 42f).

In this chapter, the history, theory, and practice of the Interactional View are considered from the Adlerian perspective.* The intention of this effort is to identify and clarify the theoretical harmony or dissonance created by the juxtapositioning of the two views of how marital/family therapy is to be conducted.

HISTORICAL DEVELOPMENT

The Interactional View is the result of the weaving together of the thinking of three men: Gregory Bateson, Donald Jackson, and Milton Erickson. This process of integration began in 1952 in Palo Alto, California and in many respects continues into the present. Perhaps

---

*There has been disagreement as to what title should be attached to the set of constructs evolved at MRI. Among the names given by MRI staff or others are family/interactional psychotherapy (Greenberg, 1977); brief problem-focused therapy (Rohrbaugh & Eron, 1982); brief therapy; focused problem resolution (Weakland, Fisch, Watzlawick, & Bodin, 1974); new communication (Weakland, 1967), and the currently accepted interactional view. Their work has also been discussed under the rubrics of the Palo Alto Group and, of course, the Mental Research Institute (MRI).

in some respects similar to Adler's Vienna, there is in Palo Alto an openness to innovation. Also similar to fin de siècle Vienna, at MRI there are frequent discussions about contemporary philosophical issues and through their introduction of systemic thinking to psychotherapy the MRI staff believe that they are participating in a Copernican shift in the way that problems of human beings can be conceptualized and addressed by therapists.

As Weakland (1982) observed, MRI started before it began. In the late 1940s Gregory Bateson, an anthropologist, attended the Macy Conferences where Norbert Wiener introduced the concepts of cybernetics. Bateson, who was the son of the eminent British biologist William Bateson, was an iconoclast who did not recognize conventional professional boundaries. From this perspective it is not surprising that Bateson became intrigued with applying cybernetic principles to communications theory.

In 1947 John Weakland, an electrical engineer studying anthropology, became associated with Bateson. In 1952 Bateson received funding from the Rockefeller Foundation to study communication patterns and moved to Palo Alto. There Jay Haley, who was working toward an MA in anthropology at Stanford, and William Fry, who had just completed a residency in psychiatry, joined Bateson and Weakland. These men made up the core of what became known as the Palo Alto Group.

Initially the group's interests ranged far and wide. They filmed, or otherwise recorded for later study, communication patterns of animals in the San Francisco Zoo, seals on Seal Island, seeing eye dogs and their trainers, hypnotists and their subjects, and eventually schizophrenics and their families. A grant from NIH for the study of schizophrenics was applied for and received.* In approaching this project, Bateson and his group set aside the conventional wisdom about psychopathology and approached their subjects with the perspective of anthropologists studying a foreign culture.

In 1954 Bateson invited psychiatrist Don Jackson, who had been trained as a Sullivanian, to join the group as a consultant. Two years later Bateson, Jackson, Haley, and Weakland (1956 [cf. Berger, 1978, pp. 5–27]) published the results of their work in an article where they presented their now famous double-bind theory of schizophrenia.

In 1959 Jackson, with private financial backing, started the Mental Research Institute (MRI) with Virginia Satir and Jules Riskin. At MRI

---

* Bateson later felt that this was a disastrous move which sidetracked the efforts of the group and he left the project in 1962 with great antipathy toward the field of psychiatry (Wilder, 1981).

it is emphasized that although Bateson's group and the MRI staff maintained a friendly coexistence (for a while sharing the same offices), the two should be considered autonomous groups (Haley, 1981; Wilder, 1978).

In 1960 Satir received a grant to begin a training program for family therapists, which she directed until 1966. In 1961 Paul Watzlawick was invited to join the MRI staff. A Ph.D. in philosophy and linguistics who is fluent in five languages, Watzlawick had studied at the Jungian Institute in Zurich. At MRI he began working on a recorded anthology of verbal communications, taken from tapes of conjoint family therapy sessions.

In 1967 the Brief Therapy Clinic at MRI was opened under the direction of psychiatrist Richard Fisch. The work of the Brief Therapy Clinic culminated in the influential books *Change: Principles of Problem Formation and Problem Resolution* (Watzlawick, Weakland, & Fisch, 1974) and *The Tactics of Change: Doing Therapy Briefly* (Fisch, Weakland, & Segal, 1982).

Watzlawick has called Bateson the "great theoretical mentor" and Jackson the "great clinician" of the Palo Alto Group (Wilder, 1978). However, the third force that permeates the work at MRI is Milton Erickson. Early in their studies of communication the group became interested in studying the communication patterns in hypnosis. Erickson was both a hypnotist and one of the few therapists at that time who treated schizophrenics. Thus in the early 1950s Haley and Weakland began to make regular journeys to Phoenix, Arizona to study with Erickson. This culminated in three books by Haley (1963, 1967, 1973) that introduced Erickson's work to the larger community of mental health professionals. Currently in the MRI work, the indirect therapeutic techniques of Erickson are very much in evidence. The staff of the Institute has long since changed, but the direction of the work continues.

Historically, advocates of both the Interactional View and Individual Psychology have pictured themselves as innovators who have broken away from "traditional psychotherapy." Both approaches have stressed developing pragmatic theories which focus on observable change as the measure of success. However, at MRI there has been more effort devoted to theoretical development than typically found in Adlerian training centers. At MRI there is the feeling that the Interactional View is still being evolved; Adlerians tend to accept their theory much in the terms originally formulated by Adler, and they focus their creative energies on developing ways of applying the ideas. Both Adlerians and the MRI staff have committed much effort to training and have attempted to express the theories in clear, simple terms that can be easily taught.

Fisch, Weakland, Watzlawick, Segal, Hoebel, and Deardorff (1975) suggested that because of its simplicity the Brief Therapy model of MRI is ideally suited to teach paraprofessionals. However, nothing has been generated from MRI which even approximates the massive commitment of Adlerians to preventive educational programs.

BASIC CONCEPTS

A senior MRI staff member commented: "Who would have ever thought that the *Interactional View* would have anything in common with *Individual Psychology.*" As with many, he had been distracted by the "individual" in the title and was not aware that IP is in every respect a social psychology. In the discussion here, the reader will discover that IP and the IV do have much in common and that although each has its own theoretical language, it will be argued that these approaches are compatible on epistemological, theoretical, and practical levels. At the same time, although from the same theoretical genus, significant differences exist which indicate that IP and the IV are clearly different theoretical species. The implications of these differences for the practitioner are explored.

Stance Toward Theory (The Meta View)

Every psychological theory, either explicitly or implicitly, suggests how it should be viewed in the context of other viewpoints. Stances range on a continuum from "ultimate truth as revealed by God or science" to "this might help us get through the day." At MRI great care is taken to emphasize the incompleteness of the Interactional View. For example, the use of the modest term "view" rather than the more pretentious "theory" reflects this inclination. In seminars senior staff members may preface their comments with "According to our mythology . . ." In other words, the IV is presented as being only one of many ways to view human beings, and "within this [the Interactional] view, theories, and assumptions do not represent 'truth' " (Fisch et al., 1975, p. 3.).

However, at MRI the role of theory in the practice of psychotherapy is considered to be of paramount importance. As Fisch et al. state:

Any theory of psychotherapy is essentially a set of assumptions and therapy without theory means only that the assumptions are not stated. Whether explicit or, even more importantly, implicit, assumptions dictate what we do and do not do with our patients (1975, p. 2).

The MRI view of the role of theory in psychotherapy is remarkably similar to the position stated in IP. For example, in terms of maintaining theoretical humility Adler reminded his colleagues that

> in approximately half of the neurotics, the call on the physician signifies their decision to get better . . . it is this fifty percent of "cures" that enables all schools of psychiatry to continue to live. (Adler in Ansbacher & Ansbacher, 1964, p. 336)

Adler recognized that there were multiple viewpoints in any profession and emphasized the importance of assumptions in guiding what is done. In 1937 he wrote the following:

> Everyone subordinates all experiences and problems to his own conception. This conception is usually a tacit assumption and as such unknown to the person. Yet he lives and dies for the inferences he draws from such a conception. It is amusing and sad at the same time, to see how even scientists—especially philosophers, sociologists and psychologists—are caught in this net. In that it also has its assumptions, its conceptions of life, its style of life, Individual Psychology is no exception. But it differs in that it is well aware of this fact. (Ansbacher & Ansbacher, 1979, p. 24)

Both approaches also discourage what Watzlawick (in Watzlawick & Weakland, 1977) has called utopian thinking. In his essay "The Utopia Syndrome," Watzlawick writes that "with the possible exception of the writings of Alfred Adler, Harry Stack Sullivan and Karen Horney, most schools of psychotherapy . . . have set themselves utopian goals" (1977, p. 305), and he quotes Adler on how neurotics can use utopian thinking to avoid accepting personal responsibility for failure (p. 304).

Paradoxically, in light of the humble positions advocated above, proponents of both approaches perceive themselves as being part of a revolutionary avant garde who have introduced a radically different way of conceptualizing the art and practice of psychotherapy. At MRI it is felt that Bateson and the Palo Alto Group introduced to psychotherapy a new epistemology with their application of systemic thinking to the therapeutic process. Likewise for Adlerians the holistic imminent teleology of IP represents a Copernican shift in the way psychotherapy is practiced. Writers from both schools of thought have filled pages criticizing psychoanalytic thinking, both asserting that "conventional" or "traditional" therapies actually become part of the client's problem. Thus both approaches position themselves as being rebels within the family of psychological theories, with IP practitioners acting in some respects like the oldest sibling who was first to rebel against an oppressive parent and now grumbles because the younger siblings do not fully appreciate the sacrifice and courage required in being the first to challenge the family rules.

Epistemology

Historically, mainstream psychology set out to prove that it, like physics, was a true science. For the most part, the model of what a science should be came from Newtonian physics, which offered a cause-effect epistemology. Freud asserted that he had discovered the "true science" of the mind which allowed the therapist to pursue the cause-effect chain that led a neurosis back to its origins in the patient's early childhood.

Any theory that attempted to set a different epistemological course has been obliged to address the popular psychoanalytic epistemology. In the literature of Individual Psychology and of the Interactional View there are extended references assaulting cause-effect thinking. For example, Watzlawick (1977) illustrates how the Newtonian cause-effect epistemology of psychoanalysis and the cybernetic epistomology of the Interactional View would lead to two very different approaches in a therapy session. Working from a Newtonian model, the therapist logically (according to the guidelines established by this epistemology) would delve into the patient's past to discover the "cause" of the current problem. The epistemological interrogative would be "Why?" Through the guidance of the therapist, the client would be led to see the cause-effect chain and thus would acquire "insight." The insight would lead to the resolution of the problem. There would be no involvement of other individuals in the patient's therapy. As Watzlawick (Watzlawick & Weakland, 1977) summarizes:

> In accordance with *this* theory of the nature of psychiatric disorders he will, quite correctly and consistently, treat the woman's case in monadic, intrapsychic isolation and on the basis of the above-mentioned epistemology of a linear, unidirectional causality. (p. xiv)

Watzlawick then contrasts this with the cybernetic epistemology:

> If, on the other hand, he takes into account the marital interaction as described . . . he will attempt to discover *what* is going on

here and now and not *why* the spouses' respective attitudes evolved in their individual pasts. He will identify their pattern of inter- action as well as their attempted solutions (the more-of-the-same quality of their escalating behaviors) and he will then design the most appropriate and effective therapeutic intervention into the present functioning of this human system. (p. xiv)

A comparison of these comments with discussions of epistemological issues found in the literature of IP shows striking similarities in the two points of view. For example, Adler (in Ansbacher & Ansbacher, 1964) wrote,

Every semblance of causality in the psychological life is due to the tendency of many psychologists to present their dogmas dis- guised in mechanistic or physical similes. At one time they use as a comparison a pump handle moving up and down, at another a magnet with polar termini, at another a sadly harassed animal struggling for the satisfaction of its elementary needs. From such a view, to be sure, little can be seen of the fundamental differences which human psychological life manifests. (p. 92)

As to the historical "Why," Adler observed:

(client) "My mother is the reason for my difficulties in life" (Adler's response) "Relations are to blame only as long as he makes them blame-worthy. He uses experiences in the environment to construct his own life style. If parents are at fault then they can point to the mistakes of their parents and on and on." (p. 340)

More recently, the late Adlerian psychiatrist Rudolf Dreikurs (1966) wrote on the implications of the "new" physics for psychology. First, he observed that quantum theory changed the conception of causality. Cause-effect relationships, in quantum theory, are the result of observing a large number of particles and using statistical probability to predict future behavior of the "average" particle. However, when one particle is observed the ability to predict its behavior deteriorates. Dreikurs asserted that this was true for any organic whole "from quantum to man," and that it is "statistical probability that gives the impression of rigid causality" (p. 60). Further he wrote: "Truth is merely a statistical phenomenon. Absolute truth cannot be perceived since all of our knowl- edge is only approximate. . . . Interpretations of facts can contradict each other and yet both be correct" (pp. 61–62).

Thus the systemic, circular epistemology of the IV and the holistic, imminent teleology of IP follow remarkably similar paths. Both forcibly reject the "old" cause-effect epistemology inherited by psychology from Newtonian physics. Both also reject the utility in psychotherapy of the historical "why," and both claim that therapists will find solutions to the therapeutic puzzle only in the "here and now." Both epistemologies lead the therapist to think in terms of patterns and to search for the unique rules of organization which would best explain current behavior. In this respect both can be considered ideographic approaches. Finally, both question the ability of any psychological theory to predict the future course that an individual or family may take, and thus call into question the value of diagnostic formulations which purport to predict future behavior based on past performance.

A significant difference between the epistemologies of the two theories would be in their focus. The term "individual" in Individual Psychology refers to Adler's assertion that the indivisible monad in psychology was the individual. Thus the theory and practice of IP are always grounded in a holistic understanding of the individual. The construct that Adler used to describe the holistic nature of the individual was the life style. The life style is defined as a "collection of inner convictions which form a permanent master plan or theme, upon which one bases his movement in life toward his self determined goal" (Dreikurs, Pew, Pew, & Stratton, 1971, p. 31). The family is seen as a group of individuals in which each member is attempting to move toward his or her unique, inner-determined goals. As with any group, the family does develop values which set guidelines for members and will develop a distinct character which includes a unique way of perceiving experiences. At this level, the IP therapist would conceptualize the family in terms similar to the therapist with an Interactional View.

At MRI the focus is almost exclusively on the family system, and "mentalistic" thinking about the private world of the individual family members is discouraged. Interventions are designed to disrupt the current maladaptive family interactions. In contrast to IP, the direction of movement of the family or its members is not considered; rather the therapist focuses exclusively on the patterns of interactions between family members in the "here and now." At MRI the therapeutic interrogative is *What,* whereas for the IP therapist it is *For What,* or as Adler phrased it, *Whither* (Adler, quoted in Ansbacher & Ansbacher, 1964, p. 9). Both approaches are systemic but the MRI epistemology focuses on the system at a given moment in time, whereas the IP epistemology focuses on the system in motion.

Insight and Equifinality

Beginning with their focus on the "here and now" and with their antipathy toward the historical "why," MRI theorists assume an uncompromising position against insight as a therapeutic tool. Citing von Bertalanffy's cybernetic concept (1968) of equifinality, MRI theorists argued that "identical final states may be reached from different initial conditions and through different developmental pathways" (Wilder, 1979, p. 173). Thus the current state of a family or individual may be arrived at via innumerable paths. It is felt that the insight-oriented therapist simply will select, from these many possible passages to the present, the one that fits his or her theoretical bias. In reality, it is argued, this "fantasy" about meaning has little to do with understanding the system being observed (cf. Fisch et al., 1975).

An Adlerian would feel comfortable with the concept of equifinality. From the teleological perspective, multiple strategies may be employed to move toward the same goal. For example, one may move toward a goal of superiority by becoming expert, oppressing others, and achieving "true" humility. The list could continue, being limited only by human creativity. Further, an Adlerian would agree that the therapist (and also the client) will select "facts" from the past that fit with his or her current private logic. However, Individual Psychology is a theory which clearly affirms the value of insight in therapy. Indeed, in Dreikurs' formulation of the phases of the Adlerian therapeutic process, the third of the four steps "is designed to give insight to the patient, not by telling what to do or not to do, but by showing him what he is doing in his life, on what principles he operates, by confronting him with his goals" (Terner & Pew, 1978, p. 245). Adler felt that a neurotic "life plan" could "be kept intact only if the patient succeeds in withdrawing it from his own criticism and understanding" (Adler in Ansbacher & Ansbacher, 1964, p. 334).

In MRI language, in IP, insight reveals to the client the rules of the game in which he or she is caught and through this "spitting in the soup" makes the game more difficult to continue. The focus of the insight in IP is to help the client understand the motivation and dynamics of his or her *current* behavior. (E.g., "Could it be that you want to show your wife that you are in charge?" vs. "Your anger toward your wife perhaps is linked to those helpless feelings you used to have with your Mother.") Additionally, IP is a psychology of use and so the possession of insight, as with all other human attributes, has no value in and of itself. Rather, insight acquires value only from the way it is utilized, and since IP focuses on positive change as the measure of success in therapy, insight without change would be considered to be of no value.

The Theory of Logical Types and the Double Bind

The initial Palo Alto Group project was "designed to investigate the nature of human communications, specifically the nature and function of paradoxical communication, as it could be understood deductively through application of the Theory of Logical Types (Wilder, 1979, p. 172). This theory was extrapolated by Bateson from Whitehead and Russell's *Principia Mathematica* (1910). Any behavioral scientist ignorant of the theory of logical types, Bateson asserted, could "claim approximately sixty years of obsolescence" (1972, p. 279).

The theory of logical types focuses on differentiating between classes and members of classes. The following discussion illustrates how this theory can be applied to the study of behavior. Bateson's group observed that the behavior of the monkeys in the San Francisco Zoo was similar when they fought and when they played (e.g., rushing at each other with teeth bared). Somehow, in a split second, the monkeys would seem to discern the intentions of another simian who rushed at them with teeth exposed. According to the theory of types, the differentiation would be made in terms of whether the manifested behavior was a *member* of the *class* of behaviors called *playing* or if it was a *member* of the *class* of behaviors called *fighting*. Obviously, monkeys that were unable to make such differentiations would create, through their inappropriate responses, many problems both for themselves and for the other monkeys.

Similarly, in humans, the Palo Alto Group speculated that schizophrenics failed to develop the ability to accurately differentiate the meaning (class) of communications sent by others and subsequently develop their own idiosyncratic formula for communicating with others. To understand this phenomenon, the group observed the interactions of schizophrenics and their families. The following is a prototype of these interactions. Father comes to visit hospitalized schizophrenic daughter; daughter runs to hug Father; Father reflexively moves away from daughter; daughter confused steps back; Father, with great concern, says, "Now don't be afraid of showing your emotions." Confusion occurs because the daughter erroneously assumes that the Father's actions belong to the class of "let's be intimate," as his entreaty that she share suggests, when in effect the "meta-message" or class of his behavior is "keep your distance." The recipients of such conflicting messages are placed in a "bind" if they do not recognize the mixed messages they are receiving. Unable to respond to the conflicting messages in the example given above, the girl could leave the field and develop her own private scheme for communicating with others. While from the girl's standpoint this could be considered an adaptation to a perceived impossible situation, to others her idiosyncratic approach to communication would be disruptive and probably labeled as pathological.

Based on numerous observations of interactions such as the foregoing, the Palo Alto Group formulated the double-bind theory of schizophrenia (Bateson et al., 1956; cf. Berger, 1978, pp. 5-27).

At MRI there continues to be a fascination with paradoxical communication patterns, such as those exemplified in the double-bind paradigm. They have identified a class of "be spontaneous" paradoxes which given the above conditions could lead to pathological communication states. (E.g., "If you really loved me, I wouldn't have to tell you to bring me flowers.") Such "be spontaneous" demands are impossible to satisfy. If the recipient of the message does not follow the injunction, his or her behavior is taken as a blatant example of purposeful rebellion. If followed, the action will be met with: "You only did it because I told you." Thus there is no way to respond successfully to the request of the sender (cf. Watzlawick et al., 1974, pp. 66-70).

An Adlerian therapist would agree with the premise implicit in the double-bind hypothesis that pathology such as schizophrenia results from the inability of an individual to cope with the demands of a social situation, and that this perceived inadequacy to cope with social "reality" results in the client constructing a private world. In Individual Psychology the symptoms of schizophrenia always have social meaning; this human problem like other human difficulties can be understood only within the context of the individual's social existence. However, from this point on, the viewpoints begin to diverge. As indicated above, Individual Psychology grounds its explanations in the subjective world which is created as the individual moves to meet the challenges of social living. There is no assumption that there are any specific biological or environmental factors that act as a "cause" of schizophrenia.* Rather, ultimately, the pathology is felt to be the result of the individual choosing to reject the demands of social "common sense" and instead to reify his or her private logic. From this viewpoint, psychotic symptoms serve a twofold purpose: first, to excuse the individual from the demands of

---

* It should be noted that such factors are not ruled out as predisposing the individual for mental pathology. However, the Adlerian would observe that there are probably millions of individuals with high levels of the neurotransmitter dopamine or millions who live in families with bizarre communication processes who live "normal" lives.

social living and second, to protect the schizophrenic's private logic, where, unconstrained by common sense, anything is possible (cf. Shulman, 1968).

Galois' Mathematical Group Theory and the Game Without End

Everyone has seen families with problems attempt many extraordinary and often heroic measures to bring about change, and in spite of these generally well-intentioned efforts, the problems remain and often even become worse. Additionally, in the mental health community, there have been many pages written on how to cope with "resistant" clients who, despite the extraordinary and often heroic efforts of well-intentioned therapists, seem to remain the same. In considering this dilemma, the MRI associates focused on the concept of change and concluded that persistence and change inevitably must be considered together. Thus in observing a problem, the first question to be asked is "How does this undesirable situation persist?" and the second, "What is required to change it?" (Watzlawick et al., 1974, pp. 1-2). To explain how problems persist, Galois' mathematic group theory was used as an "exemplificatory" analogy. A French mathematician who lived in the early nineteenth century, Evariste Galois defined a mathematical group as an entity composed of members that are all alike in one common characteristic. Galois proposed that a group has four properties. Each of Galois' mathematical propositions is now stated, followed by an example of how it can be related to phenomena observed in social systems.

1. All members of the group have a common denominator and the outcome of any combination of two or more members is itself a member of the group. Example: "The constitution of an imaginary country provides for unlimited parliamentary debate. The rule can be used to paralyze democratic procedure completely—the opposition party only has to engage in endless speeches to make impossible any decision that is not to its liking. To escape this impasse, a change of the rule is absolutely necessary, but can be made impossible precisely by what is to be changed, i.e., by endless filibuster" (Watzlawick et al., 1974, p. 15). A family is dominated by a tyrannical Father and a family rule (the common denominator) is "whatever you do don't upset Dad!" Any sign of anger by Father creates great anxiety in family members, which is calmed only when he is no longer unhappy. Thus family members may behave in many

different ways, but they will always be aware of Father's reaction
to what they do. Intense group pressure will be brought to bear
on anyone who "upsets" Father and will continue until the
offender changes to please the family patriarch.

2. Members of the group may be combined in varying sequences,
yet the outcome of the combination remains the same. Example:
"When a juvenile delinquent's behavior improves, his parents
may discover delinquent behavior in a child previously regarded
as the 'good one' " (Watzlawick et al., 1974, p. 16). In systemic
thinking this is an example of a homeostatic mechanism whereby
members of a family may change roles, but overall the basic
structure of the family remains the same.

3. Each group will have an identity member which when combined
with any other member number will result in no change. (An
example of this will follow.)

4. Any group member combined with its reciprocal or opposite
will give the identity number. Examples: "light and dark, figure
and ground, good and evil, past and future, and many other
such pairs are merely the two complementary aspects of one
and the same reality or frame of reference, their seemingly
incompatible and mutually exclusive nature notwithstanding"
(Watzlawick et al., 1974, p. 18). "One of the common fallacies
about change is the conclusion that if something is bad, its
opposite must of necessity be good. The woman who divorces
a weak man in order to marry a strong one often discovers to
her dismay that while her second marriage should be the exact
opposite of the first, nothing much has actually changed" (Watzlawick et al., 1974, p. 20). In the above example, the identity
member would be the woman's behavior in intimate relationships, which would require a "weak" mate. In societies the
identity member is tradition, which ensures continuity despite
changes that may go from one extreme to another.

In each of the preceding examples, dramatic internal changes can
occur within a system (group) and still the system remains the same.
At MRI such changes are called *first-order changes*. From this view,
all systems are trapped by the rules that ensure the continuance of the
system. Premises or rules governing a social system are generally un-
comprehended by the participants. In a family the set of rules governing
its members would be accepted as unquestioned "common sense." A
system which runs through many internal (first-order) changes without

changing the basic rules that govern the system is said to be caught in a *game without end*. Such a system "cannot generate from within itself the conditions for its own change; it cannot produce the rules for changing its own rules" (Watzlawick et al., 1974, p. 22).

Change of the rules that govern the system is called *second-order change*. Such changes do occur as an everyday phenomenon. However,

> The occurrence of second-order change is ordinarily viewed as something uncontrollable, even incomprehensible, a quantum jump, a sudden illumination which unpredictably came at the end of long, often frustrating mental and emotional labor, sometimes almost as an act of grace in the theological sense. (Watzlawick et al., 1974, p. 23)

Change in therapy from the MRI position is brought about by disrupting the sequence of first-order changes (the game without end) by which the family has attempted to correct a problem and thus in a sense force the family to violate the rules that have governed their behavior. This violation of the family rules forces the family to generate new rules in order to maintain the integrity of the family system and second-order change occurs.

Wilder comments that group theory "is a more recent formulation than Bateson's (Theory of Logical Types) and less powerful and pervasive as an explanatory metaphor" (1979, p. 177). In any case, familiarity with the language of group theory is important in that it will assist the reader in understanding the "language" spoken at MRI.

In reviewing the Adlerian literature, it is apparent that change is viewed in a way similar with the MRI constructs of first- and second-order change (cf. Kern & Wheeler, 1977). For example, a parent may stop beating a child and begin giving gifts for "good" behavior. In the MRI parlance, an Adlerian would see these two apparently opposite parental responses as still belonging to the class of "autocratic ways of controlling children's behavior," which probably would lead to a "game without end" with the parents attempting various maneuvers to gain control and the child defeating each move. Instead the Adlerian would work to change the family system from an autocratic to a more democratic one where the purpose would be to teach the child how to function cooperatively in the family group. For the Adlerian this shift would be, in the MRI sense, a second-order change.

In comparing the two viewpoints, significant differences do appear concerning how the change process is conceptualized. First, in the Interactional View (IV), there is no room for the "mentalistic" concept of choice. From the systemic perspective of IV, individuals are like actors in a play who may create an illusion of change because they may alter their lines or even occasionally change roles; in reality, however, the plot of the play generally remains the same. From this perspective, the power of the individual to bring about change is minimized, and the influence of the social system in determining behavior is emphasized.

Ironically, in some respects in IV the individual is snatched from the psychoanalytic cauldron of uncontrollable libidinal forces and plopped in the systemic oven of powerful homeostatic social rules. In contrast, in IP there is a belief that change occurs as a result of conscious or unconscious decisions by individuals and that such decisions can make a significant difference in social systems such as the family. A belief in choice leads logically to the issue of responsibility. From the perspective of IP, the individual, via moment-by-moment decisions, creates his or her role in the family or in any other social system. Thus each of us creates, as well as is created by, the social systems to which we belong and we must accept a degree of responsibility for the way these social systems function.

Second, for MRI all axiological questions are carefully avoided. There is no explicit position taken as to what the ideal family should be like and in both therapy sessions and teaching seminars, MRI staff members carefully avoid taking positions on "how things should be." In contrast, in the Adlerian literature there are clear statements about what constitutes mental health (the concept of social interest) and about how the ideal family should function (democratically).

Finally, both approaches are similar in that the therapist controls the session and utilizes strategic interventions to bring about clearly defined changes. However, at MRI the significance of the quality of the therapeutic relationship is minimized with the therapist being pictured as being a skilled technician who brings about change through clever interventions. In contrast, in individual psychology the quality of the therapeutic relationship is held to be of great importance. For IP therapists the therapeutic relationship should serve as a model to clients that the rules governing human interactions can be positive and respectful.

The Calculus of Communication

Pragmatic is a frequently used word at MRI. It is emphasized that the Interactional View arose from a composite of practical clinical considerations. Systems theory was adopted because it appeared to fit with an emerging style of therapy which seemed to differ radically from the way that the MRI staff had been taught to do therapy. All had been trained to do individual therapy which focused on changing intrapsychic dynamics. However, stimulated by their clinical experience and by Bateson, they began to shift to an interactional approach which focused on changing patterns of interpersonal communication. In this shift, it was concluded that "individual personality, character and deviance are shaped by the individual's relations with his fellows . . . and symptoms, defenses, character structure and personality can be seen as terms describing the individual's *typical interactions which occur in response to a particular interpersonal context*" (Jackson, 1977a, p.2). In terms of the theory of logical types, the individual and interactional approaches are two distinct epistemological classes and thus cannot be mixed. Among other factors, this created a problem because almost all of the vocabulary used in psychotherapy—for example, all diagnostic terms—is referenced to the individual. Thus an effort was made to develop a new language that would be consistent with the interactional view, and all "mentalistic" terms of the "old" intrapsychic individual approaches were religiously expunged. From the interactional view, Jackson (1977a) wrote: "No theoretical assumptions about the individual have been or need be invoked, only assumptions on the nature of communication *quo* communication" (p. 10).

The assumptions regarding how communication occurs within a social system are as follows:*

1. Communication always takes place within a context which must be taken into account in order to understand the meaning of messages.

To illustrate this point, we can consider a simple sentence such as "Where did you get that idea?" Said in the context of a classroom this sentence has a different import than if it were uttered in criminal court. According to Bateson, the term context describes the total situation and is used in a way similar to the way Adlerians use holism.

2. In the presence of another, all behavior is communicative. We cannot not communicate.

In another's presence before a word is spoken, an immense amount of information is exchanged (e.g., nonverbal messages such as "he looks angry").

3. Communication is an interpersonal process. Who is the sender

---

* See Watzlawick, Beavin, and Jackson (1967, Chapter 2) for a full discussion of these assumptions.

and who is the receiver is a moot point. Both participate equally in the reciprocal process of communication.

During the process of communicating there is an ongoing series of interactions with each participant acting on and reacting to the flow of information coming from the other. (E.g., "When I said that, he smiled" or "I don't think he's listening to me.")

4. Meaning depends on how the communicational sequence is punctuated. (E.g., is the rat being trained to press a lever after a stimulus, or is the experimenter being trained to deliver food after the rat presses the lever?)

How the flow of information is organized (punctuated) will determine the meaning attributed to it. (E.g., "she smiles and so she must really enjoy what I'm saying" vs. "This is amusing! He is so smug; how could anyone make such a fool out of himself.")

5. Communication is always multilevel. One of the more obvious levels is the report level, which is concerned with factual information, and the other is the command level, which indicates how the information is to be taken.

On one level the sentence in the example in Number 1 above is a simple request for information (the report level); however, by imagining it being spoken in one instance by an angry boss to an erring employee or in another by an admiring student to a teacher one can see that the sentence may carry different messages about how the message is to be taken (e.g., criticism vs. praise). This command level will reflect the relationship between the two communicators.

6. The communication process may be broken into digital and analogic components.

The digital component utilizes logic to organize information according to certain abstract rules. Digital communication is through words used symbolically to convey concepts. The analogic component is nonlogical and is expressed through imagery and figurative language. The digital and analogic processes are similar to the primary and secondary modes of thought proposed by Freud, and also to the currently popular concepts of the dominant and nondominant hemispheric functions of the brain (cf. Watzlawick, 1978, Chapters 6 and 7).

7. Communication may be either symmetrical or complementary.

In the interactional view both symmetrical and complementary relationships can be stable and functional or both can be unstable and pathological. Symmetrical interactions occur between equals where both parties assume that they have the equal right to initiate action, criticize, and so on. Complementary interactions occur when the relationship is not equal and typically there is a one-up and one-down position.

It was hoped that by studying communications, the assumptions just described would be developed into axioms that would form the basis for a "calculus of communication." This calculus would be used to study communication patterns and to identify the patterns that seemed to foment pathological behavior. Likewise there was an effort made to develop diagnostic descriptions which were focused on pathological communication patterns and not on the pathological behavior of an individual.

Originally published in *Pragmatics of Human Communication* (Watzlawick et al., 1967), the ideas formulated above have had an unquestioned impact, not only in the field of psychotherapy, but also in the emerging field of human communication where the MRI Interactional View is cited in most textbooks on the subject (cf. Wilder, 1979). However, the axioms of the new "calculus of human communication" have remained at the metaphorical level and the attempts to develop a diagnostic system grounded in the axioms have met with frustration. The multitude of variables involved in the interactional view of the communication process does not encourage academic research.

There is nothing in the literature of IP that parallels the effort at MRI to study the communication process. However, there appears to be no incongruence between the constructs developed above and the perspective of Individual Psychology.

The Family System

At MRI the family is the therapeutic monad. The major assertion of the Interactional View is that *"the family is a rule-governed system:* That its members behave among themselves in an organized, repetitive manner and that this patterning of behaviors can be abstracted as governing principles of family life"* (Jackson, 1977b, p. 6). In this perspective, the family is a social unit characterized by ongoing long-term relationships which are stabilized by commonly understood rules. The family members are generally unaware of the rules or norms that govern their family. What Jackson called homeostatic mechanisms are developed to ensure that behavior does not deviate too far from the family norms. For example, a family may have a norm that everyone should act happy. Any display of negative emotion would thus activate the homeostatic mechanisms, which might range from a directive to "cheer up" to the development of physical or psychological symptoms. In any case the family would remain in a state of agitation until the norm had been reestablished. The family norms (or rules) can be learned by carefully observing the family and noting how the behavior of the members falls into a pattern. From these patterns, the observer can infer what family rules might be.

In the Interactional View formulation, values are a homeostatic mechanism which may be used as interpersonal strategies by family members to enforce rules. In invoking a value the family member "forms an extra-familial coalition (with religion, society, culture, etc.) [to] exert leverage on relationships within the family" (Jackson, 1977b, p. 15).

For example, a family norm may direct that all members say what they think even if others disagree. However, when the discussions get out of control any member may invoke a shared family value of democratic functioning, and thus establish order.

At MRI, the concept of role is different from that commonly held. First, Jackson (1977b, p. 17) observed that the common use of role is from an individually oriented perspective, and thus deemphasizes the interaction between different members of a group or family. Jackson also observed that the role concept typically is tied to stereotypes created by cultural and theoretical viewpoints. In contrast, at MRI family roles are always an artifact of the ongoing interactions between family members. It is the homeostatic rules governing family interactions that create family roles.

An example of the process of roles emerging from rules in Jackson's concept of material quid pro quo (something for something). First, Jackson (1977a) defines marriage as a "*voluntary, permanent, exclusive, goal-oriented* relationship with many vital mutual tasks to be carried out on a long-term basis and marked by time-bound eras—each with its special problem" (p. 29). The main task of a couple is to work out how they will collaborate in meeting the mutual challenges confronting them. As they move to meet these challenges, according to Jackson, an unspoken contract emerges which outlines, among other things, how arguments will be conducted and how labor will be divided. A significant factor in this process is that each partner develops a level of trust in what he or she can expect from the other.

The view of the family as expressed by Jackson would fit comfortably with the perspective of Individual Psychology. Adler introduced to psychology the idea that a constellation of relationships will be formed in a family in which roles are partially formed by cultural expectations of parental roles and sibling positions and partially formed by how each individual creatively adapts to his or her role (cf. Adler, 1964). Thus just as each individual does, every family will develop a style of life and will move toward psychological goals negotiated through the interactions of its members. The family style of life will include values regarding how members are to act. These values are similar to the family rules described by Jackson. Additionally, each family will develop its own internal private logic which will include perceptions of the world and modus vivendi statements about what members need to do to find a place both in the family and in the outside world. The family private logic would include the quid pro quo mentioned by Jackson.

There are two differences between the views of the family held by Individual Psychology (IP) and those held by the Interactional View (IV). First, from the IP perspective the family is seen as a unit moving through time toward internally determined psychological goals, whereas from the IV perspective the family is a product of the interactions of the moment in which its members are observed. Assumptions about the past and future are avoided rigorously. Second, in Individual Psychology the creativity of the individual in formulating his or her role in the family is recognized and studied, whereas in the interactional view there is a concerted effort to avoid any "mentalistic" concepts having to do with the individual.

ASSESSING THE SYSTEM: THE MEANING OF BEHAVIOR AND GOAL SETTING

In contrast to the theory, which often soars to lofty philosophical/ scientific heights, the practice of therapy at MRI is firmly rooted in the often mundane realm of day-to-day existence. The language used in the sessions and in case conferences is free of therapeutic jargon. For example, in discussions about a case one may hear phrases such as "Who's the customer here?" (Who in the family feels that there is a problem?) As might be expected there is little concern with conventional psychiatric labeling and a focus is kept on the presenting problem. Regardless of whatever other positive changes may occur in therapy, success is always judged according to whether or not the complainant (customer) feels that the presenting problem is no longer a problem.*

For almost twenty years, the Brief Therapy Clinic at MRI has been the vat in which the ingredients of the transactional view have been formed into a distinctive approach to psychotherapy. The emergence of the approach was a slow process solidly based in the group's clinical work. A senior staff member at MRI described this growing awareness in the following terms: "Sometimes a visitor at one of our case conferences would suggest an approach; and we (the staff) would look at

---

*In the marketplace terminology used at MRI "customer satisfaction" may mean that the behavior which resulted in the complainant seeking assistance is still present, but it is no longer considered a problem.

each other and shake our heads—we seemed to know that the idea didn't fit with our style" (Fisch, 1982).

The clinic staff meets two afternoons a week; all donate their time. The first afternoon, therapy sessions are conducted with one therapist conducting the session while the rest of the therapeutic teams observe through a one-way mirror. After each session a half-hour case conference is held to process the session and to plan interventions. The second afternoon meeting is devoted exclusively to discussing cases. The interaction at these meetings is lively with participants freely advancing many ideas. Each discussion ends with the therapist in charge of the case outlining a specific strategy that will be attempted in the next session.

Clients coming to the clinic are not screened. Thus a multiproblem family replete with a veritable garden of pathological behavior may be followed by a family who are concerned because a child is not on the honor role. Therapists are assigned to families on a rotating basis. No effort is made to match a particular therapist with any family. All clients are seen for no more than ten sessions. Intervals between sessions are varied to fit the strategy being applied in the case.

A client desiring to come to the MRI Brief Therapy Clinic first contacts a secretary, who, if space is available, schedules an appointment and collects some general information. Generally, only the complainants (the family members who feel that there is a problem) come to the first session. Only in rare instances is the entire family seen. It is felt that bringing unwilling or combative family members together only complicates the therapeutic task and that much time will be wasted simply managing fights that erupt during the session. Also, from the systemic viewpoint changing one person in a family will lead to a change of the system. Thus paradoxically, "family therapy" sessions at MRI frequently involve only one person.

Upon their arrival at the clinic, clients are taken to the treatment room and introduced to the therapist who has been assigned to their case. The therapist explains to them that sessions are observed through a one-way mirror by the therapeutic team and that occasionally during the session the team will call the therapist by phone, to offer observations and suggestions. The clients are informed that there is a ten-session limit. Finally, they are told that all sessions are videotaped for educational purposes and they are asked to sign a release.

The initial interview at MRI is critical, since it provides the basis for future case planning. The first step in the initial encounter is to clarify and explore the presenting problem, which "in one package" offers what the patient is ready to work on, a concentrated manifestation of whatever is wrong, and a concrete index of any progress made (Weakland et al., 1974, p. 147). The problem is approached from the "man from Mars" standpoint: "What would an intelligent, but naive observer perceive as common and characteristic if he could look in on an adequate sample . . . of actual psychotherapy sessions?" (Fisch et al., 1982, p. 11). It is felt that in all therapeutic situations the following would be apparent:

1. A client expresses concern about some behavior—actions, thoughts, or feelings—of himself or of another person with whom he is significantly involved.
2. This behavior is described as (a) deviant—unusual or inappropriate to the point of abnormality—and (b) distressing or harmful, immediately or potentially, either to the behaver (the patient) or to others.
3. It is reported that efforts have been made by the patient or others to stop or alter this behavior, but they have been unsuccessful.
4. Therefore, either the patient or others concerned are seeking the therapist's help in changing the situation, which they have not been able to change on their own. (Fisch et al., 1982, p. 11)

In the first interview, all present are asked to state what brings them to the session and what their main complaint about the family is. Initially, an effort is made to help clients put their complaints into behavior terms (e.g., "Can you give me an example of what you mean when you say that you and your wife do not communicate?"). Clients are also asked what brings them to treatment "now" and what it is that they wish to change. An effort is made to let each client know that his or her position is heard and understood (e.g., "It seems to me that you feel that Tim taking drugs and your grandfather's alcoholism are related"—the bad seed hypothesis). When interventions are formulated each client's view of the problem is taken into account. During this process the therapist is careful not to reveal what his or her position is regarding the views offered by the clients. The purpose of this strategy is to maintain all possible options for the therapists to ensure maximum maneuverability.

A number of strategies are offered (see Fisch et al., 1982, Chapter 2), which can help the therapist avoid the pressure to assume premature stands. For example, the therapist can "take small steps" (e.g., "Before we go on, I want to make sure that I understand what you mean by . . ."). Also, qualifying language can be used to avoid being forced to take a position (e.g., "There are several possibilities which may explain what is going on . . ."). Finally, there is the classic MRI maneuver of assuming the one-down position. In the MRI lexicon, the one-down position means that the therapist "in his manner and speech, comes on as a modest person whose frailties show or are alluded to" (Fisch et al., 1975, p. 22). To illustrate, with an intellectual client a therapist may comment, "I'm sorry but I have difficulty understanding some of the philosophical ideas you talk about. Could you help me out by putting them in more concrete terms?"

After the complaints of family members have been clarified the next question asked of each is *"How have you been attempting to handle this problem?"* Again clients are encouraged to give their answers in terms of what they *do*. The answer to this inquiry is the key to the rest of the therapeutic process, because at MRI it is felt that the attempted solutions of the clients are what actually maintain problems. For example, a teenager begins talking back to her parents and they respond by demanding that she "show more respect." She not only continues her talking back but becomes even more rebellious. Her parents respond by threatening her with punishment if she continues her behavior, and on and on. Thus a feedback loop is established in which "the original difficulty is met with an attempted 'solution' that intensifies the original difficulty" (Weakland et al., 1974, p. 149). Clients are also asked how they feel about the problem. This helps clarify the family member's position regarding the problem, which can later be used in "selling" the intervention.

During the first interview the clients are also asked, "What minimum change would indicate to you that a step has been taken in solving this problem?" This question encourages the clients to begin "thinking small" and to move away from unrealistic goals. In discussing the case after the session, the therapeutic team reviews the goals stated by the clients and occasionally will modify them. In all cases, the staff makes the final judgment as to the adequacy of the statement of the goals. It is these goals which are used as measures of success/failure in the follow-up of cases.

After the problem has been defined, the behavior which maintains it is identified, and the therapeutic goals set, the clinic team begins to discuss a behavioral intervention that will break the "game without end" that the family is in. The purpose of the intervention is to disrupt the current way that the family is attempting to solve its problems. Typically, the case planning begins during the first session and the team in the observation room may converse with the designated therapist to share thinking about what interventions might be attempted.

In selecting interventions, the team begins by deciding what not to do. It is hoped that this will help avoid the "mine fields" where the therapist ends up doing "more of the same" by approaching the problem in the same way as the family has. Next, a strategic approach to the problem is formulated; this includes specific tactics on how to implement the behavioral interventions. The key to the success of the intervention is always selling the task to the clients.

At the conclusion of each session, clients are generally given a directive or homework assignment which frequently involves their continuing or exaggerating the symptomatic behavior which brought them to therapy.

STRATEGIC INTERVENTIONS

It is in the strategic interventions formulated by the brief therapy staff that the influence of Erickson can be seen. A strategic psychotherapist "acts on the basis of a specific plan, formulated in advance, for resolving the presenting problem as quickly and efficiently as possible" (Rohrbaugh & Eron, 1982, p. 251). Critics of this approach have translated strategic into the pejorative term manipulation. However, strategic therapists point out that all human relationships are manipulative and that strategic therapy is a "loving" manipulation.

At MRI, the purpose of the strategic interventions is always to disrupt the client's current unsuccessful attempts to solve a problem. Convincing a client to do something that runs counter to the way "common sense" has dictated a problem be resolved is generally achieved using the "gentle art of reframing" (see Watzlawick et al., 1974, Chapter 8).* To understand reframing one can refer back to the theory of logical types where any object generally can be seen as belonging to more than one class (e.g., a red ball can belong to the class of all red things, the class of all balls, etc.). Similarly, "facts" about a social difficulty can fit several different explanations. Thus in reframing, the therapist eventually takes the "facts" offered by the client and "reframes" them in a way that leads to the desired therapeutic outcome. Reframing always takes into account the conceptual framework of the client. For example, a rebelling teenager who is failing in school is told that he is doing exactly what a hated principal expects him to do. Each bad grade simply proves to the principal how stupid he (the client) is and the suggestion is offered that "the principal really would be angry if all of a sudden

---

* According to Weakland (1982) the word reframing was coined one day when the Palo Alto group was discussing the Gestalt notion of figure and ground and someone mentioned that besides figure and ground what appeared in a picture was determined by where the frame was placed; thus reframing results in a different picture.

you started getting passing grades." (For numerous examples of reframing, the reader is referred to the annotated bibliography at the end of the chapter.)

The therapeutic intervention made by the brief therapy team will have as its focus a directive assigning the clients some task. Again, the purpose of these directives is to get the client to stop symptom-maintaining behavior. Finding that "compliant" patients who changed at the therapist's request were rare, the MRI staff found that "behavioral instructions . . . are more effective when carefully framed and made indirect, implicit or apparently insignificant. When requesting changes, it is helpful to minimize either the matter or the matter of the request. We suggest a change rather than order it. . . . We may request only actions that will appear minor to the patient, although in our view they represent the first in a series of steps" (Weakland et al., 1974, p. 158).

Many of the directives are paradoxical in nature. For example, a symptom may be prescribed telling the client to make every effort to increase a nervous mannerism. Such paradoxical interventions create confusion. The clients puzzle as to why the therapist is suggesting such an unexpected thing. As Erickson (Erickson & Rossi, 1979, p. 4) demonstrated, when confused, an individual becomes more open to accepting suggestions made by the therapist. Again, such requests are always framed in a way that makes them palatable to the client. The literature from MRI abounds with examples of paradoxical interventions and the reader is again referred to the annotated bibliography.

SUMMARY OF COMPARISONS BETWEEN THE TWO MODELS

Like the Interactional View, Individual Psychology offers a strategic, systemic approach to family therapy. The holistic approach of Individual Psychology teaches the practitioner to identify patterns and can be applied equally effectively to the individual or to a group such as a family. It is a pragmatic therapy which views behavioral change as the ultimate measure of success and rejects cause–effect explanations of human behavior. The majority of the constructs of the Interactional View would fit comfortably within the Adlerian frame. For example, the epistemology of both viewpoints rejects linear cause–effect thinking. Both reject the historical "why?" For different reasons both believe that change can be immediate and dramatic and that many roads can lead to the same destination. Further, Adlerians could learn much by studying the theory of logical types, the double bind, first- and second-order change, and Jackson's family homeostatic mechanisms.

From the perspective of Individual Psychology, there are areas of the Interactional View which would not fit. First, the casting out of the individual from the Interactional View abode would be seen by an Adlerian as an unnecessary action with potentially troubling consequences. It would be unnecessary because in Individual Psychology the life style assessment interview developed by Dreikurs, Shulman, and Mosak (cf. Dreikurs et al., 1971) offers a systematic way, compatible with systemic thinking, of studying the phenomenological world of the individual. Just as many behaviorists found it necessary to "discover" cognition, one can suspect that avid systemic theorists will suddenly discover that their family systems are composed of individuals. It would appear that Watzlawick (1984) in introducing the concept of "constructivism" is in fact moving toward the Adlerian concept of private logic.

In the perception of the individual as simply being an artifact of the "system" the proponents of the Interactional View create an image of human beings as helpless actors in a play that is beyond their comprehension. This guiding fiction (an IP term) has some troublesome implications. For example, it fosters a feeling of helplessness. In Individual Psychology there is the conviction that the individual can change a pathological system, and in fact it is the feeling of helplessness that allows tyrants to exploit others. In Individual Psychology family therapy would include helping each member become aware of his or her role in the family and all members would be encouraged to think in terms of how changing themselves would facilitate greater cooperation. Personal responsibility for the cooperative functioning of the group would be emphasized. Also, demeaning the individual could create a tendency to dehumanize psychotherapy and encourage the "clever therapist syndrome" where facile interventions (or manipulations) become the focus of sessions, and a plethora of "cookbook" interventions are promoted.

It is important to note that all of the senior therapists at MRI have had extensive training in individual psychotherapy, and perhaps this background provides a base for the brief therapy that they now practice. Younger therapists studying systemic therapy without this background might have a tendency to apply the concepts in an inappropriately manipulative manner. To avoid this possibility, it would appear the training in life style assessment would be an excellent way to help those training to be systemic family therapists to a humanistic appreciation of the family system from the eyes of the individual.

When Individual Psychology and the Interactional View are approached as metaphors striking differences appear. The language of the Interactional View is deeply steeped in mathematics (the theory of logical types, Galois' group theory, and a calculus of communication). Perhaps one could ask if the metamessage of such language is one of a cerebral detachment. Also, this language is that of "high-powered" science and perhaps one could question whether this was simply "more of the same" in terms of using scientific jargon to convey a message of importance which may impress, but unfortunately may actually detract from the constructs.

In contrast, the language of Individual Psychology comes from a philosophical tradition and most of the terms used to describe constructs may be found in common use (e.g., goal, compensation, and purpose). The metamessage in the language of Individual Psychology would appear to be one of simplicity and humanism. Unfortunately, this message may be one of the factors that keep Individual Psychology from "selling" better in the theories marketplace—it simply seems so plain and ordinary. Further, in the scientific community the concept of teleology has a negative metamessage. Divine teleology (via Aristotle) was used for centuries to stifle scientific thinking. More recently, the biological sciences struggled against vitalism, which offered teleological explanations for natural processes. However, the reader should be aware that the imminent teleology of Individual Psychology is in a different explanatory class (in the sense of the theory of logical types) than the external teleology of religion and Aristotle. In imminent teleology the goal is constructed or created by the individual, whereas in the external teleologies, the goal is created outside the system. This inability to differentiate between these two classes of teleological approaches has created much confusion and has contributed to the lack of attention to Individual Psychology.

It is in the area of practice that the similarities between IP and IV are most striking. From the beginning Individual Psychology has clearly been a strategic therapy (cf. Adler in Ansbacher & Ansbacher, 1964, pp. 24–25).

Paradoxical interventions have long been part of the Adlerian therapeutic repertoire (cf. Mozdzierz, Macchitelli, & Lisiecki, 1976). Additionally, Adlerians apply "emotional judo" to utilize clients resistance and have a rich literature on the use of homework, metaphors, jokes, and other therapeutic techniques and tactics to bring about change (cf. Mosak & Dreikurs, 1973).

Under the theoretical umbrella of Individual Psychology there is room for many therapeutic styles, and as discussed above, Individual Psychology can be considered to be a strategic systemic approach to psychotherapy. Additionally, it offers a view of the individual which is compatible with systemic thinking and by recognizing the creative ability of the individual to make choices, Individual Psychology offers an optimistic view of the change process. In the perspective of Individual Psychology it is possible for the individual to make a difference in the way any group, including the family, functions. Individual Psychology discourages utopian thinking while not taking away hope for improvement through individual effort. In many respects Individual Psychology could be considered more of an open system than the problem-focused approach of Interactional View. In the Interactional View the system is seen as being regulated by homeostatic mechanisms. By focusing on these mechanisms that maintain the integrity of the system, the movement of the family or person is not emphasized. In contrast, imminent teleology of Individual Psychology assumes that an individual or a family is in continual motion toward goals. Thus in Individual Psychology, movement and change are focal.

The preceding comparison of IP and IV reveals that there is enough similarity to support the contention that both belong to the same general epistemological family. This would mean that communication between advocates of both theories is possible with minor translations. However, there are enough significant differences between the two views that each does maintain a theoretical separateness. Again, I hope that this chapter encourages dialogue that could be enriching to the entire field of family therapy.

ANNOTATED REFERENCES

Fisch, R., Weakland, J., & Segal, L. (1982). *The tactics of change: Doing therapy briefly.* San Francisco: Jossey-Bass.
   The practical companion book to *Change* (described below). In this book the actual practice of the MRI approach to brief therapy is clearly described using many examples from actual sessions. Of the sources listed here, this book will give the reader the best approximation of how the transactional view is applied in therapy.

Haley, J. (1973). *Uncommon therapy: The psychiatric techniques of Milton H. Erickson, M.D.* New York: Norton.
   Possibly the best description of the strategic approach used by Erickson. The book is organized around the life cycle, giving many examples of Erickson's work with clients of all ages.

Watzlawick, P., Weakland, J., & Fisch, R. (1974). *Change: Principles of problem formation and problem resolution.* New York: Norton.
   Probably the most frequently cited book of those written by the MRI Associates. The first two chapters are concerned with theory and require effort to read. The remainder of the book discusses paradoxical interventions and other therapeutic strategies developed at MRI. A must for those who want to understand the transactional view.

Weakland, J., Fisch, R., Watzlawick, P., & Bodin, A. (1974, June). Brief therapy: Focused problem resolution. *Family Process, 13*(2), 141–168.
The best *brief* description of the MRI style of brief therapy.

Wilder, C. (1979). The Palo Alto group: Difficulties and directions of the interactional view for human communication research. *Human Communication Research, 5*(2), 171–186.
An overview of the work of the MRI staff. Presents a brief history and among other topics covers the double-bind hypothesis and first- and second-order change. Attempts to assess the theory and suggest areas where research could be done.

ADDITIONAL REFERENCES

Adler, A. (1964). *Problems of neurosis: A book of case histories* (P. Mairet, Ed.). New York: Harper Torchbooks. (Original work published 1929)
Ansbacher, H., & Ansbacher, R. (Eds.). (1964). *The Individual Psychology of Alfred Adler: A systematic presentation in selections from his writings.* New York: Harper & Row.
Ansbacher, H., & Ansbacher, R. (Eds.). (1979). *Superiority and social interest.* New York: Norton.
Ashby, W. (1956). *An introduction to cybernetics.* London: Chapman and Hall.
Bateson, G. (1972). *Steps to an ecology of mind.* New York: Ballantine.
Bateson, G., Jackson, D., Haley, J., & Weakland, J. (1956). Toward a theory of schizophrenia. *Behavioral Science, 2,* 154–161.
Berger, M. (Ed.) (1978). *Beyond the double bind: Communication and family systems, theories and techniques with schizophrenics.* New York: Brunner/Mazel.
Bertalanffy, L. von (1968). *General systems theory: Foundations, development, applications* (rev. ed.). New York: George Braziller.
Coeguyt, G. (1979). *The double-bind technique in Adlerian family counseling.* Unpublished manuscript.
Dreikurs, R. (1966). The scientific revolution. *Humanist, 26,* 8–13.
Dreikurs, R. (1969). The scientific revolution. In C. Smith, & O. Mink. (Eds.), *Foundations of guidance and counseling: Multidisciplinary readings.* Philadelphia: Lippincott.
Dreikurs, R., Pew, W., Pew, M., & Stratton, V. (1971). *Manual for life style assessment, Part 1.* Minneapolis, MN: Hennepin County Court Services.
Ellenberger, H. (1970). *The discovery of the unconscious: The history and evolution of dynamic psychiatry.* New York: Basic Books.
Erickson, M., & Rossi, E. (1979). *Hypnotherapy: An exploratory casebook.* New York: Irvington Publishers.
Fisch, R. (1982). Personal communication.
Fisch, R., Weakland, J., Watzlawick, P., Segal, L., Hoebel, F., & Deardorff, C. (1975). *Learning brief therapy: An introductory manual.* Palo Alto: Mental Research Institute.
Fisch, R., Weakland, J., & Segal, L. (1982). *The tactics of change: Doing therapy briefly.* San Francisco: Jossey-Bass.
Frankl, V. (1970). Fore-runner of existential psychiatry. *Journal of Individual Psychology, 26*(1), 12.

Greenberg, G. (1977). The family interactional perspective: A study and examination of the work of Don D. Jackson. *Family Process, 16*(4), 385-412.

Haley, J. (1963). *Strategies of psychotherapy.* New York: Grune & Stratton.

Haley, J. (1967). *Advanced techniques of hypnosis and therapy: Selected papers of Milton H. Erickson, M.D.* New York: Grune & Stratton.

Haley, J. (1973). *Strategies of psychotherapy.* New York: Grune & Stratton.

Haley, J. (1973) *Uncommon therapy: The psychiatric techniques of Milton H. Erickson, M.D.* New York: Norton.

Haley, J. (1981). *Reflections on therapy and other essays.* Washington, DC: Family Therapy Institute.

Haley, J. (Ed.) (1979). *Advanced techniques of hypnosis and therapy: Selected papers of Milton H. Erickson, M.D.* New York: Grune & Stratton.

Jackson, D. (1977a) Family rules: Marital quid pro quo. In P. Watzlawick & J. Weakland (Eds.), *The interactional view.* New York: Norton.

Jackson, D. (1977b) The study of the family. In P. Watzlawick & J. Weakland (Eds.), *The interactional view.* New York: Norton.

Kern, R., & Wheeler, M. (1977). Autocratic vs. democratic childrearing practices: An example of second-order change. *Journal of Individual Psychology, 33*(2), 223-232.

Mosak, H., & Dreikurs, R. (1973). Adlerian psychotherapy. In R. Corsini (Ed.), *Current psychotherapy.* Itasca, IL: Peacock.

Mozdzierz, G., Macchitelli, F., & Lisiecki, J. (1976). The paradox in psychotherapy: An Adlerian perspective. *Journal of Individual Psychology, 32*(2), 169-184.

Pew, M., & Pew, W. (1972). Adlerian marriage counseling. *Journal of Individual Psychology, 28*(2), 192-202.

Rohrbaugh, M., & Eron, J. (1982). The strategic systems therapies. In L. Abt & I. Stuart (Eds.), *The newer therapies: A workbook.* New York: Van Nostrand Reinhold.

Schramski, T. (1981). Individual psychology and brief therapy. *Individual Psychologist, 17*(3-4), 15-20.

Shulman, B. (1968). *Essays in schizophrenia.* Baltimore: Williams & Wilkins.

Terner, J., & Pew, W. (1978). *The courage to be imperfect: The life and work of Rudolf Dreikurs.* New York: Hawthorn.

Watzlawick, P. (1976). *How real is real?* New York: Vintage.

Watzlawick, P. (1978). *The language of change: Elements of therapeutic communication.* New York: Basic Books.

Watzlawick, P. (1984). *The invented reality.* New York: Norton.

Watzlawick, P., Beavin, J., & Jackson, D. (1967). *Pragmatics of human communication.* New York: Norton.

Watzlawick, P., & Weakland, J. (1977). *The interactional view.* New York: Norton.

Watzlawick, P., Weakland, J., & Fisch, R. (1974). *Change: Principles of problem formation and problem resolution.* New York: Norton.

Weakland, J. (1967). Communication and behavior: An Introduction. *American Behavioral Science, 10,* 1-4.

Weakland, J. (1981). One thing leads to another. In C. Wilder-Mott & J. Weakland (Eds.), *Rigor and imagination: Essays from the legacy of Gregory Bateson.* New York: Praeger.

Weakland, J. (1982). Personal communication.

Weakland, J., Fisch, R., Watzlawick, P., & Bodin, A. (1974). Brief therapy: Focused problem resolution. *Family Process, 13*(2), 141–168.

Whitehead, A. N., & Russell, B. (1910). *Principia mathematica* (2nd ed.). Cambridge: Cambridge University Press.

Wilder, C. (1978, Autumn). From the interactional view—A conversation with Paul Watzlawick. *Journal of Communication, 28*(4), 35–45.

Wilder, C. (1979). The Palo Alto group: Difficulties and directions of the interactional view for human communication research. *Human Communication Research, 5*(2), 171–186.

Wilder-Mott, C. (1981). Rigor and imagination. In G. Wilder-Mott & J. Weakland (Eds.), *Rigor and imagination: Essays from the legacy of Gregory Bateson.* New York: Praeger.

Wilder-Mott, C., & Weakland, J. (Eds.) (1981). *Rigor and imagination: Essays from the legacy of Gregory Bateson.* New York: Praeger.

8

Strategic Family Therapy and Adlerian Psychology: A Comparison

F. Donald Kelly

DEFINITION, HISTORICAL DEVELOPMENT, AND PERSPECTIVE

Strategic family therapy is a pragmatic, problem-centered approach to family intervention which emphasizes behavior change and problem resolution. It is less an organized theory of family therapy than it is a metaconstruct employed to describe a range of approaches to family intervention. Strategic therapists seem less concerned with family theory per se than with a theory of human behavior change and the mechanisms that account for that change. Despite this theoretical looseness, in their review of family therapy Madanes and Haley (1977) grouped the strategic approaches under the general theoretical umbrella of the communication therapies. A central figure associated with this approach was Gregory Bateson, trained as an anthropologist, who was influenced by concepts from general systems theory, communication theory, and the field of cybernetics. In 1948, Bateson initiated an ambitious communications research project at the Palo Alto, California Veterans Administration Hospital and was joined there by Jay Haley, John Weakland, William Fry, and, eventually, Don Jackson. Out of their work came the double-bind theory of schizophrenia (Bateson, Jackson, Haley, & Weakland, 1956) and a search for therapeutic strategies to deal with schizophrenics in the family milieu. This search led to a collaboration between Haley and Milton Erickson, who was developing innovative approaches to psychotherapy through the use of hypnosis and paradoxical intention

---

F. Donald Kelly, Ph.D., is Associate Professor, College of Education, Florida State University.

(Erickson, 1954). Many of the tactical approaches now employed by strategic family therapists have their origins in his work.

Other influential people and groups who are associated with strategic family therapy include the Mental Research Institute (MRI) group, Gerald Zuk, Lynn Hoffman and Peggy Papp, and Mara Selvini Palazzoli of the New Center for Family Studies in Milan, Italy.

Alfred Adler was a Viennese psychiatrist, a colleague of Freud and Jung, who developed his theory of Individual Psychology in the early 1900s. Adler was one of the first psychological theoreticians to conceptualize human problems in a social systems context. He emphasized the social embeddedness of human experience and believed that individual behavior could be understood only within the social context. "The child has interlocking relations with the mother and family which could never be understood if we confine our analysis to the periphery of the child's physical being in space" (Ansbacher & Ansbacher, 1956, p. 127). Thus Adler and his followers undertook a detailed exploration of the social context within which problem behaviors manifested themselves. He paid particular attention to transactions among siblings as well as interaction between parents and among parents and their children. Adler's emphasis on the family constellation for understanding personality development as well as the current family situation was a landmark contribution which continues to have an impact on modern-day family systems therapists.

Adler recognized the difficulty which parents and families experienced in raising cooperative, responsible, and encouraged children. He believed that the roots of many of the psychological and behavioral problems of children (and adults) could be found in faulty child rearing and disturbed family relationships. To remedy these deficiencies in child rearing and the negative consequences of destructive family relations, Adler established a series of child guidance clinics in Austria. This child guidance clinic philosophy was brought to the United States by Rudolph Dreikurs, one of Adler's principal adherents. This movement stimulated a shift from individual treatment to family treatment, and thus was part of the impetus for modern-day family therapy.

BASIC CONCEPTS

Feedback Mechanisms

Strategic therapists view families as interactive social systems as opposed to collections of discrete individuals. This system is governed by sets of rules and tolerance limits which serve to maintain a homeostatic balance. When an individual family member's behavior breaks

existing rules or exceeds the tolerance limits, then feedback mechanisms
are initiated to restore the homeostatic balance (Fraser, 1982). For
example, a mother, father, and child are sitting at the diningroom table
eating dinner. Mother complains to father about the long hours he is
working and the burden she feels at home. Father responds angrily that
she does not appreciate his efforts. She shoots back with an even
stronger rejoinder. At this point, the child begins to cry, the parents
shift their attention to him, and the argument abates. The child's
behavior (crying) served as the feedback mechanism which operated to
restore the homeostatic balance when the parents' behavior exceeded
the tolerance limits allowed by the system. Following from this example,
it is the strategic therapist's focus on repetitive interactional sequences
between and among people that is the important unit of study. Individual
behavior then is understood only as part of a complex array of behaviors
set within the social system. Behavior is not explained in a traditional
cause and effect linear sense, but is understood as part of a larger,
interlocking pattern that operates in a cyclic fashion.

An example of one of these repetitive interactional sequences is
represented by a marital relationship between a controlling, demanding
husband and a meek, dependent wife. The wife experiences periodic
but severe bouts of depression. When these episodes occur, the husband
becomes more understanding, tolerant, and sensitive to his wife's condition and acts in a more cooperative manner. Gradually the wife's
symptoms of depression subside and the relationship drifts back to its
"normal" or modal state. After a certain period of time, the cycle repeats
itself with a set of rather predictable behavior exhibited by both husband
and wife. In this case the depressive behavior communicates the wife's
plea "Pay attention to me and be nice to me." The husband enters
into an implicit contract to behave in a milder, more cooperative manner
when and if the wife exhibits sufficiently severe depressive symptoms.
The wife fulfills her end of the contract by displaying the symptoms
which will then trigger the husband's role in the interactional cycle.
Thus the depressive behavior of the wife periodically stabilizes the
marital relationship when the tolerance limits are exceeded. However,
she often pays the price of being labeled as the problem person or the
identified patient, when in reality her behavior is just one part of the
total marital or family process. It is significant to note here that the
system is evaluated as dysfunctional when there is a rigid or repetitive
use of one method of problem resolution (in this case depression) to
the exclusion of more constructive alternatives.

Negative feedback loop. With its roots in the theoretical fields of
communication theory and cybernetics, strategic family therapy quite

naturally would focus on the system's processes of negative and positive feedback. A negative feedback loop is one which operates to limit or minimize deviation from the tolerance limits or rules of the system. The previous example of marital depression represents the operation of a negative feedback loop that serves to maintain a (relatively speaking) steady state or balance between the two partners. Her depression prevents his control/domination from becoming too extreme or exceeding the implicit mutually agreed on tolerance limits. His increased cooperation and sensitivity, albeit temporary, prevent her from exceeding the tolerance limits on weakness and dependency. Thus the system is kept in balance through this complementary regulating mechanism. The difficulty in this situation is not the negative feedback loop process itself, but the strategies employed within that process to enforce compliance to the limits set by the system.

Positive feedback loop. Another aspect of system dysfunction which shows itself in a much more dramatic fashion is the positive feedback loop. This mechanism increases deviation from existing tolerance limits even though behavior of systems members may have the overt intention of decreasing it. This typically involves corrective measures which are designed to ameliorate a problem situation actually having the opposite effect of intensifying the original difficulty (Weakland, Fisch, Watzlawick, & Bodin, 1974). An example derived from a parent–child context may help to clarify the vicious positive feedback loop and point the way to its reversal. In a family situation a youngster may be identified as not sufficiently responsible in attending to his household chores and school homework. Thus the father may ask for more initiative and self-direction in these areas. The father's request, typically delivered or heard as a demand, may be met with halfhearted compliance on the part of the child. If even more initiative and responsibility are demanded (feedback), the youngster is put in the bind of offering more compliance or of taking initiative by rejecting the father's demands. Thus the more pressure the father exerts on the child to perform his assigned duties and chores, the more energy the child may exert to "be his own person" and do the opposite. In this situation, the original *solution* becomes an integral part of the problem as it serves to amplify and intensify the original problem behavior. One way for this vicious cycle to be reversed is for father to withdraw his "demand" that the child take initiative in doing chores. Only then does the child have the perceived freedom to take true initiative rather than merely doing father's bidding.

Similarly, in the case of depression mentioned earlier, the wife's intensified depressive symptoms may trigger the husband's anger, resentment, or withdrawal rather than increased cooperation and sensitivity. In response, she may intensify the depression even more and thus receive even greater anger and/or emotional withdrawal from the husband. This vicious positive feedback cycle continues to escalate as one element leads to an intensification of the other.

Adlerian Principles

In comparison to strategic therapy, Alfred Adler's theory is both individual and interpersonal in nature. It emphasizes such important internal states as subjective perceptions, unconscious personal goals, individual life style, inferiority feelings, and a compensatory striving to overcome one's felt inferiority. In terms of these theoretical issues Adlerian therapists and strategic family therapists are a study in contrasts. The latter group regards internal dynamics as relatively unimportant to the task of understanding and treating disturbed behavior and a significant hindrance to the adoption of a systems perspective.

The interpersonal dimension of Adler's theory, however, proposes a number of propositions which seem particularly congenial to the systemic view of the strategic therapist. First, Adler emphasized the social embeddedness of all human experience and believed that individual behavior could be understood only within the existing social context. "Individual psychology regards and examines the individual as socially embedded. We refuse to recognize and examine an isolated human being" (Ansbacher & Ansbacher, 1956, p. 2). Certainly, Adler considered the social history of the individual in the context of relations with parents, siblings, and significant others. But he also considered the current social milieu to have a significant bearing on an individual's presenting problem situation. This assumption leads to the second important interpersonal proposition of Adler's theory. "All important life problems, including certain drive satisfactions, become social problems. All values become social values" (Ansbacher & Ansbacher, 1956, p. 2). He believed that all human difficulties could ultimately be boiled down to problems of human cooperation.

While not using the language of communication theory, Adlerian family therapists recognize the "positive feedback loop" dynamic operating in many parent–child interactions. For example, Dreikurs and Grey (1968) observed the escalating and cyclical fashion of interpersonal power struggles which commonly occur between parents and their children. They observed that the more parents tried to *make* a child do his chores or clean his room, the more resistant and oppositional the child would become. This resistance typically was met with more force exerted by the parent and again with greater resistance from the child. The common result of an escalation in power struggles, according to Adlerians, is an increase in anger, frustration, and potentially punitive, hurtful behavior on the part of both parties in the conflict.

Adlerians see the endpoint of these repetitive, yet progressive inter-personal cycles culminating in frustration and deep discouragement where the child seemingly has given up on self and the world and wants only to retreat from defeat, humiliation, hurt, and rejection. The parents may have a similar reaction, giving up on themselves as good parents.

VIEW OF SYMPTOMS

Haley (1976), as a major proponent of the strategic approach, con-ceptualized symptoms as "a style of behavior adapted to the ongoing behavior of other people in the system" (p. 98). In essence they are acts of communication within the social system. Thus, whether the symptomatic behavior is defined as depression, anxiety, obsessive-com-pulsive disorder, or acting out, it is viewed as an adaptive act of communication. It is believed that symptoms appear when people find themselves stuck in an impossible situation and are trying to break out of it. More constructive approaches to resolve the situation have not worked. The trapped person, almost out of desperation, resorts to symptomatic means. Thus symptoms serve a functional purpose within the interpersonal system of marital and family relationships.

Function of Symptom: Balancing

One of the important functions which symptoms serve, according to strategic therapists (Madanes, 1981), is the balancing of power in family and marital relationships. The sharing and dividing of power (control and responsibility) is an issue over which all couples must struggle through the development of their relationship. In some relationships the issue may be resolved by the husband taking control of all decisions involving money and social contacts, while the wife may take control of all decisions involving child rearing and the management of the home. Sometimes the struggle over power becomes unbalanced with one partner dominating the relationship by assuming the major share of the control and responsibility over most of the significant issues. Under these circumstances, the dominated partner may resort to symptoms as a means of balancing the power. For example, the psychosomatic symptom of migraine headaches may operate to achieve this purpose. A symptomatic wife would already be in a "one-down" position with respect to the distribution and sharing of power. The symptom, however, clarifies and even magnifies this inferior position, thus making the position of the "one-up" partner even more superior. The logical extension, and explicit demand, of this situation is for the controlling and dominating husband to assume responsibility for the weaker spouse's symptoms. The symptomatic partner (wife) encourages this process by requesting help, advice, and comfort from the dominant partner (husband). It is at this stage that the balancing of power takes place. While the wife requests help to relieve the symptoms, she simultaneously resists that help, refuses to be influenced, and tenaciously holds on to the symptoms. As a consequence, the husband is defeated in his effort to help and the wife is successful in her effort to expose his helplessness in this situation. Thus both partners are simultaneously powerful and powerless in their relationship to one another around the symptom.

If the symptomatic behavior is abandoned or if the husband succeeds in helping the symptomatic wife get over her problems, then the shaky balance of power will be altered. This couple will probably return to struggle over the issue and the division of power (control and responsibility) that preceded the appearance of the migraine headaches. If this struggle does not lead to a more equitable division of power than in the past, then it is quite likely that symptomatic behavior will return again. This process is often seen as a repetitive cycle that may remain unchanged over a course of many years.

Symptom as Metaphor

Another perspective on symptoms proposed by Madanes (1981) is that they serve as a metaphor or analogy for a family or marital struggle that people are unable to resolve. For example, a husband and wife may find themselves disagreeing over finances, child rearing, careers, sex, or any number of important relationship issues. Continual battling over these issues without some satisfactory resolution could significantly endanger the future of the relationship. Rather than face the immediate prospect of the dissolution of the relationship, one spouse (typically the one in the less powerful position) may develop a symptom. Then, rather than argue about finances or sex, the couple can shift their struggle to her depression and what should be done about it. This couple's style of interacting on the symptom of depression is a mirror reflection of their style of interaction regarding important relationship issues. Thus they are able to interact and test where they stand with one another without tampering with the sensitive and unresolved topics that may threaten the relationship.

Adlerian Perspective of Symptoms

Adlerians view symptomatic behavior as they do all other behavior. It is goal-directed and purposive in that it serves the individual in his or her striving to achieve subjectively developed goals. More specifically, Adlerians view symptoms as serving to safeguard self-esteem or as an excuse to exempt one from the demands of life. Mosak and Shulman (1967), in their discussion of various purposes of symptoms, classified a variety of common functions which they observed in clinical practice. Several of these functions are (a) securing a triumph over another, (b) providing an exemption from the demands of reality, and (c) forcing the environment into one's service (p. 80).

Adler's notion of neurotic symptoms as the "weapon of the weak" (Ansbacher & Ansbacher, 1956, p. 269) is strikingly similar to the strategic view of symptoms serving to balance power in the relationship. The neurotic, weak person is in a one-down position with respect to the distribution of power, and has given up on any reasonable hope of regaining a share of that power through constructive means. Thus the discouraged individual may resort to the use of neurotic symptoms as weapons to give him or her a tactical advantage in the battle for power in the relationship. For example, depression may serve to intimidate and neutralize an overly critical spouse. In like fashion, impotence may represent a man's rejection of his wife's power to arouse him sexually.

The strategic view of symptoms serving as metaphors for unresolved interpersonal struggles is a perspective quite congenial to the Adlerian position. Madanes (1981) suggested, for example, that "a wife who vomits compulsively may be expressing disgust with her husband" (p. 32). In similar fashion, Mosak and Shulman (1967) representing Adlerian theory suggest that vomiting may communicate the message "I can't swallow that." Adler referred to this use of physical symptoms to accomplish a psychological purpose as "organ dialect" (Adler, 1963). In these situations involving psychosomatic symptoms, he believed that people who could not directly speak their minds, allowed their bodies to do their speaking for them.

FUNCTIONAL VERSUS DYSFUNCTIONAL FAMILIES

The primary focus of strategic therapists has been and continues to be families experiencing severe dysfunction. Perhaps this is understandable in light of the historical emphasis on schizophrenics and their families by such people as Haley, Jackson, and Bateson. Recent analyses of family therapy (Stanton, 1981) suggest that the strategic approach may be more effective than other approaches in dealing with the severely disturbed families of the schizophrenic, the addict, or the personality-disordered patient.

Despite the emphasis on unhealthy, dysfunctional families, strategic therapists do present a perspective on the functional behavior manifested by healthy families (Haley, 1973). In general, they tend to be more actively involved with life and less involved with analyzing their own feelings, motivations, and interpersonal behavior. Healthy families, like healthy individuals, direct the majority of their energy toward a full and productive involvement with life's challenges as opposed to an avoidance of those challenges.

Some of these challenges severely test the capacity of families to cope, adapt, and change. For example, most families must face the developmental hurdles posed by the birth of a child, career or job changes, the child's eventual leaving home, and the retirement of parents. Healthy families will come to grips with these hurdles using basically constructive and adaptive means. These hurdles will be dealt with as opportunities for growth, development, and greater maturity. Unhealthy families, on the other hand, are recognized by their inability to deal with these developmental hurdles. In the face of these pressures their means of coping can often become disorganized, effective problem solving diminishes, various symptoms appear, and scapegoating of family members may emerge (Haley, 1980).

Another aspect of healthy families, according to Haley (1976), is the congruence between family structures and rules and those promoted by the society and culture at large. Most cultures promote parental authority over and responsibility for their children, just as they discourage cross-generational alignments of one parent siding with a child against the other parent. Healthy families reflect this assumption of parental authority and find both parents cooperatively working out joint positions when dealing with the generation of children.

Adlerian therapists, with their emphasis on child guidance and family education as well as therapy, subscribe to a specific and concrete set of values regarding functional and dysfunctional family behavior. The functional family is more likely to have a democratic rather than an autocratic atmosphere. In this context parents recognize and accept their responsibility to guide, direct, and discipline their children. However, they are also aware of the importance of giving children choices, allowing participation in family decisions, and providing freedom and responsibilities commensurate with their age.

The healthy family demonstrates a reliable and consistent order to its functioning. The pattern and routine of daily activities, while not overly rigid, adheres to a relatively predictable schedule. Order is also demonstrated through a clear and explicit communication of general family rules, as well as individual privileges and responsibilities. The healthy family will find its members cooperating with these rules or working to change rules in a way that might better serve the common good.

Adlerian and strategic therapists are alike in promoting cooperation and unity between husband and wife in dealing with child-rearing and family management issues. Similarly, both orientations encourage husband and wife to assume more traditional parental roles in which they will set limits, promote specific values, and provide human discipline when limits are transgressed. The general philosophical positions of Adlerian and strategic therapists are compatible. However, Adlerians have explicated a much more concrete and specific set of parenting strategies which they postulate will contribute to the development of healthy family functioning.

MODEL OF BEHAVIOR CHANGE

Outcomes

Any discussion of change first requires an elaboration of the goals or outcomes of that change process. The primary goal of strategic therapy is to block the sequence of repetitive negative cycles of inter-action between family members and to replace them with "beneficent cycles" (Weakland et al., 1974, p. 150). All presenting problems are conceptualized as involving a negative sequence of interactions between two or more people. This, then, becomes the primary focus of the therapist and provides definition for the direction of change.

A secondary goal of strategic therapy is to help families make the sometimes difficult transition from one stage of family life to the next (Madanes, 1981). One of these stages, the time when children leave home, is a particularly difficult period in the family cycle. It is a time when problems and symptomatic behavior are very likely to appear.

Role of the Presenting Problem

For the strategic therapist, such symptomatic behavior is thought to be an analogy of a relationship problem between two or more family members. However, rather than focusing on the relationship problem directly, strategic therapists initiate the change process by zeroing in on and clarifying the presenting problem. Then they use the presenting problem as a *lever* to stimulate change in family relationship. Thus behavioral sequences are changed not by discussion and promoting insight into one's interpersonal behavior, but rather through directively adjusting people's behavior vis-à-vis the presenting symptom.

In clarifying the strategic approach to change, Madanes & Haley (1977) present the case of a middle-aged accountant who is severely depressed and who has not attended to his business for several years. He constantly worries about his work, wishes to get on top of it, but is prevented by his depression. This symptom of depression and the manner in which this man and his wife deal with it are conceptualized as analogous to the manner in which they deal with relationship problems between them. Thus the symptom is serving as a solution, albeit a poor solution, to their difficulties at relating to one another. The strategic therapist would initiate the change process by focusing on the depression and what they can do about it. The symptom becomes a *lever* for stimulating change in the way husband and wife relate to one another. The therapist might suggest that the wife help the husband and monitor his day-to-day approach to work. At an obvious level, this directive would be designed to help solve the problem of depression. At the more important relationship level, it is intended to change the pattern of interaction between husband and wife by allowing her to adopt a more helpful and appreciative stance toward the husband and his work and make the solution of this problem an arena of shared cooperation rather than antagonistic bickering.

Substituting Positive Interactional Sequences

The principal vehicle of therapeutic change in this case, as in all strategic therapy, is the "interactional processes set off when a therapist intervenes actively and directively in particular ways in a family system" (Haley, 1971, p. 7). The therapist's intervention is designed to substitute positive interactional sequences for the negative ones that already exist. However, all aspects of the negative sequence need not be altered; the change can be confined to those aspects that are most destructive and those that are critical to the overall change process.

First-Order and Second-Order Change

Finally, any discussion of change from the strategic perspective must include Watzlawick et al.'s (1974) distinction between first-order and second-order change. The former involves various changes in the individual behavior of family members within a relatively stable, unchanging family system. While behavior changes, the pattern of family interaction remains approximately the same. A classic example of this first-order change is represented by a family whose 11-year-old son is performing poorly in school. Intervention is initiated and results in improved performance. However, the identified patient's 9-year-old brother starts exhibiting academic or behavior problems during the course of treatment. Although the presenting problem had improved, the family system had not really changed since the younger sibling took over the problem role. Second-order change would have occurred in this family system if the identified patient's school performance had improved and his sibling had continued to demonstrate the presumably constructive behavior that had existed before the initiation of treatment. Thus second-order change requires change in the system itself, as well as change in the problem child's position in the system. Successful therapy involves change at both levels.

Adlerian Model of Change

Adlerian psychology proposes three basic ingredients which are assumed to account for the major proportion of behavior change. These are insight, encouragement, and consequences. Insight is a crucial ingredient because of the purposive and goal-directed nature of all behavior (Mosak & Dreikurs, 1973). All people are striving toward some individually developed and subjectively determined goal such as pleasing, controlling, getting. Yet for most people these goals remain outside the conscious level of awareness. Thus people systematically play out the dominant goal(s) through a variety of behavior, all of which lead in the same direction. Insight helps raise one's consciousness about these goals and purposes. It allows the individual to exercise conscious control over the more extreme or maladaptive aspects of these goals and to channel behavior toward more productive ends.

While insight is important in the Adlerian system, it is neither the only nor the most important mechanism for change. The process of encouragement holds the place of being the most significant ingredient in the behavior change process (Dinkmeyer & Losconcy, 1980). This is the case because its psychological counterpart, discouragement, is believed to be the basis for all disturbed behavior. Discouragement is reflected in three basic attitudes: (1) I am worthless; (2) I don't have a place of significance in my family or social group; and (3) I am not competent or skilled. The process of encouragement is designed to ameliorate these negative attitudes so as to restore people's faith in themselves and the realization of their strength and ability. The therapist promotes encouragement through a nonjudgmental, warm, and accepting response toward all family members. It is also promoted through a variety of additional strategies which include special relationship time between parents and children, family council meeting, appreciating the individual differences among family members, and recognizing individual members' strengths and competencies.

The final ingredient in promoting behavior change, natural and logical consequences, recognizes the reality that behavior is largely controlled by its effects (Dreikurs & Grey, 1968). In many families, individuals (often parents) intervene to prevent another family member from experiencing the negative consequences of various misbehavior. A prime example of this is the "enabler" wife of the alcoholic husband whose overly responsible behavior allows the alcoholic to avoid the negative consequences of his alcoholism. Thus parents are instructed to recognize and take advantage of all naturally occurring opportunities to allow children (and spouse) to experience the consequences of their behavior. For example, if a child chronically forgets his lunch as he leaves for school, mother is instructed not to rescue him by taking the lunch to school for him. This behavior would wind up "enabling" the child's forgetfulness and in the long run his dependency and incompetency.

In summarizing the Adlerian and strategic positions on behavior change, it is safe to say that the two orientations differ dramatically on the role of insight and awareness. The former considers it very important, whereas the latter judges it to be useless at best and counterproductive at worst. Other mechanisms of change derived from the two orientations, for example, consequences (Adlerian) and use of the symptom as a level (strategic), are quite compatible theoretically. Furthermore, many of the Adlerian tactics described by Dreikurs and Grey (1968) and Dinkmeyer and McKay (1973) have a decidedly strategic flavor.

ASSESSING THE SYSTEM

Strategic therapists typically draw a clear distinction between the processes of diagnosis and assessment. The former, which is derived from medical approaches to treatment, involves assigning a label to a symptom or a constellation of symptoms experienced by an individual patient. Thus an individual who is feeling sad, tired, lethargic, and hopeless might be assigned the diagnostic label of depression. According to Haley (1979) the use of diagnostic labels such as depression, schizophrenia, and borderline personality serve to conceptualize the problem as an individual phenomenon separate from the interactional context of significant others. In addition, he believes that these labels often define the problem in a manner which makes it more difficult rather than easier to solve.

Definition

The process of assessment is an ongoing process designed to help the therapist gain a precise operational understanding of the problem. In a way, assessment is a continuous process that never really ceases because the therapist is always deepening and refining his or her understanding of the family and their problems.

Phases of the Assessment Process

Strategic therapists use the clinical interview as their primary method for assessing the meaning of the presenting problem and the social system within which it occurs (Haley, 1976).

1. *Observation during initial contact.* The initial phase of assessment begins when the therapist first meets the family. Important issues such as the mood of the family, parent–child relationships, how the family organizes itself in the therapy room, how parents correct their children, interaction among the adults, and how family members deal with the therapist, must be noticed. Such observations are important because they reveal to the therapist how a particular family deals with itself and with a novel situation (therapy). Presumably, a family's style of interaction will begin to mainfest itself in these early stages of therapy.

2. *What brings the family to therapy?* The next phase of assessment begins when the therapist shifts gears from comfortable social exchanges to the question of what brings the family to therapy. Haley (1979) suggests asking about the problem in a very general and ambiguous way to allow family members maximum freedom of expression. Furthermore, he believes that such a general inquiry allows clients to speak in a more metaphorical way so that a wife who talks about her son's lack of cooperation may also be communicating the same about her husband.

Observing the manner in which family members express themselves allows the therapist to assess the meaning of the problem from their different perspectives. Sometimes people will view a problem in terms of what is wrong with the identified patient, or how the identified patient should change, or even what I (parent) might do to cope with the identified patient. Each of these perspectives has different implications for intervention.

Once the general inquiry has been conducted, the therapist must nail down a concrete, operational statement of the problem. Weeks and L'Abate (1982) suggest a series of specific questions relating to the who, what, when, where, and how often dimensions of the problem. Inquiring about the reactions of other family members, especially parents, to the problem behavior is very important also. Such questions help reveal for the strategic therapist the central issue of repetitive patterns of destructive behavior. To discern these patterns, the therapist must acquire information about the sequence of antecedent events that led up to the problem behavior, the escalating chain of actions (especially interpersonal) which involve the problem behavior itself, and the consequences which follow. In systems language, the antecedents would be "problem-initiating feedback," whereas the consequences would serve as "problem-maintaining feedback" (Weeks & L'Abate, 1982).

3. *Interaction stage.* A third phase of assessment within the initial interview is termed the interaction stage (Haley, 1976). This involves getting family members to talk with one another about the problem and their views of the problem. The therapist might ask two family members to discuss discrepancies which emerged earlier in their individual points of view. In this important phase, the therapist begins to get a picture of how family members interact with one another using the problem as a point of focus. The therapist may also propose that family members "enact" the style they typically use to deal with a problem. For example, the identified patient might be asked to demonstrate temper tantrum behavior and father may be asked to show how he responds to it. Sculpting and family choreography are among the many other enactment techniques that can be employed.

4. *Statement of desired changes.* The concluding phase of assessment within the initial interview requires a statement of desired changes, or the goals for therapy. This focuses the family's attention on the question of "Where are we going?" and provides some relatively objective criteria for establishing what the therapist and family have accomplished when therapy concludes. Haley (1976) emphasizes the importance of operationalizing goals in terms that are objectively measureable. For example, the goal of curing a family member's "depression" is not tenable. On the other hand, targeting certain behavioral manifestations of the presumed depression and changes in other family members' reactions to

the depressed person do provide workable goals which serve as the basic therapeutic contract between therapist and client system.

Adlerian Approach to Assessment

Adlerian family therapists approach the task of assessing the system in ways that are both similar to and different from those of the strategic therapist. With respect to the former, Adlerians eschew the use of heavy diagnostic labeling in favor of developing a descriptive and functionally operational analysis of the problem. This operational analysis is initiated with an interview of all family members because it is presumed that a problem with an individual family member is a function of interpersonal relationships within the family group. It begins with a similar opening question of what brings the family to therapy; behavior is observed through enactments within sessions and in homework tasks.

Another method employed by Adlerians to assess the interactional dynamics of a behavior problem is an interview strategy designed to track a "typical day" in the life of a family (Rosenberg, 1959). The typical day is examined from the moment the first person rises in the morning until the last person retires in the evening. The therapist focuses most specifically on those situations in which family members interact with one another so as to assess the nature and interpersonal dynamics of those interactions. Some of the most revealing family situations involve awakening children for school, mealtime, chore time, play time, homework time, bedtime, and how parents spend their alone time together. The data from this interview strategy not only broaden the contextual information base about the family but, more important, reveal the patterns of interaction that repetitively occur between and among family members.

Finally, Adlerians would assess dynamics of family functioning through an examination of the family constellation. This is accomplished by noting the relative position of siblings to one another and also exploring the psychological position of parents in their families of origin. Data derived from this analysis assist the therapist in understanding the current interactional sequences as well as in developing intervention strategies to alter those sequences.

These three Adlerian approaches to assessment would fit comfortably within the theoretical framework of strategic family therapy since their focus is on uncovering repetitive family themes and current transactional dynamics between and among family members. Other Adlerian assessment techniques, such as early childhood memories (Mosak, 1958) and dreams (Ansbacher & Ansbacher, 1956), would not fit with the strategic perspective of behavior because of their focus on individual personality dynamics.

STRATEGIES AND TECHNIQUES

The therapeutic techniques employed by strategic therapists are decidedly pragmatic, symptom-focused, and behaviorally oriented. All interventions are designed to alter negative sequences of interpersonal behavior between and among family members. Consequently, the focus of therapy is on the present rather than the past and on behavior as opposed to feelings, perceptions, and motivations.

Therapeutic Directives

As a result of this behavioral orientation to change, one of the chief therapeutic methods of the strategic therapist is the use of directives. As the term implies, this strategy involves both direct and indirect requests for the client(s) to engage in a specific set of behaviors either in session or during the time between sessions. Haley (1979) emphasizes the crucial importance of giving therapeutic directives and explicates a three-point rationale for their use. First, they promote behavior change by requiring an experiment with new ways of acting. Second, they provide a vehicle for the intensification of the therapist–client relationship. By giving directives, the therapist becomes involved and thus a more significant figure in the client's life. This increase in significance typically results in an increase in influence. Finally, client response to directives provides valuable and immediate data about motivation, cooperation, resistance, and typical response style to requests for changes. The positive resolution of these issues is crucial for the successful outcome of therapy.

Strategic therapists give straightforward as well as paradoxical directives. The former involves asking the client(s) to behave in a particular manner when the therapist expects the client to comply with the directive. Haley (1976) offers an example of a straightforward directive as follows: "A father who is siding with his son or daughter against the wife may be required to wash the sheets when the daughter wets the bed. The task will tend to disengage daughter and father or cure the bedwetting" (p. 60).

A paradoxical directive involves asking clients to perform a particular task when the therapist expects rebellion and resistance against the directive. This resistance to change may exist when clients are seeking confirmation of their own appraisal that conditions are hopeless and therefore cannot change. Clients also resist directives when the family is experiencing a relatively steady state of homeostatic balance. The directive itself, at least implicitly, asks for change and therefore injects an element of instability into the family system. It is the instability suggested by change that is resisted. Paradoxical directives are designed to bypass this resistance. An example of this strategy provided by Haley (1976) involved an overprotective mother whose actions denied her son the freedom to make decisions or take responsibility for the consequences of his actions. The goal in this situation was to help mother disengage from her son. However, it was anticipated that she would respond to a straightforward request to do less for her son by doing even more. Thus the paradoxical approach was used. The mother was asked to spend the next week hovering over her child. The directive required her to exhibit more extreme hovering and overprotective behavior than she had typically been showing. It was presumed that she would balk at doing more and begin emphasizing how the child should be doing more for himself.

The Go-Between Process

Another strategic technique, developed by Zuk (1971), is the "go-between" process. This tactic involves the therapist assuming a go-between role when he or she observes "tension-producing, malevolent, intimidating patterns of family members toward each other and the therapist" (Zuk, 1971, p. 15). The goal of this technique is to alter the negative, destructive patterns of interaction so that more positive and constructive patterns may develop. The go-between role of the therapist is operationalized through such behaviors as side-taking, mediating, and aligning.

Stanton (1981) describes the process of this go-between strategy as involving four distinct phases. First, the therapist makes an assessment of what is wrong and shares this assessment with the family. Second, this shared assessment is expected to catalyze conflict and be tested or resisted by the family. Next, the therapist chooses a conflictual issue which has polarized the family and moves into a mediator role. Finally, the side-taking aspect of the go-between role emerges as the therapist aligns with one side of the conflict in an attempt to disrupt the homeostatic relationship balance and force new and, it is hoped, more adaptive means of relating. In this side-taking phase of intervention, the therapist may shift alternately between both sides of the conflict, selectively supporting one family member and then another.

Positive Interpretation

Positive interpretation (Soper & L'Abate, 1977) is intended to help people relabel or reframe their perceptions of experience from negative to positive, and thus reduce antagonistic and oppositional forces which inevitably obstruct the therapeutic process. For example, the fighting and arguing behavior of father and son may be relabeled as reflecting concern for and commitment to the relationship rather than efforts to hurt and punish one another. Similarly, the symptomatic behavior of a younger sibling may be reframed as a sacrificial effort to take parental pressure off of an older brother or sister who is struggling with issues of independence and leaving home (Selvini Palazzoli, Boscolo, Cecchin, & Prata, 1978).

Rituals

Family rituals (Selvini Palazzoli, Boscolo, Cecchin, & Prata, 1977) involve prescribing a specific set of behaviors which family members are to act out in certain specified circumstances. The purpose is to alter the rules and the pattern of a negative transaction into which they become frequently locked. For example, a husband and wife may have difficulty putting to rest an issue from the past which they bring out and fight over during times of conflict. This issue from the past becomes the primary focus of conflict while the contemporary issues get lost or ignored. A ritual might involve each partner writing his or her side of the argument on paper and then placing their "sides of the argument" in a fancy box on the mantle in the living room. This treats the old conflict issue as a valuable heirloom from the past. If this issue gets resurrected in any future arguments, the couple is instructed to immediately go into the living room, open the box, and spread their written positions out on the table *before* they can resume the argument. Complying with the ritual requires cooperation with one another and with the therapist toward a comon goal. Compliance with the specifics of the ritual typically results in the disruption of the old pattern of interaction.

Adlerian Intervention Strategies

The techniques of therapy derived from Adlerian theory represent both similarities and contrasts to those employed by strategic therapists. Since some of the fundamental concepts underlying each approach are quite different, it is not surprising that the operational approach to intervention would show significant differences also.

The therapeutic relationship. Since most emotional and behavioral problems are thought to stem from discouragement and a deficiency in social interest, Adlerians emphasize the establishment of a strong, friendly, and cooperative therapeutic relationship as the basis for the correction of this deficiency. Therapist behaviors which promote this positive relationship involve the communication of genuine respect for the client as an equal as well as an empathic understanding for the client's private world of experience. The Adlerian emphasis on the therapeutic relationship is much stronger than that given in strategic therapy. Haley (1979) and Stanton (1981) briefly address such issues as "motivating" family members and "joining" the family system. However, the limited overall treatment of relationship issues seems to reflect a relatively lesser importance of these variables in contributing to change from the perspective of strategic family therapy.

Psychological interpretation. Another aspect of therapy which Adlerians consider crucial to the initiation and maintenance of change is insight gained through psychological interpretation. Interpretive comments are designed to raise clients' consciousness about the purposes and goals which motivate their various behaviors. Emphasis is placed on beliefs, intentions, and the individual's private logic (Dinkmeyer, Pew, & Dinkmeyer, 1979) because these internal states are presumed to control and direct overt behavior. Thus family therapy is partly a reeducative process. But traditionally the clear focus of this learning experience is on self *in relation to others,* and how one's beliefs, convictions, and intentions direct interpersonal behavior. More recently, as in this book, the family is also viewed as a holistic entity.

This emphasis on awareness and insight by way of interpretation marks a significant difference between Adlerians and strategic therapists. The latter use interpretation only to reframe a situation. Furthermore, Haley (1976), Weeks and L'Abate (1982), and Madanes (1981) seem to suggest that interpretation designed to raise one's consciousness about self often promotes resistance to change and an avoidance of growth.

Reorientation. The final phase of therapy in the Adlerian system is referred to as reorientation. This is the time to move from awareness to action. The focus here is on the present, immediate situation and what clients must do to alter this situation. In this phase, Adlerian therapists strike a posture similar to that of strategic therapy. Their emphasis is concrete, specific, and behavioral. For example, concrete directives are typically given to family members regarding such issues as communication (Dinkmeyer & McKay, 1973), child discipline and limit setting (Dreikurs & Grey, 1968), defusing conflict (Nikelly, 1971), and effective problem solving (Corsini & Painter, 1975).

Changing minuses to pluses by reframing and assigning good intention are also typical of both theories. Two additional strategies employed by Adlerians in dealing with more resistant and well-defended clients are paradoxical intention (Adler, 1964) and acting "as if" (Adler, 1963). These techniques have a decidedly strategic flavor. The second is employed to defuse the common client refrain "If only I could do this, or that." The therapist here suggests an experiment for the couple or family to act "as if" a different perceived reality were existing. This maneuver opens the possibility for old patterns of interaction to be broken and more rewarding ones to be established. Therapeutic paradoxes are employed in much the same way and for the same reasons (bypassing resistance) as those used by strategic therapists.

SUMMARY

Through the preceding review it is apparent that the Adlerian and strategic approaches to family therapy have some striking similarities as well as contrasts. These extend from the basic theoretical concepts all the way to methods of assessment and intervention. At a conceptual level, Adlerian psychology is individual as well as interpersonal in nature. Accounting for both dimensions of human experience is considered important to developing a holistic view of clients and the interactional milieus in which they operate. Neither alone is sufficient for a complete understanding of human behavior. However, internal variables (goals, perceptions, beliefs) are considered more important than external variables (family constellation, parent–child hierarchy, sibling rivalry) in the explanation of behavior and the change of that behavior.

Strategic therapy focuses almost solely on externally observed interpersonal transactions occurring among family members. The emphasis is on the family as a rule-governed system and the tolerance limits established to maintain a homeostatic balance in that system. Internal dynamics of systems members are considered to be irrelevant with respect to the goal of systems change. This is perhaps the most fundamental difference between the Adlerian and strategic approaches to family therapy.

When translating this conceptual difference into applied practice, one observes strategic therapists treating the system while Adlerian therapists simultaneously treat the individuals *and* the system. For example, strategic therapists would attempt to alter a repetitive sequence of negative transactions among family members and thus effect a systems change. Adlerians would also attempt to change negative interpersonal transactions. In addition, however, they would try to "educate" individual family members as to the purposes and goals underlying their contribution to the negative transactional process. Thus the importance of insight or awareness as a contributor to change remains a significant point of departure between the two schools of thought.

Both approaches view symptoms as acts of communication, and as misguided efforts to deal with an existing difficulty. In practice, Adlerian therapists focus more on the purposive, goal-directed nature of the symptom as it expresses an intention of the symptomatic family member. It is important to note, however, that Adlerians would also deal with the manner in which that symptomatic behavior is cooperatively and complementarily reinforced by other family members engaged with that behavior. Awareness of one's goal is thought to aid in modifying that goal and the symptomatic behavior it expresses.

The strategic therapist focuses more on the consequences of the symptom as it contributes to an intensification of negative interpersonal sequences of behavior. This focus on consequences leads the strategic therapist into behavioral interventions designed to block the need for the symptom, replace it with a more adaptive response, and thus alter the sequence of interaction. Similarly, the Adlerian therapist would also use natural and logical consequences to interfere with existing dysfunctional patterns.

The general approaches to assessment and treatment offer both contrasts and similarities. Strategic assessment focuses on what transpires between people. Therefore, observation of behavior is the primary assessment tool. Inferences about the meaning of the observed behavior are derived from general systems theory, communication theory, and cybernetics theory. Adlerians balance their assessment between the observation of external behavior and the observation of internal events (purpose, goals, beliefs) revealed by the direction of the interpersonal patterns of behaving. Internal events are also assessed through the use of projective devices (dreams, early recollections). However, the primary methods of assessment in family therapy for both sets of variables come through the use of observation, verbal interview data, role playing, sculpting, and the family constellation.

In conclusion, the Adlerian and strategic approaches to family therapy share many similarities at both the conceptual and practical levels. The language employed to describe these concepts and procedures is quite different. Similarly, the differential emphasis placed on certain concepts versus others in the two approaches is at variance. These differences in language and emphasis might lead one to conclude greater contrasts in the conceptualization and practice of family therapy than, in fact, exist. Despite some very real theoretical differences, it appears that the degree of overlap is such that a case can be made for integration and synthesis between the Adlerian and strategic approaches to family therapy.

REFERENCES

Adler, A. (1963). *The practice and theory of Individual Psychology.* Paterson, NJ: Littlefield, Adams.

Adler, A. (1964). *Problems of neurosis.* New York: Harper and Row.

Ansbacher, H. L. & Ansbacher, R. R. (1956). *The Individual Psychology of Alfred Adler.* New York: Harper & Row.

Bateson, G., Jackson, D., Haley, J., & Weakland, J. (1956). Toward a theory of schizophrenia. *Behavioral Science, 1,* 251-264.

Corsini, R. (1953). The behind-the-back technique in group psychotherapy. *Group Psychotherapy, 6,* 102-109.

Corsini, R. (1966). *Roleplaying in psychotherapy.* Chicago: Aldine.

Corsini, R., & Painter, G. (1975). *The practical parent.* New York: Harper and Row.

Dinkmeyer, D., & McKay, G. (1973). *Raising a responsible child.* New York: Simon & Schuster.

Dinkmeyer, D., & Losconcy, L. (1980). *The encouragement book.* Englewood Cliffs, NJ: Prentice-Hall.

Dinkmeyer, D. C., Pew, W. L., & Dinkmeyer, D. C., Jr. (1979). *Adlerian counseling and psychotherapy.* Monterey, CA: Brooks/Cole.

Dreikurs, R. (1958). *The challenge of parenthood.* New York: Hawthorn.

Dreikurs, R., & Grey, L. (1968). *Logical consequences.* New York: Meredith.

Dreikurs, R., & Soltz, V. (1964). *Children: The challenge.* New York: Hawthorn.

Erickson, M. (1954). Indirect hypnotic therapy of a bedwetting couple. *Journal of Clinical and Experimental Hypnosis, 2,* 171-174.

Fraser, J. S. (1982). Structural and strategic family therapy: A basis for marriage or grounds for divorce? *Journal of Marital and Family Therapy, 8,* 13-22.

Haley, J. (1971). A review of the family therapy field. In J. Haley (Ed.), *Changing families.* New York: Grune & Stratton.

Haley, J. (1973). *Uncommon therapy.* New York: Norton.

Haley, J. (1976). *Problem solving therapy.* San Francisco: Jossey-Bass.

Haley, J. (1979). Ideas that handicap therapy with young people. *International Journal of Family Therapy, 1,* 29-45.

Haley, J. (1980). *Leaving home: The therapy of disturbed young people.* New York: McGraw-Hill.

Kelly, F. D. (1984). Social interest. In R. J. Corsini (Ed.), *Encyclopedia of psychology* (Vol. 3, p. 338). New York: Wiley.

Madanes, C. (1981). *Strategic family therapy.* San Francisco: Jossey-Bass.

Madanes, C., & Haley, J. (1977). Dimensions of family therapy. *Journal of Nervous and Mental Diseases, 165*, 88-98.

Mosak, H. (1958). Early recollections as a projective technique. *Journal of Projective Techniques, 22*(3), 302-311.

Mosak, H., & Dreikurs, R. (1973). Adlerian psychotherapy. In R. J. Corsini (Ed.), *Current psychotherapies* (p. 3583). Itasca, IL: Peacock.

Mosak, H., & Shulman, B. (1967). Various purposes of symptoms. *Journal of Individual Psychology, 23*, 79-87.

Nikelly, A. G. (Ed.) (1971). *Techniques for behavior change.* Springfield, IL: Charles C Thomas.

Rosenberg, B. (1959). The counselor. In R. Dreikurs, R. J. Corsini, R. Lowe, & M. Sonstegard (Eds.), *Adlerian family counseling* (p. 33-40). Eugene: University of Oregon Press.

Selvini Palazzoli, M., Boscolo, L., Cecchin, G., & Prata, G. (1977). Family rituals: A powerful tool in family therapy. *Family Process, 16*, 445-453.

Selvini Palazzoli, M., Boscolo, L., Cecchin, G., & Prata, G. (1978). *Paradox and counterparadox: A new model in the therapy of the family in schizophrenic transaction.* New York: Jason Aronson.

Sonstegard, M. (1964). A rationale for interviewing parents. *School Counselor, 12*, 72.

Sonstegard, M., & Dreikurs, R. (1975). The teleoanalytic group counseling approach. In G. Gazda (Ed.), *Basic approaches to group psychotherapy and group counseling* (pp. 468-510). Springfield, IL: Charles C Thomas.

Soper, P. H., & L'Abate, L. (1977). Paradox as a therapeutic technique: A review. *International Journal of Family Counseling, 5*, 10-21.

Stanton, D. (1981). Strategic approaches to family therapy. In A. S. Gurman & D. P. Kniskern (Eds.), *Handbook of family therapy* (pp. 361-402). New York: Brunner/Mazel.

Watzlawick, P., Weakland, J., & Fisch, R. (1974). *Change: principles of problem formation and problem resolution.* New York: W. W. Norton.

Weakland, J., Fisch, R., Watzlawick, P., & Bodin, A. (1974). Brief therapy: Focused problem resolution. *Family Process, 13*, 141-168.

Weeks, G. R., & L'Abate, L. (1982). *Paradoxical psychotherapy.* New York: Brunner/Mazel.

Zuk, G. H. (1971). *Family therapy: A triadic-based approach.* New York: Behavioral Publications.

9

Structural Therapy and Adlerian Family Therapy: A Comparison

Steve Hirschorn

PURPOSE

The purpose of this chapter is to compare and contrast structural family therapy and Adlerian family therapy. It was noted by Burck (1972) that there is a tendency among followers of a psychotherapy theory, both individual and family, to utilize the practice of "theory seizure." Adherents of a theory zealously attempt to motivate others to accept the "rightness" of their particular frame of reference, claiming other theories are "wrong"! Defraia (1984) wrote a humorous article in which the idea of theory seizure is taken to its ludicrous extreme. His protagonist, although wanting to be accepted into the family of family therapists, has been found guilty of finding value in intrapsychic propaganda. He is labeled a "systems thought criminal . . . a closet individual psychotherapist" (p. 32), whose punishment is to read every issue of *Family Process.*

Sprenkle, Keeney, and Sutton (1982) attempted to identify the relation between theory and clinical practice. The study found that older clinical AAMFT members regarded individual psychodynamic theorists as most influential. Those between the ages of 28 and 46 regarded family theorists as most influential. This study suggests that family therapists are utilizing ideas of individually oriented as well as family theorists. It is my belief that therapy follows theory. However, more than one theory can be followed if, after examination, the basic premises of others are compatible. Structural and Adlerian family therapy are examined in this chapter to assess their possible compatibility.

Steve Hirschorn, Ph.D., is in private practice in Pensacola, Florida.

DEFINITIONS OF PROCESS AND EXPECTATIONS

Structural family therapy is most closely identified with Salvatore Minuchin (1974). While others at various times in its formation and growth contributed heavily, Minuchin has remained structural family therapy's most consistent spokesperson. Its principles and techniques are contained in his writings (1974, 1984) and in his work with colleagues (Minuchin & Fishman, 1981; Minuchin, Rosman, & Baker, 1978). There are also important articles by Aponte and VanDeusen (1981) and Stanton (1981).

Structural family therapy reflects a general systems frame of reference, with the intent being to transform the family system. Minuchin has developed a theory of family therapy that specifically focuses on the family structure. While structural family therapists do not ignore the symptoms or presenting problems of identified patients, it is their belief that whatever is causing the symptoms will cease when the family structure and its interactions are corrected. The continuing and mutually reciprocal interactions between an individual and his context form the basis for the theory (Minuchin, 1974). Structural theory does not totally disregard communications or individual personality, but it emphasizes the family structure: its hierarchy, boundaries, affiliations, and coalitions.

> This emphasis on structural change permeates all aspects of the theory and technique, and it can be considered the primary differentiating factor from other theories. . . . Treatment programs are then designed to restructure the family and thereby change or modify individual member's behavior. (Walsh, 1980, p. 41)

Minuchin (1974) asserts that structural family therapy is built on three principles. The first is that the individual psychic life of the family members is not wholly an internal process. The individual both influences context and is in turn influenced by it in constantly occurring sequences of interactions. The second is that changes in a family structure can contribute to the behavior of the inner psychic processes of the system's members. Finally, the therapist, when interacting with a patient in the patient's family, becomes part of the context (p. 9).

Structural family therapists assess the effectiveness of a family system as it attempts to fulfill its function. Individual family members interact in accordance with the function that is to be fulfilled. Functions are the modes of action by which the system carries out its purpose (Aponte & VanDeusen, 1981, p. 312). The functions, family rules, and organizational structure of the family have a predeterministic quality as "there is in man an innate, genetically transmitted determined mechanism that acts as a structuring force" (Lane, 1970, p. 15; quoted in Aponte & VanDeusen, 1981, p. 311). Accordingly, the structure of an individual family member and the social context is linked and interdependent. To intervene effectively, the structural therapist needs to know and understand the social context in which the behavior occurs, as well as those structural dimensions that indicate more positive functioning. There are five major structural dimensions: subsystems, boundaries, alignments, power, and stress.

Subsystems

Minuchin (1974) emphasizes the interactions of the subsystems, the necessary parts of a family that are utilized to fulfill a particular function. A family's structure and its organizational characteristics originate with the parents. As a new couple, the parents developed mutually satisfying means of meeting each other's needs. In the process, it is probable that disparate values and expectations had to be reconciled. These means of mutual satisfaction became spouse functions and the basis of their interactions with each other. However, the birth of children necessitated changes, new transactions, and additional functions. Discipline, for example, became a necessary parenting function.

As familes grow, subsystems develop. These subsystems are defined not only by membership but also in terms of functioning. Although each individual in the family may belong to several subsystems, composition is usually set by generation, sexual identity, interest, or specific functions. In addition to the marital and parental subsystems, sibling subsystems develop. These latter subsystems can also be divided by sex, age, and interest. Each subsystem has a critical role to play in development. Individuals within each subsystem, as well as the subsystems themselves, must learn methods of cooperation and negotiation. The subsystems help in the development of a child's sense of belonging, individuation, and identity.

Boundaries

Minuchin (1974) states that because each subsystem of a family has functions that make specific demands on its members, rules are needed to dictate how people will be involved in fulfilling that function.

The boundaries of a subsystem are the rules defining who participates and how. . . . The function of boundaries is to protect the differentiation of the system. (Minuchin, 1974, p. 53)

Without clearly defined boundaries, interference would occur and the separateness that subsystems need to fulfill their function would not be present. The lines of authority and responsibility must be clear. Boundaries are necessary as they mandate which family members will participate in a given function, how they will relate to each other, and how they relate to others outside the family.

Families are divided into a continuum of types based on the kind of boundaries maintained. Minuchin (1974) identifies three general types: the very rigid or disengaged, diffuse or enmeshed, and clear. The first two are extremes on a continuum with aspects of each probably being present in all families. Families characterized by extreme disengagement or rigid boundaries are lacking in mutual support, nurturance, sharing, and togetherness. Members feel isolated and seem to be unified only during a crisis. Families at the other end of the continuum are characterized by diffuse or enmeshed boundaries. Prominent among members of such a family are (a) overinvolvement, (b) lack of individuation, separation, and differentiation, and (c) confused and muddled lines of command.

Clear boundaries are considered the most effective. They are indicated by individual family members knowing who is to be involved in an operation and in what manner. For example, effective parenting mandates a separation of sibling and parental subsystems. Each parent supports the other as an executive, thereby increasing the influence of each on the children. Sufficient levels of nurturance, support, and discipline can therefore be obtained.

Alignment

Alignment is the "joining or opposition of one member of a system to another in carrying out an operation" (Aponte & VanDeusen, 1981, p. 313). Structural family therapists assess this organizational dimension to understand the family patterns in fulfilling activities. Haley (1976) presents examples of alignments when discussing coalitions and alliances. The former is "a process of joint action against a third person." The latter occurs "where two people might share a common interest not shared by the third person" (p. 109). Whereas boundaries are concerned with who is participating in a function and in what manner, alignment refers to the agreement or lack of agreement one family member displays to another in the carrying out of an operation.

Power

Power is defined by Aponte as "the relative influence of each family member on the outcome of an activity" (1976, p. 134). The amount of power is relative and specific to the operation and is somewhat dependent on the motivation of the other family members involved to either oppose or cooperate. These dimensions are present in all transactions, and are particularly apparent when discipline is the presenting problem. Among the many scenarios that can lead to a discipline problem is one in which the parents, although appropriately included in the executive boundary, are not in agreement as to what defines misconduct and subsequent consequences. Their lack of consensus leads to the covert and overt joining with the children by one of the parents. Which of the parents will prevail is determined by the power each possesses relative to the issue.

Degree of Stress

Another key concept of structural family therapy is the adaptability of a family to stress. Minuchin (1974) identified the following four major sources of stress: a family member's stressful contact with extrafamiliar forces; the entire family's stressful contact with extrafamiliar forces; stress at transitional points in the family life cycle; and the stress around idiosyncratic problems.

Each source of stress is different, and the effects depend on the family's ability to adapt its structure. Although every family will react differently, each will attempt to preserve the integrity of its structure. Milestones in measuring an individual's and family's movement from pathology to health are the degree of rigidity and willingness to accept outside input while engaged in a stressful situation (Walsh, 1980, p. 50).

Structural family theory and therapy rest on the "understanding of the individual and the family in their social context" (Aponte & VanDeusen, 1981, p. 358). The emphasis is clearly on the family, its interactions, functions, and structure, not the individual and his personal dynamics. A family and its individual members' ability to do well depend on the degree to which the family's structural organization is clear, specific, well defined, flexible, and cohesive.

All of these dimensions are compatible with Adlerian theory. Adlerians, however, add the need to develop respect and democratic methods as essential ingredients in the interactions among the subsystems. Place, function, and goal are major concerns in both theories. Adlerians carefully examine the power dimension in the family as a central issue.

The existence of boundaries between parent and child, with parents as
the family leaders, is emphasized in the Adlerian parent study groups
as well as in therapy. Both theories recognize the importance of observing
the movement among the family members and between the family and
its external context. However, Adlerians emphasize that the individual
members actively create the family system and do not merely react to
it.

HISTORICAL DEVELOPMENT AND PERSPECTIVE

Structural family therapy was developed during the 1960s. The preceding decade, 1952 through 1961, could be termed the founding decade
of family therapy as pioneers were initiating their own styles and
theories. While these pioneers were experimenting with the inclusion
of the entire family in treatment, general systems theory was being
developed by Von Bertallanfy (1968). "This was a general theory of the
organization of parts into wholes . . . a complex of interacting elements"
(p. 55). The family therapies that originated utilized many of the broad
principles of general systems theory but were not based entirely on
these ideas. Gurman and Kniskern (1981), in a review of family therapy,
state:

> The reality of the situation is that there have evolved a number
> of family systems theories, with a wide range of adherences to
> and deviation from the language and logic of general systems
> theory. (p. 507)

Structural family therapy, however, is a family therapy which has a
definite systems perspective. Salvatore Minuchin, an Argentinian psychiatrist, began formulating concepts of structural family therapy during
the later 1950s and 1960s while working at the Wiltwick School for
Boys, a psychiatric facility. Here he worked with Ernest Papanek, who
had been a student of Alfred Adler. He and his staff were working
mainly with a lower socioeconomic population of Blacks and Puerto
Ricans, and although the facility was an institution for boys, treatment
soon began to include families. The distressing social conditions of the
families and the need to swiftly address the survival issues that surfaced
led to a structural orientation to therapy. An approach was necessary
which blended immediate specific action in solving problems within the
social context in which they occurred. In this setting, as in other
settings, Minuchin demonstrated his sense of social purpose. Simon
(1984) states that "Minuchin has persisted in drawing the attention of

the mental health field to the problems of the poor" (p. 22). This may in part be due to his own experiences as a cultural outsider, growing up as a Russian Jew in Argentina and then immigrating to the United States. In 1965 Minuchin became director at the Philadelphia Child Guidance Clinic. His intent was to initiate a project similar to Wiltwick's, again attending to the urban poor.

Jay Haley joined Minuchin, bringing with him a family developmental framework (Haley, 1971; Minuchin, 1974). Although Haley is more closely affiliated with strategic therapy, his contributions to structural family therapy are considerable.

Structural family therapy, which originated with the treatment of poorer families, has since been successfully used with families of all socioeconomic backgrounds. In addition, the structural approach with psychosomatic families has received a very favorable response (Minuchin, Rosman, & Baker, 1978).

Structural family therapy has many similarities with Adlerian family therapy, both in origin and perspective. Structural therapy is a systems approach. Adler, although his ideas predate the formal construction of general systems theory, is noted to be the "psychological theorist who most closely approximates an application of systems concepts to the individual level" (Amerikaner, 1981, p. 33). Categorizing structural family therapy as a family systems approach and Adlerian psychology as an individual systems approach speaks not only to the similarities in perspective but also to their differences. Each theory carries the systemic approach to its extremes within its own parameters.

Both Adlerians and structuralists formulated ideas that ran counter to what then was accepted and prevalent. Minuchin's experiences as an outsider in two different cultures may have initiated his focus on the environmental context within which behavior occurs. Adler's principles—in fact, his decision to be a doctor—were initiated by his own life experiences. Adler's focus on one's subjective perception and overcoming perceived inferiorities was stimulated by his difficulties in overcoming his own initial academic and health difficulties. Adler's experiences fueled his interest in the connection between mental and physical processes, the total personality. The individual was not to be treated in isolation, but with a full understanding of his relationships. In that sense, all life problems became social problems. Adler's concepts, frequently called Individual Psychology, stress the individual's attitude in relation to the world and how he interacts with others.

While there have been some ethical concerns generated by professionals opposed to techniques that change family patterns and structure with less emphasis on insight and choice, a serious splitting of professionals such as occurred with Adler and the Vienna Psychoanalytic Society has not occurred. For the most part, Minuchin's ideas have been widely used, particularly his awareness of effects of cultural, social, and economic issues on the family. Both Minuchin and Adler recognized the importance of the social context in which behavior occurs and emphasized the continuing recurring and reciprocal interactions of the individual and his social systems

Despite the similarities in their general systems approach to therapy, there are differences in their perspectives. Adlerians are more interested in the individual dynamics of family members, their purpose and motivation, how each member perceives his and the family's situation, and how individuals gain their sense of belonging. Special emphasis is placed on the family constellation and the presenting of ideas from within a specific philosophical framework which will lead to an increase in social interest. Personal understanding and insight are more likely to be offered, whereas structural family therapists strive to alter relationships between family units and members without necessarily sharing awareness or discussing purpose. They attempt to alter perceptions by changing the family organization in such a manner that the experiences of all family members change. The target of intervention is the family. While its individual members are not ignored, the primary goal is to change the family's structure. Much less emphasis is placed on the individual's ability to adapt and overcome or to make changes that reflect a greater display of social interest. Much more emphasis is focused on the resistance of families to change, the self-perpetuating nature of transactions, and the behavioral stages of a family.

Structural family therapy has been known as a specific family therapy, with its major area of concern being child-related difficulties and drug and psychosomatic problems. Stanton (1981) has extended its applicability to marital problems, but the primary focus continues to be family therapy.

Adler and his followers use open demonstrations in child guidance clinics, parent study groups, and Adlerian institutes, attempting to expose the general population and professionals to the concepts of Adlerian theory. Adlerians have also devoted a great deal of effort toward prevention, as the philosophy is presented in many forms to all individuals interested in personality development. This is most apparent in the many books that have been prepared for parents and teachers as a philosophy for cooperative living.

Minuchin and his colleagues also demonstrate their techniques, but with professionals concerned with remedying family problems. Thus structuralists refine working within the developmental context. Each enriches the other.

COMPARISON OF BASIC CONCEPTS

Adlerian family therapy is basically a systems approach which emphasizes the family constellation, the individual's psychological/ordinal position in the family, and his subjective perception of his life experiences, all of which affect the construction of his life style. The family is seen as a total system, with each member attempting to establish his place. Needs of individual members are viewed as family group needs, with the behavior of one family member affecting all family members (Croake & Hinkle, 1983). This creates a new identity, the family. Just as the individual is whole, the family is whole, and both are parts of larger wholes. Structural family therapy is a pure family systems approach, emphasizing the totality of the system rather than its individual members. Subsequently, less importance is placed on the individual dynamics or an individual family member's perception of his world. This is the major difference between structural and Adlerian family therapy, and it is present in every aspect of comparison. Despite this difference, similarities exist when each theory's position regarding the relationship between man and his environment, family boundaries, purposiveness of behavior, and social interest are examined. The differences seem to be more of emphasis than of beliefs, which would lead to incompatible theoretical positions.

Relation Between Man and Environment

The primary focus of each theory is on the belief that the individual can be understood only in terms of his relationships, his interactions with his environment and family. Both theories recognize that an individual's psychic life is not entirely an internal process, but a product of his relationship with others. Minuchin (1974, p. 9) states that "the individual influences context and is influenced by it in constantly recurring sequences of interactions." Mosak and Dreikurs (1973, p. 39) note the similarity when they write that "man is born into an environment in which he must engage in reciprocal relations. . . . Man can not be studied in isolation."

While both theories recognize the necessity of studying man in terms of his relationships, the emphasis is different. Adlerians are attempting to understand how the individual family member is gaining his sense of belonging, his significance within his family and environment. Structural family therapists do not address individual dynamics—neither their development nor the basic nature of man. The emphasis is on the relations that exist between the parts of the system. Individual dynamics are developed in accordance with the rules that govern the nature of human relationships. More specifically, Aponte and VanDeusen (1981, p. 311) state that

> the nature of the human being and society are seen as bearing within them certain predetermined dynamics that strongly influence directions and ranges of the rules that govern human relationships.

The family organization and structure subsequently are the devices which are highly significant in helping individual members develop responses that will fulfill the rules that govern behaviors. While structural family therapists do not deny the existence of subjective or idiosyncratic individual beliefs, the medium for understanding is the family. By changing the relationship between a person and the familiar context in which he functions, one changes his subjective experiences (Minuchin, 1974, p. 13). An individual family member's mental status or idiosyncratic beliefs are not directly addressed unless it is in the service of assessing or transforming family structure and social organization. Appropriate family structure will lead to appropriate individual performance. The foremost need is to change or alter the family structure.

The Adlerian view is different. The subjective beliefs of family members need to be understood. While formal life style inventories are not completed on the parents, the Adlerian therapist does attempt to understand their subjective beliefs about parenting and family life. Establishing appropriate structure is conducted through discussion of the individual needs of family members. As individual family members change their motivations and behavior, family structure is transformed.

Despite the difference in emphasis, whether to first alter family structure or individual beliefs, the two theories present an important similarity, the belief that man cannot be studied without understanding the context of his behavior.

Boundaries

Boundaries and subsets are emphasized in each theory. The organization of a system is of utmost importance to the structural therapist as it is the primary determinant of an individual's performance. It is necessary to understand the relations that exist between subsets comprising the system since it is the interaction among these parts that forms the basis for all social expression. The medium through which an individual expresses himself is the system's structure, with the "psychological structure of the individual being viewed as interdependent with the person's social structure" (Aponte & VanDeusen, 1981, p. 311).

The concept of boundaries and subsets is also important in Adlerian family therapy, since appropriate boundaries between the parents and siblings or between siblings within a subunit will increase the chances for the development of a life style which reflects greater degrees of social interest, cooperativeness, and responsibility. The relationships between siblings as well as the individual's subjective interpretation of events are stressed. Appropriate boundaries are not the primary intended outcome of therapy. They are necessary but not sufficient as the change agent. Adlerian philosophy incorporates ideas and beliefs which not only encourage the maintenance of appropriate structure but suggest educative ideas and principles that will increase the likelihood of a more positive life style.

With regard to structure, the most obvious differences between the two theories is the belief in arranging appropriate structure to allow predetermined dynamics to occur, versus the importance given to the individual's creation of a life style based on his subjective perceptions. While this difference is significant, it need not precipitate techniques which are mutually exclusive. The family structure and the type of relations between and within family units that are encouraged by both theories is similar. Additionally, it can be argued that the presentation of Adlerian ideas might be enhanced by initial attempts at reordering structure.

Purposiveness

Purposefulness of behavior is another key concept of both theories. Each theory emphasizes the necessity to assess the purpose of the symptom. However, structural family therapists are more likely to gauge the effect of the symptom on the family's function and its impact on the family's developmental stage. To understand the full scope of the problem and the purpose of the symptom, structural family therapists believe it is necessary to be aware of what family functions are being blocked, primary functions being those activities which encourage the learning of independent, self-reliant behaviors and the management of intimacy. Despite these family functions being consistent with Adlerian philosophy, Adlerians are more likely to assess the purpose of a symptom in terms of its affect upon others in relation to an individual family member, they do not explicitly utilize the concept of developmental stages within a family. The heavy emphasis upon explaining the four goals of misconduct in preadolescents (domination, attention, revenge, and helplessness) is evidence of the Adlerian practice of pinpointing the purpose of the symptomatic behavior in individuals. It is rarely tied to a developmental crisis or stage or viewed as a manifestation of a marital problem. Emphasis is on understanding the purpose of a symptom for an individual as it has developed within his family. However, the incorporation of objective individual stages within the Adlerian framework can be utilized if it is seen not as a cause and effect relationship but as an individual's or family's subjective reaction to a transition or crisis.

For example, the teen years are common sources of stress in a family. It is a transition period for both the adolescent and parents, particularly if the teen is the last child in the family. Structuralists would view this situation as a developmental issue for the family as they will soon be composed of one subunit, the marital couple. If mother has been the primary caretaker of the children, she may have to find other interests, and the marital union may be stressed. Appropriate individuation of the teen needs to be encouraged. The purpose of the family stress may be to deflect marital conflict or mother's hesitancy to begin pursuing less family-oriented activities. It might be seen as mother's need to find new paths for personal significance. Adlerians might assess the situation as a power struggle but would be less likely to tie the behavior to a developmental stage.

Social Interests

The concept of social interest is included in each theory. Adlerians are divided as to the orgin of social interest. Is it innate and needing to be nurtured, or is it entirely developed and encouraged within the family? However, Adlerians do agree that an individual's display of interest, his willingness to cooperate, is an indicator of positive mental health. Increased social interest is a goal of family therapy. Structural family therapists do not directly address the Adlerian concept of social interest. However, Minuchin refers to an individual's necessity to display a community mindedness when he discusses man's relationship with the environment, the need for individuals to work together for survival in a world where resources are limited and dwindling. The encouraging of community mindedness is more apparent when he quotes Ortega and Gasset, "I am myself plus my circumstances, and if I do not save it, I can not save myself" (Minuchin, 1974, p. 5). While the author is reflecting on man's relationship with his environment, he is also pointing out the necessity for an individual to improve his environment and circumstances. The latter is a key ingredient in the Adlerian concept of social interest.

CONCEPTUALIZATION OF WELL-FUNCTIONING AND DYSFUNCTIONAL FAMILIES

There are many similarities between the two therapies when well-functioning and dysfunctional families are described. What is different, however, is the manner of observation. Adlerians emphasize subjective perceptions and group dynamics, whereas structuralists are more concerned with the family's relational patterns. Aponte and VanDeusen (1981) state that

> functional and dysfunctional levels are determined by the adequacy of the fit of the system's structural organization to requirements of an operation in a set of circumstances. (p. 313)

They elaborate by defining a family's structural organization as its pattern of relationships, that which is common to each family, and that which makes each family unique such as its special values, circumstances, traditions, and idiosyncrasies. The circumstances refer to the specific context in which the family or family members will attempt to fulfill a function by utilizing the structure. Functions are the actions by which the purposes of a system are accomplished. In discussing function, structural family therapists are concerned with family purposes or family developmental stages. For the structural family therapist, the degree of a family's effectiveness is determined by the symptoms and difficulties encountered by the family as it meets developmental needs of individuals and fulfills family functions. Structural family therapists describe better functioning families as being flexible, able to transform and adapt themselves to the continually occurring changes that result from internal and external stresses.

Dysfunctional families are more likely to adhere to structures and patterns which no longer meet the needs of individual members of the family as a whole, and do not display the ability to develop transactional patterns without disrupting family continuity. Better functioning families have clear, but not rigid, boundaries between each of the subunits, with an appropriate hierarchy. Structural family therapists, in conceptualizing a well-functioning family or dysfunctional family, emphasize the family's structure, subsystem pattern of interacting, and the meeting of the needs of all family members. Attempts to understand a family's dysfunctional pattern are made by assessing the structural components of boundaries, alignments, and power. This is based on the belief that dysfunction is more likely to occur when one structure dominates, thereby decreasing the family's ability to adapt to an individual's or family's developmental need (Aponte & VanDeusen, 1981, pp. 313–314.).

The concepts of enmeshment and disengagement (Minuchin, 1974) are utilized by structural family therapists in their attempt to assess the degree of differentiation, permeability, and rigidity between and among individual and family subunits, and the family and its environment. These transaction styles, enmeshment and disengagement, are on opposite ends of the structural boundary continuum. While all families have such components, according to function and developmental level, operating at either extreme of the continuum indicates possible difficulties.

Enmeshment

The enmeshed family has diffuse and blurred boundaries with family members being overly concerned with each other. Frequently a problem in one member is overreacted to by other family members. Differences are often equated with being wrong, and individual autonomy is sharply curtailed. Family loyalty and protection take priority over autonomy and mastery of skills. Age-appropriate privacy, individuation, and responsibility are negated by intrusiveness and hypervigilance. Dependency is fostered under the cloak of excessive concern. Shame and guilt often occur when the child does not meet parental expectations and somatic complaints are frequent as appropriate problem-solving skills are not learned. The children become extremely hesitant and demonstrate little initiative for fear of receiving criticism. The child acts as the family expects and often holds himself responsible for any family difficulties.

While boundaries between family members are very permeable, the boundaries with the community may be very rigid. If there is extended interaction with the community, new and different ideas can provide the impetus for disagreements since there are no ways to express the differentness without being blamed. Frequently the family member who expresses a desire for change is accused of not caring for the other family members. Many times the purpose of misconduct is to create more distance.

Adlerians also recognize the dysfunction of the enmeshed family, addressing many of the concerns through the teaching of parenting skills which lead to structural changes. Frequently the idea of the "good" versus the "responsible" parent is used to illustrate the point. The former is usually a parent who fosters dependency by doing for her children what they can do for themselves, negating her children's mastery of skills. The responsible parent encourages self-sufficiency and attempts to work out of his parenting role at the earliest possible opportunity. The responsible parent precipitates an outcome favored by structuralists, the individuation of family members.

Disengagement

At the other end of the continuum are families characterized by overly rigid boundaries. These family members remain disengaged, having little to do with each other unless there is a severe crisis. The disengaged family system is much more likely to tolerate a wide range of individual behaviors and differences. Members of these families may experience less nurturance than desired and family responses to a member's serious need for aid are not answered. Many times the purpose for misconduct is more closeness.

Boundaries

The structural concept of boundaries refers to a transactional style of a family, with the possibility that there may be different combinations. The Adlerian concepts of equality, mutual respect, and democratic problem solving enhance the development of independent, responsible families with boundaries similar to those desired by structuralists. The Adlerian concept of equality specifically states that while all family members are equal by virtue of being human beings, there is a differentiation by knowledge, role, and purpose (Dreikurs & Soltz, 1964). Adlerians consider the parents to be the leaders of the family. Structuralists similarly define the parents as responsible for the executive functions of the family.

Alignments

The structural component of alignments is described in terms of stable and detouring coalitions and triangulations (Minuchin, Rosman, & Baker, 1978). According to Aponte and VanDeusen,

> a stable coalition is the joining together of family members against another so that the pattern becomes a dominant, inflexible characteristic of their relationship. . . .
> The detouring coalition is a form of stable coalition distinguished by its intent to diffuse the stess between the members of a coalition

by designating another party as the source of their problem and assuming an attacking or solicitous attitude toward that person.

In triangulation, each of two opposing parties seeks to join with the third person against the other, with the third party finding it necessary, for whatever reasons, to cooperate now with one and now with another of these opposing parties. (1981, p. 314)

In these types of transactional patterns a child can be inappropriately included in the parental boundary. Minuchin (1974) states that

this difficulty results in a rigid triad where the boundary between the parental subsystem and the child becomes diffuse, and the boundary around the parents/child triad, which should be diffuse, becomes inappropriately rigid. (p. 102)

A stable coalition occurs when one of the parents joins the child in a rigid generational dyad against the other parent. A frequent detouring coalition occurs when a child is designated as a source of stress. Discussions of possible marital disharmony are avoided and the partners live as if harmony existed. The spouses submerge their conflict and focus on the difficulties of the child by complaining about his behavior, protecting him, or defining him as the source of family difficulties. Triangulation occurs when each of the parents seeks to enlist the same person, frequently the child, against the other parent. The child is immobilized because by taking one side, he is automatically against the other.

Adlerians do not explicitly discuss the structural concept of alignments. The nature of the marital relationship is not openly probed initially. However, if the educational parenting approach does not produce positive results, the purpose of the continuing family conflict is examined via "the question" (Adler, 1964). For example, "What would life be like for the two of you, what could you be discussing, and what would be taking place if Tommy's behavior improved?" are examples of examining the purpose of the child's symptomatic behavior upon the marriage. Again, it is a matter of emphasis. The goal of therapy remains similar, the establishing of appropriate boundaries and alignments.

Power

Power is the third ingredient considered by structural family therapists in their assessment of family functioning. Difficulties in power occur when those in the parental boundary are not able to exercise the influence or force necessary to carry out appropriate functions. Adlerian family therapists primarily address power from an educative standpoint. The appropriate use of power in a manner consistent with equality, mutual respect, and democratic principles is promoted (Sherman, 1983). Adlerians are very process oriented, encouraging family discussions, use of natural and logical consequences, and communication techniques which teach effective uses of power as well as produce an outcome in which an appropriate structure is built and maintained. Structural family therapists are not as concerned with how the executives become appropriately elevated, just so they can accomplish the functions necessary for development.

THE ROLE OF THE THERAPIST

The role of the Adlerian family therapist and structural family therapist is consistent with the premises of each theory regarding which will best promote change. The structural family therapist is a very active and directive leader who attempts to influence family transactions by selectively altering his behavior and intervention, depending on the session's structural goals. The structural family therapist's task is

> to develop a relational context that will allow, stimulate, and provoke change in transactional patterns around issues that are associated with the problems. How the therapist carries out these actions is reflected in the kinds of personal involvement he/she engages in and with whom. (Aponte & VanDeusen, 1981, p. 325)

The structural family therapist believes that changes will occur if new family structures are formed. Consequently, it is the responsibility of the structural family therapist first to discover alternative transactional patterns that are more effective and then to promote their use. Since the structural family therapist must be the leader, he utilizes a number of techniques that will keep him in that position.

From the initial meeting, the structural family therapist uses techniques which are intended to change the family's faulty transactions. This is accomplished via facilitating engagements, which encourage interaction among family members, and centralizing engagements, which promote interaction between family members and the therapist and discourage interactions between family members (Aponte & VanDeusen, 1981). Whether to use a facilitative or centralizing engagement depends on the session's structural goal.

Centralizing Engagements

During centralizing engagements, the therapist interacts with one member at a time, without the family present, conducting a series of individual sessions concurrent with family therapy, or interacting for a long period of time with a specific member while others observe. Centralizing engagements are more likely to be used when emotions are so intense that the therapist's encouraging of family members to speak directly to each other would lead to further blaming or scapegoating. This is particularly true in many initial sessions where the identified patient is an adolescent.

Facilitating Engagements

Facilitating engagements seem more appropriate when issues of intimacy, nurturance, and misperceptions are prominent or after centralizing interactions have diminished hostilities. Facilitating interactions are accomplished by the therapist's encouraging or directing family members to speak with each other or by the withdrawal of the therapist.

The therapist is never structurally neutral as she actively and continuously utilizes her personality, experience, and techniques to achieve structural changes. The therapist "will have to accommodate, seduce, submit, support, direct, suggest, and follow in order to lead" (Minuchin & Fishman, 1981, p. 29). The structural therapist is also assessing her personal experience of the family as she attempts to understand patterns. As therapy progresses, the therapist becomes less actively involved, allowing the new or reinforced family structures to act with increasing autonomy.

The Adlerian family therapist is more of a democratic leader who tries to promote a therapeutic relationship which is a collaborative one among equals, with the patient having an active role in therapy. The Adlerian therapist believes that "psychotherapy is a cooperative educative enterprise involving one or more therapists and one or more patients. The goal of therapy is not to rescue the patient from illness, but to develop and liberate the patient's social interest" (Mosak & Dreikurs, 1973, p. 53). It is a process of reeducation. In an attempt to promote social interest and improve family harmony, the Adlerian philosophy is discussed, modeled, and practiced. However, the role of the Adlerian leader is different in family counseling, family therapy, and parenting groups—the three major modalities in which Adlerian family therapists are involved. While she is always attempting to model the principles of her philosophy, the techniques vary in each of the three modalities.

When conducting a parent study group, the Adlerian is a facilitator. The goal is to encourage parents to explore the principles of Adlerian child-rearing techniques through group discussion, and then to put them into practice. The role of the leader is to guide the participants, ensuring that the group discussions are based on the course material. Structural family therapy may involve an educational component; however, parenting groups with a specific parenting philosophy are rarely included as a part of therapy.

Family counseling is conducted in public with volunteer families for the purpose of disseminating Adlerian mental health principles, providing resources for troubled families, and teaching others to work more effectively with children. It is normally conducted at a family education center or child guidance clinic. The role of the Adlerian family counselor is to interpret the dynamics of the family situations to parents, to reveal to the child his goal, to help parents acquire new methods of solving conflicts, and to establish better relationships (Rosenberg, 1959).

Pew and Pew (1976) seem to espouse the belief that Adlerian family counseling is more for the child since life style analysis or reorganization of the personality is usually unnecessary. It is their opinion that most parents are able to utilize a simple commonsense approach toward changing family relationships. This is a position which is also favored by Dreikurs and Soltz (1964), who state

> that effective influence on the children does not depend on the relationship with the mates, provided mother—since she is around the most—does not use the children against the father or does not let him use them against herself. Very few people realize to what extent the children decide the role they want to play, they stimulate the appropriate reaction on their parents. (p. 260)

During Adlerian family therapy more emphasis is placed on the family system and its interactions. The parents review the presenting problem and explain the "typical day." Throughout, the Adlerian family therapist is a listener, building rapport and giving the parents every opportunity to explain their parenting rationale and its effectiveness. The Adlerian leader models mutual respect and encouragement, reframes meanings from negatives to positives, validates each member, and promotes the family's use of Adlerian principles.

Both Adlerian and structural family therapists are extremely active, hopeful, and directive. They demonstrate a basic respect for their patients, who are not seen as fragile, mentally ill, or sick. The basic difference in their behavior is related to their beliefs regarding how to be most influential with a family. The structural family therapist is more outcome oriented, doing whatever he feels necessary to alter a family's pattern of relationships. The Adlerian therapist is more likely to provide an explanation of dynamics and model behaviors consistent with facilitating changes within individual family members which will lead to changes in structural outcome.

ASSESSING THE SYSTEM

Adlerian family therapists and structural family therapists do not use standard diagnostic interviews or instruments. However, assessment is an essential part of each therapy as both utilize what can be defined as working hypotheses. The usual psychiatric procedure involves a gathering of pertinent information about the patient, either from him or family members, and then assigning a diagnosis in accordance with DSM-III (American Psychiatric Association, 1980). This is not the assessment procedure that Adlerian and structural family therapists follow. In addition, psychological testing is not normally utilized since it places a greater emphasis on the identified patient. Adlerians are more likely to use art therapy, sculpting, or psychodrama than would their structural counterparts, who most often have the family members enact a discussion which then discloses their interpersonal patterns. This structural procedure of enactment is also frequently used by Adlerians.

The goal of structural family therapy is to alter the family's underlying systemic structure. Whatever is said or done between the therapist and family members, or among family members, is used toward assessing the family's structure. From the initial telephone call regarding the requesting of an appointment an assessment of how to restructure has begun since "whatever the history of the problem, the dynamics that maintain it are currently active in the structure of the system, manifesting themselves in the transactional sequences of the family" (Aponte & VanDeusen, 1981, p. 315).

The goal of Adlerian family therapy is not necessarily limited to altering family structure. While pursuing an understanding of family rules and dynamics, patterns of transactions, and determining the purpose of psychological movement, there is an individual nature to assessment, as family members become aware of their beliefs, goals, and purposes. The goal is to increase the self-esteem of individual members of the family while stimulating their social interests so they will participate in the give and take (cooperation) of family life (Dinkmeyer

& Dinkmeyer, 1983, p. 117). Since the goals are different, what is assessed is different. Yet the outcome often is similar.

During the initial stages of therapy, the structural family therapist is very active, intervening directly in the family as attempts are made to identify the problem, determine the systems within the family that are involved, and define the structures within the system that are sustaining the problem. The emphasis is always on the system's structure, a major difference from Adlerian theory. While both modalities pursue the purposefulness of behavior, the structural family therapist is attempting to uncover the family functions that are being blocked by the symptom. The Adlerian is looking more at individual purposiveness and its effects on the behavior of others, again not necessarily taking the family's developmental stage into account.

"The structural family therapist's collection of data and his assessment are achieved experimentally in the process of joining the family" (Minuchin, 1974, p. 89). However, there is no specific period of data collection which is separate from the promotion of change. The structural therapist analyzes the transactional field initially by conducting conjoint family interviews and then constructing a family map, an organizational scheme which allows him to formulate a hypothesis about areas of well functioning and dysfunctioning. During this assessment stage, the structural family therapist is concerned with the following six areas of the system: (1) the family structure, its preferred transactional patterns and available alternatives; (2) the system's flexibility and capacity for restructuring in response to changing circumstances; (3) the family system's resonance or sensitivity to individual members; (4) the family's sources of support in stress; (5) the family's developmental stage and its performance of tasks appropriate to that stage; and (6) how the index patient's symptoms are being used to maintain the family's preferred transactional pattern (Minuchin, 1974). Recognizing that problems do not occur in isolation, their assessment includes the relationship of the problem to other family functions, family developmental stages, and stresses inside or outside the family such as ill health or unemployment. During this assessment stage, the emphasis is always on discovering how the family structure is sustaining the problem and not on the structure in which it originated.

The therapist's assessment tools "are the observation and experience of the transactions among the members of the ecosystem connected with the problems as they act to solve the problem with the therapist" (Aponte & VanDeusen, 1981, p. 318). The structural family therapist is very active in this stage, as he acts and reacts in order to complete his understanding.

The therapist's presence alone is sufficient to cause the family to organize in relation to him. In addition, tasks may be imposed for the specific purpose of probing. Joining and accommodating techniques are used during this initial period to create a therapeutic system.

> Joining is used when emphasizing actions of the therapist aimed directly at relating to family members or the family system. Accommodation is used when the emphasis is on the therapist's adjustments of himself in order to achieve joining. (Minuchin, 1974, p. 123)

There is an interpersonal focus to a structural assessment as the therapist is gauging the family's reaction to him and he is also assessing his impact on the family. The joining and accommodation techniques are used deliberately, as the therapist may wish to join in a close, medium, or disengaged manner, depending on the goal of the session. The range of behaviors associated with the structural family therapist's joining techniques includes the acting in coalition, confirming, neutralizing, observing, tracking, and directing of transactions. Joining in a close position is often demonstrated when the therapist empathizes, reflects, supports, confirms a family member's feeling, or reframes a negative experience more positively. "You seem discouraged . . . annoyed . . . angry." When in a medium position, the therapist is more neutral, gathering information, tracking dynamics, exploring, and listening to individual and family beliefs and values. "Can you tell me . . . how does that effect . . . and then what?" are frequently used questions. This conflicts with the disengaged position where the therapist uses his authority more directly as he "creates scenarios, facilitating the enactment of familar movements or introducing novelty" (Minuchin & Fishman, 1981, p. 40). "That sounds like something you need to say to your husband" and "Perhaps the two of you need special time this week" are examples. In each case, this will lead to further restructuring.

For the Adlerian family therapist, the presenting problem, no matter the topic, is also one of an interpersonal nature. However, disturbed relationships and inappropriate behaviors are more reflective of the individuals' beliefs, goals, and purposes than of structural defects or developmental stages in the family.

Adlerians also use joining and accommodation techniques as the therapist models respect for the family and their patterns of transacting. In addition, all of the previously mentioned joining behaviors, in close, medium, and disengaged positions, are utilized. For example, the Adlerian is a "tracker" when requesting information about the "typical day," in coalition when speaking only to the parents, and nurturant when he confirms feelings during the identification of mistaken goals. Structural information is gained but not emphasized.

Boundary intrusions, misalignments, coalitions, and triangles are noted, but spoken of in terms of the goals of misconduct, equality, lack of mutual respect, and discouragement. The younger the child, the more the assessment focuses on parenting. With adolescents, life style concepts, perhaps assessed by interpreting early recollections, are used more frequently.

The Adlerian use of self is also different. It is limited initially to assessing the therapist's feelings to help in his conceptualization of the life style of the parents and children. In a very neutral manner, he attempts to model mutual respect and facilitate cooperation. His usual stance is encouraging, emphasizing understanding and acceptance. The Adlerian family therapist is attempting to connect with each family member and then set goals to which all family members can agree, so that participation in therapy will continue. Resistance is seen as a nonalignment of goals between therapist and family members.

Both modalities attempt to extend the focus from the identified patient to the entire family, highlighting the interpersonal nature of problems. During this assessment stage, the structural family therapist convenes the entire family, sometimes including grandparents, uncles, aunts, and more, to ferret out the structural dynamics which are maintaining the problem. A lack of parenting education or knowledge of problem-solving skills is not generally assumed to be the problem.

Adlerians often focus on the importance of place in the system and obtain a multigenerational view of the family by getting data on the family constellation. (See Chapters 3 and 4 for a description of this process.)

As assessment unfolds, the theoretical differences between the therapies is evident in the expressed goals and conduct of the therapist. Whereas an Adlerian usually requests historical data that allow him to assess parenting goals, purposes, lines of movement toward goals, the structural therapist does not. More frequently, he will have the family enact a transaction, perhaps around historical information that will allow for assessment of the family's differentiation, flexibility, and delineation of boundaries. The factual answer is less important than the family process it discloses. Also Adlerians frequently disclose goals of misconduct to the clients; structuralists do not.

The major similarities rest in the outcome of therapy. Adlerians are concerned about structure in terms of place and its effect on dynamics, rather than structure for its own sake. Although not emphasizing structure, they restructure through the recommended procedures of child rearing, problem solving, and mutual respect. Flexibility, proper boundaries, and appropriate displays of power are utilized to fulfill individual and family functions.

STRATEGIES AND TECHNIQUES

Strategies and techniques reflect the therapist's theoretical beliefs regarding how to best promote change in the individual, marriage, or family system. Structural family therapists, based on their belief that troubled families suffer from an inappropriate or otherwise dysfunctional structural organization, use strategies and techniques that will transform a family's organizational patterns. Their techniques are purposeful, attempting to accomplish the specific end of restructuring the faulty system which is not effectively fulfilling a function. The primary emphasis is on the structure of the family system. Adlerian family techniques attempt to increase the social interest of individual family members and their transactional skills such as negotiation and problem solving. Democratic methods are taught and modeled to help the family organize as a more democratic institution. Therefore, altering family structure is a usual outcome of the therapy. The change agent is contained in the Adlerian philosophy.

The three major categories of structural family therapy techniques are the creating, joining, and restructuring of transactions.

Creating Transactions

Creating a transaction is accomplished by structuralization, enactment inducement, or task setting within the family. Aponte and VanDeusen (1981) define each as follows:

> Structuralization is the therapist's purposeful organization or his/her part in the sequences of a transaction with family members to influence the pattern of their interactions. Enactment inducement is the process through which the therapist promotes in the session the family members' transacting their habitual pattern of relating. Task setting within the family is the assignment by the therapist to the family members to carry out among themselves an operation within prescribed transactional parameters. (p. 328)

Structuralization. Via structuralization, the therapist attempts to directly influence a family member's behavior within a boundary (a husband and wife) or between boundaries (such as parents and children). This may be done through a task, the negotiation of a task, or the therapist's interactions with the family member. For example, the structural family therapist may wish to elevate a parent to a status equivalent to his spouse by having them discuss an adult issue without using the children. This will alter not only the marital relationship, but also both partners' interactions with the children.

Structuralization also occurs in Adlerian family therapy, although it is not labeled as such and it is done differently. In Adlerian family therapy relationships and structure are altered as family members change their pattern of relating to each other, the result of practicing Adlerian philosophy. Further structuralization occurs during the separately conducted interviews of parents and children. This establishes or reinforces the appropriate distance between the separate subsets of parents and children. More conjoint interviewing is conducted with adolescents, with the effect of establishing the appropriate distance not only between but also within subsets. During these interviews, further structural change occurs as the Adlerian family therapists stress equality and mutual respect, having family members speak for themselves and directly to each other. Adlerian structuralization is consistent with its belief that "a faulty equilibrium between the members of the family is the real basis of family maladjustment and conflict" (Dreikurs, 1967, p. 242). This belief is similar to that of structural family therapists whose premise is that the root of all family conflict is faulty structure and organization.

Enactment inducement or task setting. The use of enactment inducements, having the family demonstrate its habitual pattern of relating, is an essential part of both family therapies. They encourage full interaction to better assess goals and purposiveness of behavior. Enactment procedures are also useful in enabling families to begin problem resolution, while the appropriate family structure is reinforced by the therapist. The Adlerian family council, initiated during therapy, is a form of enactment inducement, as is task setting in both theories. The purpose of task setting for the structural family therapist is to erect or encourage an intended structure through a task. Adlerian tasks are also designed to change structure but are tied to Adlerian philosophy. More specifically, the task may be to use a logical or natural consequence, to have a parent withdraw from an argument, or to encourage the child to handle his own responsibilities.

The structural technique of creating transactions is compatible with Adlerian beliefs. What is different is the procedure, as structural family therapists accomplish their goal without necessarily focusing on insight or discussing a philosophy of human relations. Their purpose is to influence family transactions so that functions can better be fulfilled.

Joining with Transactions

Joining with transactions, the second major set of structural family techniques, involves the therapist's interacting with the family in a manner that will allow him to be totally accepted on professional and personal levels. These techniques include the procedures of tracking, accommodation, and mimesis.

1. *Tracking.* During tracking the structural family therapist "adopts symbols of the family's life through which to communicate to the family and around which to build relationships" (Aponte & VanDeusen, 1981, p. 330). Upon hearing the family's themes and values, the structural therapist relates in a manner similar to the family's, thereby increasing chances for acceptance.

2. *Accommodation.* In accommodation, the therapist, respectful of the family's transactional patterns, attempts to communicate with them in accordance with their pattern. The therapist needs to recognize the family hierarchy as well as verbal and nonverbal relationships or transactions and adjust his style to accommodate the family. As an example, the therapist, recognizing the power of the husband, may ask his permission to speak with the wife.

3. *Mimesis.* In mimesis, the structural family therapist joins the family by acting like a member. The therapist can become like the family or one of its members through adopting the manner of speaking, body language, tempo, or other behavioral modes of communication of the family (Aponte & VanDeusen, 1981, p. 331).

Joining techniques are designed to aid the therapist in fitting into the family system, minimizing resistance and making him more appealing so that change can be facilitated. While these structural joining techniques are specific, they incorporate the usual accepted counseling techniques of genuineness, interest, and understanding, which facilitate the development of all interpersonal relationships.

Adlerians also emphasize the establishing of a therapeutic relationship. However, the relationship between the therapist and family is based more on the Adlerian beliefs in mutual respect and equality than on the use of techniques such as tracking, accommodation, and mimesis. During the initial stages of therapy, the Adlerian family therapist is likely to establish rapport by empathic listening, understanding, and one-to-one communication, rather than through structural techniques. This relationship is further enhanced by the Adlerian therapist's understanding of the individual family member's sense of belonging. Adlerian theory, despite its individual systems perspective, does not contain any beliefs that would preclude the use of structural joining techniques. The structural family therapist is modeling equality and respect as he does not intrude on the family's style.

Both modalities are concerned with fully understanding family values and decreasing resistance. Differences in joining techniques are a matter of emphasis, with the structural family therapist attempting to join with the system while the Adlerian family therapist, in contrast, is more likely to join with individual family members through active listening techniques and the understanding of goals, themes, and life styles.

Restructuring Transactions

Restructuring transactions are intended to address difficulties that result from system conflict and structural insufficiency. System conflicts are difficulties that occur from contrary functional demands within the individual or between family members which seemingly can be resolved only with a dysfunctional compromise. Subsequently, functional needs are not satisfied. Structural insufficiencies stem from a lack of structural resources, thereby not allowing the functional demands of the system to be met. The lack of resources may be located within the family or the social system, a diminished opportunity to develop resources, or a lack of system supports necessary to take advantage of the opportunities that are present (Aponte & VanDeusen, 1981).

System recomposition, symptom focusing, and structural modifications are the restructuring techniques which are utilized in treating both types of problems. While these techniques are not mutually exclusive, the tendency is to utilize more confrontation than support in problems of a system conflict nature, with support more appropriate in problems of structural insufficiency (Aponte & VanDeusen, 1981, p. 332).

1. *Systems recomposition.* This restructuring technique involves the adding or deleting of systems or subunits from those that are involved in the problem. A common scenario is one in which a single parent has begun to rely too heavily on her parents or a brother for emotional

support. An inappropriate boundary between the separate families and between mother and children has been erected. Structuralists would be likely to elevate mother to her executive position, negating the intrusiveness of her parents and brother. She might also be encouraged to seek support from a single parents' organization. Although systems recomposition is not specifically addressed by Adlerian family therapists, it can be accomplished. More specifically, the Adlerian emphasis on democratic problem solving, mutual respect, independence, and self-responsibility leads to an altering of family structure in such cases. Solving problems by seeking support from external systems is a frequent device.

2. *Symptom focusing.* Symptom focusing techniques, including the use of paradox, have been widely used by Adlerians (Mozdzierz, Macchitelli, & Lisiecki, 1976). The purpose in both theories is to facilitate change through the use of the symptom. Among the symptom focusing techniques that structural family therapists utilize are exaggerating the symptom, deemphasizing the symptom, moving to a new symptom, relabeling the symptom, and changing the affect of the symptom (Minuchin, 1974).

There are many similarities in the two modalities' applications of these change techniques, although Adlerians more often apply them to individual members.

Using symptom exaggeration or prescription, Adlerian and structural family therapists attempt to diminish the symptom's effectiveness and ultimately lead the individual and/or family to seek to fulfill needs in a more positive manner. For example, having a worried, depressed family member agree to worry for a specific time and in a specific place, despite assertions that he cannot control his thoughts, eventually will have him assume responsibility, demonstrate control over the symptom, and block its compensating purpose for the family. The structural family therapist would block its compensating purpose. The Adlerian would more likely interpret the purpose as a means of "spitting in the client's soup," making the behavior less palatable, thus acting as a blocker.

There are also similarities in the use of symptom deemphasis. Structural family therapy borrows from strategic therapy in moving from the original symptom to a new one in an effort to restructure the family. The purpose is to focus on a family problem which has the same supporting structure but is more solvable initially because the family is not as rigidly opposed to intervention. Adlerians also use this technique of symptom deemphasis. For example, the initial Adlerian interview includes a heavy emphasis on the family constellation, pointing out how the children cooperate in their mischief or how the good child may be encouraging negative behavior from a sibling. The identified patient's behavior is seen as a cooperative venture having an interactional quality as he seeks his identity or sense of belonging through the pursuit of faulty goals. In reviewing "the typical day" the Adlerian therapist usually finds a pattern of irresponsible behavior, with subsequent remediation often beginning with other than the presenting problem, since the family's transactions may be too well entrenched. The effectiveness of the Adlerian approach may be demonstrated first with a similar problem, which offers encouragement to the parents that the original presenting situation can also be resolved.

Relabeling the symptom or altering the affect of a symptom, other techniques used by both theories, are akin to deemphasizing the symptom. By giving an alternative, more positive explanation to the family, the therapist tends to alter old perceptions that make this symptom unsolvable. New modes of responding are more easily encouraged and motivation for change is increased. When describing a problematic child as discouraged, or when reframing an oppositional child as independent minded or an undue attention seeking child as one who values his parent's attention, the Adlerian family therapist is relabeling symptoms. The result is altered perceptions, opening new means for problem resolution.

3. *Structural modification.* Structural modification is the third category of structuring transactions. It is characterized by techniques which disassemble, construct, reinforce, and reorganize structure. These structural techniques are not incompatible with those found in Adlerian family therapy. The primary difference is the emphasis the Adlerians place on the use of educational principles. Structural family therapists minimize their use of educational or instructive material, unless a family seems highly deficient in specific information. Minuchin (1974) makes that point quite clear when stating, "The therapist joins the family not to educate it or socialize it, but rather to repair and modify the family's own functioning so that it can better perform these tasks" (p. 14). Subsequently, structuralists are more eclectic, using a greater variety of tasks and directives to tranform a family's structure.

SUMMARY

The purpose of this chapter has been to compare Adlerian and structural family therapy. It has been shown that the basic premises of each allow for clinical integration. Adlerian family therapy has been categorized as an individual systems approach, with structural family therapy being labeled a family systems approach. Each modality focuses on or emphasizes different aspects of the family system. While both recognize the importance of examining and understanding the individual within his family and social context, structural family therapists emphasize the structure of a family more emphatically. Adlerians stress the subjective and idiosyncratic nature of beliefs, how they were created, and their eventual impact on all interactions.

The basic objective of structural family therapy is to effect a change in family structure that will produce a concomitant change in functioning. "This basic tenet of the rationale for change in structural family therapy rests upon the premise that all functioning is the product of the stucture of the system from which it springs" (Aponte & VanDeusen, 1981, p. 337). Adlerians would not find that premise acceptable, unless altered to include the powerful effect of the individual upon the system which is the product of each member's subjective convictions about himself, others, and the world, and his beliefs as to what needs to occur so that he can feel significant. "The person behaves as if these convictions were true and uses his life style as a cognitive map with which he explores, comprehends, prejudges, predicts, and controls the environment" (Mosak & Dreikurs, 1973, p. 74). The family as a discrete entity develops similar kinds of convictions and goals.

The goal of therapy is to promote social interest and to increase individual cooperation. Appropriate boundaries, alignments, and uses of power will be formed in accordance with the task or function. Both theories are in complete accord with that outcome.

The structural family therapy approach can be used as a framework for the utilization of many therapeutic approaches, especially Adlerian psychology. The use of Adlerian family techniques and educational material provides a consistent, clearly defined manner of attaining the structure needed by structural family therapists to promote favorable behavior. Adlerians are concerned about the family constellation and each person's place in the system. Both kinds of theorists are interested in the purpose of the interactions. However, structuralists focus on the purpose for the system, whereas Adlerians examine the purpose for the system and for each interacting member.

The Adlerian philosophy is to educate and help families adopt a more egalitarian manner of living. Structural changes as such are less apt to be noted. If the philosophy of egalitarianism is viewed as a psychological basis for producing structural change, then the compatibility of the two theories is greatly increased.

Both theories use many of the same type of techniques for assessment and behavior change. Tracking, enactment, respect for patterns existing in the system, joining with the system as a leader, assigning tasks, describing existing roles and behavior in metaphoric terms, and sculpting are among the many examples which are evident.

Although the differences between the theories cannot be minimized, it does appear that they are reasonably compatible. The differences are more complementary than opposing; for example, looking at patterns of organization and attending to individual contributions to system functioning.

ANNOTATED REFERENCES

Aponte, H. J., & VanDeusen, J. M. (1981). Structural family therapy. In A. Gurman & D. Kniskern (Eds.), *Handbook of family therapy*, New York: Brunner/Mazel.
The authors have compiled an exhaustive and comprehensive review of structural family therapy. All facets of the theory are addressed, so that it is an ideal source for academicians or practitioners, regardless of their experience level.

Minuchin, S. (1974). *Families and family therapy*. Cambridge, MA: Harvard University Press.
The author presents lengthy transcripts of cases, accompanied by his interpretation of what is occurring. The case histories illustrate the theoretical material that is presented, with emphasis being placed on models of effective and ineffective family functioning, methods of diagnosis, and the determining of therapeutic goals and strategies.

Minuchin, S., & Fishman, C. (1981). *Family therapy techniques*. Cambridge, MA: Harvard University Press.
The authors focus on the specific techniques of structural family therapy. They include understanding and joining the family, enactment, reframing, and changing boundaries, as well as more direct strategies that will precipitate change. The presentation of these practical techniques makes this book invaluable.

ADDITIONAL REFERENCES

Adler, A. (1964). *Problems of neurosis.* New York: Harper & Row.
Amerikaner, M. J. (1981). Continuing theoretical convergence: A general systems theory perspective on personal growth development. *Journal of Individual Psychology, 37*(1): 31–53.
American Psychiatric Association (1980). *Diagnostic and Statistical Manual of Mental Disorders (3rd ed.).* Washington, DC: Author.

Aponte, H. (1976). Diagnosis in family therapy. In C. B. Gemain (Ed.), *Social work practice.* New York: Columbia University Press.

Aponte, H., & VanDeusen, J. (1981). Structural family therapy. In A. Gurman & D. Kniskern (Eds.), *Handbook of family therapy.* New York: Brunner/Mazel.

Barker, P. (1981). *Basic family therapy.* Baltimore: University Park Press.

Burck, H. (1972). Personal communication.

Croake, J., & Hinkle, D. (1983). Adlerian family counseling/education. *Individual Psychology, 39*(3): 247-258.

Defraia, G. (1984). *The Family Therapy Networker, 8*(4): 29-32.

Dinkmeyer, D. & Dinkmeyer, J. (1983). Adlerian family therapy. *Individual Psychology, 39*(2): 116-124.

Dreikurs, R. (1967). *Psychodynamics, psychotherapy, and counseling.* Chicago: Alfred Adler Institute.

Dreikurs, R., & Soltz, V. (1964). *Children: The challenge.* New York: Hawthorne.

Gurman, A., & Kniskern, D. (1978). Research on marital and family therapy: Progress, perspective, and prospect. In S. L. Garfield & A. E. Bergen (Eds.), *Handbook of psychotherapy and behavior change: An empirical analysis* (2nd ed.). New York: Wiley.

Gurman, A. S., & Kniskern, D. P. (Eds.). (1981). *Handbook of family therapy.* New York: Brunner/Mazel.

Haley, J. (1976). *Problem-solving therapy.* San Francisco: Jossey-Bass.

Lane, M. (1970). *Introduction to structuralism.* New York: Basic Books.

Minuchin, S. (1974). *Families and family therapy.* Cambridge, MA.: Harvard University Press.

Minuchin, S. (1984). *The family kaleidoscope.* Cambridge, MA: Harvard University Press.

Minuchin, S., & Fishman, H. C. (1981). *Family therapy techniques.* Cambridge, MA: Harvard University Press.

Minuchin, S., Rosman, B., & Baker, L. (1978). *Psychosomatic families.* Cambridge, MA: Harvard University Press.

Mosak, H. (1979). Personal communication.

Mosak, H., & Dreikurs, R. (1973). Adlerian pscyhotherapy. In R. Corsini (Ed.), *Current psychotherapies.* Itasca, IL: Peacock.

Mozdzierz, G., Macchitelli, F., & Lisiecki, J. (1976). The paradox in psychotherapy: An Adlerian perspective. *Journal of Individual Psychology, 32*(2): 169-184.

Orten, J. (1978). Organizing concepts in family therapy. *International Journal of Family Counseling, 6*(1): 9-16.

Pew, W., & Pew, M. (1976). Workshop. South Carolina.

Rosenberg, B. (1959). The counselor. In R. Dreikurs, R. Corsini, R. Lowe, & M. Sonstegard (Eds.), *Adlerian family counseling.* Eugene: University of Oregon Press.

Sherman, R. (1983). The power dimension in the family: A synthesis of Adlerian perspectives. *American Journal of Family Therapy, 11*(3): 43-53.

Simon, R., (1984). Stranger in a strange land: An interview with Salvador Minuchin. *Family Therapy Networker, 8*(6): 21-31.

Sprenkle, D., Keeney, B., & Sutton, P. (1982). Theorists who influence clinical members of AAMFT. *Journal of Marital and Family Therapy, 8*(3): 367-369.

Stanton, M. D. (1981). Marital therapy from a structural/strategic viewpoint. In P. Sholevar (Ed.), *Marriage is a family affair*. New York: Spectrum.

Von Bertallanfy, L. (1968). *General systems theory: Foundations, development, application*. New York: George Braziller.

Walsh, W. (1980). *A primer in family therapy*. Springfield, IL: Charles C Thomas.

10

Ellis' Rational Emotive Therapy and Adlerian Family Therapy: A Comparison

James W. Croake

DEFINITION OF PROCESS AND EXPECTATIONS

This chapter compares Alfred Adler's Individual Psychology (IP) with Albert Ellis' Rational Emotive Therapy (RET) as they are applied to family therapy. Definition of terms and concepts concentrates on RET, since other chapters define these in IP. The exceptions are those instances where the writer defines these terms and concepts in a differing way from others who write, theorize, and practice IP.

It will become evident that Ellis bases much of his theory on the writings of Adler. He cites writers other than Adler for the basis of his philosophy, but it will be seen that the two philosophies are in concert. The theory and practice of the two systems are similar to a degree. However, family therapy, more than any other therapy mode, emphasizes two major differences between IP and RET. First, Ellis focuses on the self-interest of the individual family member, which is an intrapsychic rather than interpersonal method of therapy. Second, he does not recognize a systems approach to family therapy. He works with individuals, dyads, and occasionally the entire family. Even when seeing the entire family, he works intrapsychically with each family member and not with the familial–interpersonal dynamics.

James W. Croake, Ph.D., is Professor of Psychiatry & Behavioral Sciences, University of Washington, School of Medicine, Seattle, Washington.

HISTORICAL DEVELOPMENT AND PERSPECTIVES

Ellis' Attraction to Adler

Adler and Ellis share a common background of exposure to Freudian psychology and psychotherapy. Both reject the nineteenth-century reductionistic, dichotomistic, causalistic view of human behavior which Freud espoused. Ellis is one of the few theorists to acknowledge his debt to Adler, even to the extent of stating that there might not be a Rational Emotive Psychotherapy were it not for the teachings of Adler (Ellis, 1962). Ellis often refers to Adler's ideas as the foundation for his own theory; for example,

> I am convinced that a person's behavior springs from his ideas.
> . . . The individual relates himself to the outside world in accordance with his own interpretation of himself and of his present problem. He does not relate himself in a predetermined manner as is often assumed. It is his attitude toward life which determines his relationship to the outside world. (Adler, 1964a)

Wessler and Wessler (1980) trace the origin of RET to Alfred Adler, whom they see as being the first to attempt to change mistaken beliefs and fallacious discouraged attitudes in his patients.

Ellis sees the similarity of Woodworth's (1929) theory of learning with his own and that of Adler. Woodworth, as a learning theorist, rebelled in 1921 against the dominant behaviorist model of human behavior. Woodworth saw more than the stimulus–response. He postulated an organismic theory of learning: The organism always mediates between the stimulus and the response. This corresponds directly to Ellis' *ABC* model of human behavior, which is described later in detail, and Adler's (1931) comment,

> No experience is a cause of success or failure. We do not suffer from the shock of our experiences, the so-called trauma, but we make out of the experience just what suits our purposes. We are self-determined by the meaning we give to our experiences, and there is probably something of a mistake always involved when we take particular experiences as the basis of our future life. Meanings are not determined by situations, but we determine ourselves by the meanings we give to situations (p.14).

Ellis further quotes Adler, "everything depends on opinions" (Ellis,

1973) and adds, "I would be hard put to state the essential tenets of RET more succinctly and accurately" (Ellis, 1973a).

Education

Both Adler and Ellis see counseling and therapy as a process of reeducation. Adler believes that it is the job of the therapist to do the correct teaching, which should have been done by the mother, since she is usually the one who has primary responsibility for raising the children (Adler, 1964a). To this end Adler established child guidance centers in Austria in 1922; eventually the number grew to a total of thirty-one including those in Germany. It was in these clinics that Adler initiated family therapy (Dreikurs, 1959).

Ellis believes that people are born with a proclivity to think irrationally, and from birth we are further steeped in irrational thinking by our family and society at large (Ellis, 1979). To rectify this situation Ellis not only provides psychotherapy for the purpose of reeducating people but also conducts adult education courses, workshops, and seminars; writes publications for laymen and for professionals; and has an institute in New York for the training of therapists, educators and others, in the principles and practices which he espouses. Both theories have extended their work into the school system.

BASIC CONCEPTS

Philosophy

In Europe psychology and philosophy are accepted as intertwined disciplines; North America has made a practice of separating the two. Ellis and Adler soundly base their theories in philosophy. Ellis makes specific reference to Stoicism: Zeno of Citium in the fourth century B.C., Panaetius of Rhodes, Chrysippus, Cicero, Seneca, Epictetus, and Marcus Aurelius. Most of the philosophy of the Stoics is presented in Epictetus' *The Enchiridion,* in which he states that "Men are disturbed not by things, but by the view which they take of them" (Ellis, 1962). This reads as if it could have been written by Adler.

Marcus Aurelius was a disciple of Epictetus. He was the Roman emperor who wrote *Meditations,* a work which influenced later philosophers such as Spinoza, Kant, and Russell (Ellis, 1971a). Ellis, unlike Adler, gives credit to these stoic philosophers, but the similarity of their beliefs to those of Adler is remarkable. Ansbacher notes the similarity of Adler's ideas to those of Kant and Nietzsche (Adler, 1956). Adler does acknowledge his debt to Vaihinger's text, *The Philosophy of As If* (1956). Vaihinger believes that we never know what is fact within ourselves, but we are convinced that our distorted views are correct. Therefore, we act fallaciously, and this fictitious movement gives us direction in our behavior: We behave "as if" we ourselves, other people, and the world are constructed according to our apperceptions. This of course is a phenomenological view of human behavior: Our percepts reflect not reality, but rather our biased apperceptions.

Phenomenology

Ellis (1979) is in agreement with Adler regarding phenomenology: Reality is seen as subjective, there is a full appreciation of consciousness, the self is central; holism, field theory, functional relativism, perception, *Gestalt* psychology, organismic conception, and soft determinism are emphasized (Ansbacher & Ansbacher, 1956). For both Ellis and Adler biased apperception of the stimulus, whether consciously perceived or not, provides direction for behavior.

For Adler (1964b) unconscious is that part of the fictive goal which is not understood by the individual. The fictive goal pulls all behavior in its direction. People can be comprehended only in terms of their fictive goal. All emotions, values, thoughts, and behavior are only aspects of a unified relational system. The unifying aspect of their life style is the fictive goal (Ansbacher & Ansbacher, 1956). It is fictive because it is constructed in the limited social environment, mainly the family of the young child. For the remainder of their lives people strive toward this goal as if it would give them a significant or safe place in society were the goal fully achieved. However, the goal is insatiable, illogical, irrational, and unachievable. Ellis (1971c) accepts the idea of a fictive goal, but he does not give it the importance that Adler gives to it. Rather he sees it as one of the many irrational beliefs held by humans. He would probably agree that it is one of the beliefs that are most resistant to change. Ellis (1962) like Adler does not believe in the Freudian concept of the instinctual unconsciousness but contends that any material which is unconscious can usually be readily brought into awareness by a quick examination of the belief system of the patient. This information is not deeply hidden but is just below conscious awareness.

The Nature of Humans

1. *Gemeinschaftsgefühl versus Gesellschaftsgefühl.* Adlerian theory holds that people are inherently good and have a natural concern for the welfare of others. This characteristic, although present at birth, must

be developed for it to be made manifest; hence the importance of early training within the family. This tendency to care about the group, of which the individual is a part, Adler referred to as *Gemeinschaftsgefühl*, which is roughly translated as "social interest," "community interest," or "social feeling" (Dreikurs, 1950). Ellis takes more of a centralist position with respect to the basic nature of humans. He sees people being born with a distinct tendency to think and behave in ways that are self-defeating and subsequently deleterious to the greater society, as well as having a proclivity to enjoy life and to think in their own best interest. Ellis urges people to think of their own welfare first. He concedes the importance of positive interaction with other people, but he would conceive of this as more of a partnership or corporation of individuals coming together for their individual benefit. The German concept of *Gesellschaftsgefühl* would more appropriately fit his philosophy.

This differing view may be more apparent than real. Ellis (1977d) states that when one considers his own long-term best interest, there must follow the welfare of others; for example, if I steal from my neighbor, I set myself up to be stolen from in return by my neighbors or others. Ellis (1975) refers to immediate gratification as "self defeating, short-range hedonism."

2. *Worth.* In keeping with the idea of social interest, Adlerian philosophy believes in the concept of social equality or equal worth to human existence (Adler, 1964b). RET (Ellis & Abrahams, 1978) discards the concept of equality by stating that humans neither have nor lack worth; humans are just human beings. We all have a proclivity to think irrationally. That is, we all tend to place self-damning "shoulds," "oughts," and "musts" upon ourselves and other family members; becoming more socially interested will not improve our worth as human beings. Conversely, Dreikurs, speaking from the IP position, criticizes this intrapsychic focus of Ellis for ignoring the social needs of people (Terner & Pew, 1978).

3. *Conceptualizing the problem.* Adler and Ellis would both agree that often the problems within a family result from inadequate education or misinformation (Dreikurs, 1953). According to Ellis (1975), the more difficult problems within the family arise from "irrational beliefs," "shoulds," "oughts," and "musts." Family members mistakenly believe that whatever behavior another member engages in which displeases them ought not, should not, must not exist. Ellis calls this "magical" thinking. These people are confusing their demands on others with

universal laws. If the family member really ought to be acting in a different manner, then there would be a natural law in the universe which would bring forth this desired behavior. However, since the given family member behaved or continues to behave in a manner which is displeasing, it proves that there is no such law in the universe (Ellis, 1957).

Similarly, "basic mistakes" are the root of serious problems within family members and the family as a group in Adlerian thinking (Dreikurs, 1946). Mistaken beliefs and basic mistakes distort reality, which results in family discord. Ellis always sees the root of the family problem as demands upon self and other family members to behave in a manner different from that which exists. This leads to various misplaced expressions of emotion and to magical thinking; for example, "Because I don't like something it shouldn't exist."

4. *Emotions.* Both RET and IP theory view emotions as a form of thinking. Family members create and control their emotions through their thinking. Dreikurs (1969) very much agreed with Ellis on the role of emotions. Family members create those emotions that will support their cognitive intent. Emotions supply the energy which moves people toward their goals (Adler, 1969). Whereas it is helpful to identify the emotion as a clue to cognitive intent, it is more efficient to work with the cognitive purpose. Because emotions are irrational, when the family therapist deals with the family's emotions, everyone, including the therapist, is engaging in irrational behavior.

5. *The life tasks.* For the Adlerian family therapist the three life tasks of love, work, and community are essential to the therapeutic process. Ellis would strongly disagree with the necessity of the life tasks (Ellis & Abrahams, 1978). Ellis contends that there is no evidence to support the notion that family members need to successfully satisfy anything like the Adlerian notion of life tasks. He goes further and states that there are relatively few human needs, and the few that do exist would be confined to basic necessities for maintaining life: food, water, and the like. He contends that there are no such needs as love, work, friendship, or a feeling of self-worth. To believe that one needs these would be evidence of irrational thinking, mistaken beliefs (Ellis, 1971a). Ellis does recognize that we live in this world with other people, and unfortunately we are innately prone to try to rise above and be superior to others, try to obtain the approval of others, fulfill the expectations of others, and demand that everyone like, if not love us. It is helpful because we live in a world with other people, that they

value us and that we have sufficient social skills to obtain friends and lovers. Even if we don't need friends and lovers, they do make life more enjoyable; therefore, they are worth cultivating.

Dreikurs and Mosak (1966, 1967) have suggested a fourth and fifth life task, getting along with oneself and a spiritual need. Ellis would see getting along with oneself as helpful but not essential. He would see it as more important than the other tasks which Adlerians think of as needs.

The spiritual, expressed in terms of religion, has drawn considerable attack from Ellis (1970a). He contends that belief in a deity, life after death, or any of the other traditional expressions of religion is irrational, fanciful thinking. Adler (1931) considers religion an important and useful component with the family. Mosak and Dreikurs believe that coming to some personal understanding of one's purpose on earth and the nature of the universe is necessary for optimal development. Usually families meet this task through an organized religion, but it can also be accomplished through a personal commitment and feeling of belonging which does not necessitate belief in an organized religion or even the typical ideas of a deity or life after death (Dreikurs & Mosak, 1967).

6. *Parental modeling.* Both theories see the importance of parental modeling in the formation of children's development, but they also believe that the child has choice and is not the victim of the parental modeling. Adlerians note that individuals always decide what they will use from heredity and the environment, including the parental modeling, to form their own unique pattern of movement through life (Dreikurs, 1948). Ellis (1975) is in agreement with this position unless people are in a severe psychotic state such as mania, in which case they may not have free choice over their behavior.

7. *Family system.* There is a basic difference between RET and IP family therapy when it comes to the idea of a family system. Adlerian psychology is a systems theory which places emphasis on the family constellation (Croake & Hinkle, 1983). This notion includes homeostasis as an important aspect of the family system. For example, if one family member very freely spends money, another is likely to be extremely frugal; or if one member is extremely socially outgoing, another will be highly introverted. IP does not ignore the individual, but it is the individual's actions as they affect the family system which is attended.

Ellis (1978) has been negative in his criticism of those schools of thought which support a systems theory. He believes that a systems theory neglects the individual volition and actions of each of the family members. Therefore, he opposes any consideration of a family system.

IP believes that a change in the behavior of one of the family members means a change in the total family dynamics. When one member of the family changes the interaction with another member, the recipient of that behavior will no longer be able to respond in the previous interactional pattern. This changed interaction between two members means that the holistic function of the family unit has been altered (Dreikurs & Soltz, 1967).

As indicated, IP and RET are in agreement (with the exception for Ellis of some psychotic states) that people mediate between any given stimulus and response. The therapeutic implication of this freedom to choose one's reaction to stimuli is the idea that "everything can be different" (Terner & Pew, 1978). There is always the possibility of change no matter how difficult the problem within the family. The family can always see the situation differently. Condemnation is discouraging and acceptance is encouraging. Furthermore, acceptance never means forsaking desire, only the demand that the situation be different in order for the family members to be happy (Croake & Rusk, 1980; Ellis, 1973b).

8. *Inborn tendencies.* RET places considerable import on the family environment for young children whom Ellis sees as being most vulnerable to the influence of others as a reaffirmation of strong, innate, self-defeating tendencies. In addition to an inborn tendency toward short-range hedonism, irrational beliefs, wishful thinking, intolerance, and perfectionistic demands, young children readily ascribe to these and other self-defeating demands due to the inculcations of their parents and others close to them during the early years of their existence (Ellis & Knaus, 1977). Ellis agrees with IP and Maslow (1963) that humans have a proclivity to self-actualize. According to Ellis (1971a), humans also tend toward behavior which is intolerant, dogmatic, and superstitious. Adler (1969) contends that the life style is formed in the first four to six years of life. RET sees the importance of the family milieu in fostering the tendency for social interest. Adler would not subscribe to inborn tendencies to be self-destructive and to hate as does Ellis.

Ellis believes people are naturally lazy and procrastinating (Ellis & Knaus, 1977). This view is in sharp contrast to the IP position, which ascribes lazy and procrastinating behavior to "overambition." People exhibiting such inertia from an Adlerian perspective are discouraged. They desire superiority, and they view this self-ideal as being so distant from their present being that they give up or become the best at being the worst (Dreikurs, 1961b).

Both schools consider the mediating apperception of people to their biological composition as more important than the biological condition per se. Adler speaks of the importance of organ inferiority and organ specificity in neuroses (Adler, 1927). Ellis (1984) acknowledges that humans innately tend to become physically impaired when they emotionally upset themselves with their irrational thinking or inappropriately emote. Those are the various forms of irrational thinking to which RET attends most directly.

Physiologically based self-defeating behaviors include wishful thinking; confusing needs with wants, demands with desires; self-condemnation rather than critical assessment of behavior; overgeneralization and distortion as to the extent and depth of undesirable behavior in self and others; inertia because change requires persistent hard work; indulging in obviously harmful consumption of too much or of harmful substances; cleaving onto irrational family, religious, political, philosophical, cultural myths; overvigilance and cautiousness when reasonable scrutiny would be more helpful; and forgetting that some action is noxious even when noted previously. Adlerians would agree with all of these, with the possible exception of the last item, but would see them as learned rather than biologically grounded. With reference to forgetting self-defeating behavior, and hence repeating it, IP posits that behavior continues only as long as it serves the individual's purpose (Dreikurs, 1951). This position would be in disagreement with Ellis' biological proclivity and socially learned position.

Open Forum

Unlike most schools of psychotherapy, both IP and RET frequently treat families in a public setting. Adherents of both IP (Dreikurs, Corsini, Lowe, & Sonstegard, 1959) and RET (Ellis & Grieger, 1977) believe in the parsimony of the public forum; those in the audience can learn effective methods for dealing with their own family problems by noting the help given to the family in focus, who may have similar difficulties. Ellis appreciates the efficiency of an entire audience learning to think and behave more rationally. IP therapists likewise see the value in exposing everyone to typical basic mistakes. Ellis notes these as self-defeating and not in the individual's best interest. IP points to the mischief-making purpose and the deleterious effects on the family. Effectiveness is greater according to IP (Croake, 1983) for an additional reason: the community life task as well as the love task is being attended. If a family works out its problems within its greater community, there is an increased understanding and acceptance not only within the family, but within the community as well.

CONCEPTUALIZATION OF WELL-FUNCTIONING AND DYSFUNCTIONAL FAMILIES

Self-interest/Social Interest

Ellis advocates a democratic model for the family which is very similar to the Adlerian position. However, Ellis places the individual in advance of the group, including the family group. As will be discussed later in this chapter, his method of family therapy does not emphasize the family unit. Attention is given to individuals as they interact with other family members. The concept of self-interest versus social interest is a key point for Ellis (1962) as one differentiates the RET system from Adlerian psychology. Adler (1931) believes that the purpose of life is to serve others. Ellis (1977c) believes that the purpose of life is to have a "ball." Ellis is not advocating throwing caution to the wind. He advocates hedonism, but long range, not short range. When people act in a manner that will be conducive to their long-range best interest, they will behave cooperatively and have a feeling of belonging within the family. The democratic model is the best solution for meeting the desires of each family member. Therefore, the functional family in both IP and RET is cooperative, democratic, and works for the common good.

Rational Thinking

Rational thinking is characteristic of good functioning. Each of the family members' belief systems would be characterized by self-acceptance and nondemanding acceptance of the other members of the family. This is very similar to the Adlerian notion of concordance between the self and the self-ideal (Ansbacher & Ansbacher, 1956).

Irrational thinking would typify dysfunction. Irrationality is seen in language which is filled with "shoulds," "oughts," and "musts." These demanding words are damning of self and other family members and act as a restriction on freedom of expression. Adlerians also see the benefit of eliminating "the tyranny of the shoulds," as Karen Horney (1951) put it. When all family members accept one another, including all their human imperfections, the atmosphere in the home is one of encouragement. Each family member is free to pursue activities without fear of failure. Adler and Ellis agree that demanding perfection in self or another family member only interferes with successful living. The result of demands is maladaptive behavior.

Self-acceptance

RET places much emphasis on self-acceptance, to be inner directed. IP is in agreement in this regard. Self-blame only interferes with happiness and impedes progress toward one's goals. Self-blame also promotes a family atmosphere of blame which is discouraging to everyone. Ellis and Adler are further in agreement with a problem-solving attitude within the family. When difficulties do arise, seeking solutions, not blaming or self-elevation at the expense of another, is emphasized. The family moves forward in life "without ego involvement" (Ellis, 1973a).

Life Style

Adlerians believe that no one life style is any better than any other (Mosak, 1979); rather, it is the use one makes of what one possesses. This concept would be accepted by Ellis. He would not express the language of life style or the "psychology of use," but would speak of rational thinking and freedom from demands. Ellis would speak of the absence of "shoulds," "oughts," and "musts," rather than goals of misbehavior.

Neurotic goals, in Individual Psychology, are self-centered and aimed at elevating the self above others. RET would not tend to such a notion, preferring to see healthy goals as long-range hedonism and short-range hedonistic goals as self-defeating and thus neurotic. Passing up a second dessert in order to maintain a normal body weight would be an example of long-range hedonism. Conversely, eating the second helping of dessert may be rationalized, but the deleterious result will not be in one's best interest.

The healthy family in IP shows as much concern for others as for themselves. The result, from an RET point of reference, is the same but the motivation comes from self-interest first. In this respect Ellis (1975) has referred to Adlerians as a "bunch of boy scouts." Ellis may be making this comment without fully understanding the concept of social interest, incorrectly equating it with altruism. Altruism seems to place the interest of the group ahead of any individual. The individual is also a member of the group. The individual's desires, therefore, are always a consideration in any decision making, as is his need for self-actualization.

The dysfunctional family viewed by Adlerians is burdened by over-ambition, discouragement, and an inferiority complex. The overambition is a striving for personal superiority rather than the welfare of the family as a whole. Discouragement is giving up the search for proactive solutions to family problems and a retreat into avoidance or aggression. The inferiority complex is the exaggeration of realistic feelings of inferiority which are felt by all people but seen as being unique and impossible to contend with in the dysfunctional family. They totalize from a given deficiency, real or imagined, to the person and family as a whole being defective and needing to be greater than it can be. From an RET point of view, dysfunction results when negative nonsense (irrational beliefs) is present in all family members. It is then possible for a family to be functional if only one person, probably an adult, thinks rationally and behaves in a fashion which promotes self and family welfare. The promotion of family welfare would follow from the individual member thinking in a selfish, long-range, hedonistic way that the better functioning of the family will be beneficial to his or her own best interests.

THE ROLE OF THE THERAPIST

Acceptance

Ellis (1973a) is above all accepting of the patient. He is never condemning. His aim is always to challenge self-defeating beliefs and to reinforce those that are in the patient's self-interest. To accomplish this aim the RET therapist is extremely active and directive. The therapist elicits from the family that which is troublesome to them and then proceeds to indicate the negative nonsense (basic mistakes) which the individual family members are using to make life difficult for themselves. The RET therapist very much controls the direction of the family interview.

Adlerian family therapists also are very active and directive, but there is more of an emphasis on serving as a model in democratic leadership, for example, modeling for the parents proper ways of interacting with children or showing respect as family members might respect each other. The Adlerian therapist certainly believes in accepting the patient, but this is not as focal as in RET.

Encouragement

The RET therapist pushes the family members to try on new behaviors which will be in their own personal best interest. Failures are expected. The attempts are applauded. In Adlerian terms "encouragement" means to continually search for answers to family problems. This is characteristic of each Adlerian family therapy session and serves as a model for the family's day-to-day interaction. As in RET, the IP therapist may make suggestions for actions which might improve the family atmosphere. Both schools of therapy encourage family members. Ellis emphasizes individual self-acceptance, effort, and personal happiness (Ellis, 1982a). Adlerians place a premium on family cooperation and mutual problem solving. See Chapters 3 and 11 in this book for a more elaborate discussion of the encouragement process in IP.

Therapist Characteristics

RET therapists are unique in their attitudes and manner. They do not feel that it is necessary or even important to like the family or its members in order to be of help to them. The emphasis is on helping them rid themselves of the irrational beliefs that are making life unpleasant for them. If one of the family members comments that the therapist seems not to like or is disinterested in him or her personally, the therapist uses this as an opportunity to point to the extreme need by the family or its member to be liked and esteemed. The therapist might say, "Why is it necessary that I like you in order to help you?" This response by the therapist would likely be forthcoming even if the therapist did like the family or the concerned member. Further, "Where is the evidence that it is awful, that you can't stand it if I don't like you?"

Individual Psychology places the relationship of the therapist to the family as the first order of business. Adler (in Ansbacher & Ansbacher, 1956) sees psychotherapy as an exercise in cooperation and believes that success can result only when the therapist is genuinely interested in the family. Both RET and IP would agree with cooperation between therapist and family, but they differ sharply when it comes to the therapist's interest in the family: Adlerians see it as essential and Ellis sees it as unimportant (Ellis & Grieger, 1977).

Neither school of therapy would tie the therapist's success or significance as a person to the patient's behavior. It is assumed that the RET therapist is inner-directed, and any elevation or devaluation of self by the therapist would be seen as undesirable, irrational, inappropriate, and neurotic (Ellis, 1963). Similarly, Adler believes that most important, after winning the family's cooperation, is to never worry about one's own success as a therapist: "The psychotherapist must lose all thought of himself and all sensitiveness about his ascendency, and must never demand anything of the patient" (Adler, in Ansbacher & Ansbacher, 1956, p. 341).

The RET therapist is informal in appearance and manner and supposedly free of most irrational thinking. The therapist's language is probably colloquial and often colorful. This therapeutic demeanor would serve to model rational behavior. A concretized example would be the therapist's speech, which would be free of "shoulds," "oughts," "musts," and the verb "to be." (The verb "to be" will receive elaboration further along.) The Adlerian therapist would not be in disagreement with the appearance, manner, and expected role model. It is a fact within both theoretical frames that the therapists tend to vary greatly in their appearance and demeanor. However, Adlerians do not do as well as RET therapists in avoiding the use of "shoulds," "oughts," "musts," or the verb "to be," even though they would theoretically agree on the importance of eliminating their use in language. Ellis (1977d) is more firm in the elimination of these words. Once Adlerians understand the implications of their use they will likely eliminate them from their vocabularies, perhaps modeling themselves after Mosak (1977), who chides patients who " 'should' on themselves" or others.

Educational Role

As indicated, both schools of psychology emphasize education and reeducation. Ellis is more vociferous in his educating, especially when it comes to challenging the patient's irrational beliefs. Virtually all the therapy conducted by RET and IP could be considered within the education model. Even when either type of therapist is acting in a negotiating role between family members, they are educating the family as to the use of this method. An Adlerian therapist typically asks each family member if he or she is willing to act a new pattern of behavior for one week, at which time it would be reevaluated. If all family members agree, the new behavior is given a one-week trial. Ellis would feel free to use the same method or borrow more directly from behavior therapy: "What are you willing to do for your wife if she makes dinner for you?" Dreikurs ended the family session by asking all members of the family what they had learned during the session. He would start the next family therapy session with them by asking the same question: "What did you learn last time that we met?" He believed that eliminating those questions would limit the learning that takes place (Dreikurs, 1967).

ASSESSING THE SYSTEM: THE MEANING OF BEHAVIOR AND GOAL SETTING

Adlerian family theapy is a systems theory which also pays attention to the needs of the individual family member. RET is not a systems theory. Therefore, comparisons within this section of the chapter are limited by the conceptual differences of the two approaches. IP assesses behavior of family members as it affects them and the family system.

The Initial Question

The Adlerian therapist will ask what the family's purpose is in coming for treatment. The one who speaks first frequently attempts to take the overt or obvious leadership or power position in the family (Dreikurs & Grey, 1968). IP therapists ask each family member his or her view of the problem presented or the home situation in general. This method models equal respect as well as noting each family member's version of the current situation.

Ellis (1979) also asks the family members in turn how they see the problem. He listens very briefly to each member's version of the situation and then proceeds to show each person how his own beliefs are causing him to be upset. It is not the family situation or the actions, but each individual family member's own irrational thinking about what is going on which is the problem. This is similar to Adler's ideas of private logic. Each person behaves as if his opinion of the situation is correct. In turn his opinion is based on the beliefs within which he attaches meaning to the experience.

Purposive Goal Behavior

Both theorists recognize the purposive intent of all behavior, but the way in which they use this knowledge is very different. In IP the specific purpose of the individual family member's behavior as it affects the system is determined. For example, a teenage daughter may stay out beyond curfew time for the purpose of maintaining a reputation as a rebel and to be free from the responsibilities and obligations which come with keeping agreements that she sees as arbitrary and unfair. This action upsets the family system. The father, in this instance, feels that he must maintain his position of authority, so he denies the daughter the use of the car for one week. This angers mother, because now she does not have someone to do the shopping. Therefore, she assigns the shopping to the 10-year-old, who dutifully, with downtrodden look, walks to the store three times to bring home the groceries. Rebellious and martyred patterns are reinforced in the children, and conflict between the parents and the entire family is furthered. The IP therapist, using the stochastic method (Dreikurs, 1962), attempts to guess at the purpose of the behavior of each of the family members.

As the guesses become increasingly accurate, family members see their own behavior and that of the others in a new way, and the system changes. Because all members now realize their purpose, they are not as likely to continue the dysfunctional behavior. Adler (1931) termed this "spitting in the soup." The family can continue to behave in the old manner, but the payoff is not as great: One can continue to drink the soup, but it no longer tastes as good.

Ellis (1978) would recognize the purposiveness of the behavior and use it to make guesses as to the self-defeating beliefs of each of the family members without necessarily mentioning the purpose of the behavior. For example, he would proceed to show the adolescent girl that her irrational thinking and short-range hedonism not only upsets her parents but, more important, makes life difficult for herself as well. Besides getting herself into difficulty, she invariably puts herself down for her ineffective behavior. Similarly, he would show each of the parents how they, not their daughter, were upsetting themselves with their demands on her and probably their own self-condemnation as parents because of the irresponsible behavior of their child.

Private Logic

Individual Psychology notes that no matter how illogical people's behavior may appear, once the therapist understands the basic premise upon which the behavior is based, the behavior and the premise are in concert. Adlerians refer to this idiosyncratic thinking which justifies behavior as "private logic." By its nature "private" means that it is not thinking that is open to consensual validation. It is the unique production of the individual (Dreikurs, 1961a). In the example above, the logic of the adolescent for staying out until 2:00 A.M. rather than returning home by the 11:00 P.M. curfew time could be something like: "I shouldn't have to be in at 11:00 P.M. I am the oldest in the family, and ought to be able to set my own time. Therefore, it is only reasonable that I stay out as late as I like." Adler (1956) referred to what Dreikurs termed "private logic" as "private frame of reference." It is seen in all neurotic behavior. It is a method for avoiding the solution to life's problems. It makes sense from the individual's internal frame of reference but not to the objective observer.

Ellis (1971c) believes that people not only form false premises based upon their, in Adlerian terminology, "basic mistakes," they additionally make illogical deductions from these premises. Therefore, not only is their basic premise neurotic, but their reasoning based on the neurotic premise is also irrational. This, then, is a basic theoretical difference between IP and RET. In the foregoing example, Ellis would see all of the behavior as self-defeating, irrational, and mostly illogical on the part of each family member who is upset.

Life Style Assessment

This is an important aspect of family therapy in IP with those of adolescent age and older. By assessing the life style of each of the family members, everyone is more clearly aware of the purposes of positive and negative behavior. Family members see how the various individual life styles mesh in a reinforcing manner. The one, for example, who has the need to suffer requires another family member who has a desire to dominate. One can't suffer if another is not willing to cooperate in helping the individual suffer. When all of the family members' life styles are assessed in the presence of the entire family, the family life style is also clarified. This includes biased apperceptions, values, methods of operation, and fictive goals which are characteristic of all of the family members. Not only are they unique as individuals, but they are also unique as a family with respect to their style of confronting the tasks of life.

Ellis does not make use of the life style assessment in his therapy. He might recognize the validity of many of the conclusions, but he would feel that the time taken from the assessments could be better spent directly attacking each family member's irrational beliefs. Adlerian therapists do on occasion make use of Ellis' method of attacking irrational beliefs. On these occasions they find the life style assessment to be of much help in pinpointing the basic mistakes.

Ellis would not object to, but would typically not choose to utilize such Adlerian diagnostic techniques as early recollections, the family's day, or the family constellation.

Stochastic Method

Diagnosis is readily achieved within RET by using the stochastic method. Ellis (1963) observes that most human beings suffer from common forms of irrational thinking (basic mistakes). He quickly shows people that learning occurs through an S-O-R rather than S-R pattern. It is "O" and not "S" to which the individual is responding inappropriately. The family members emotionally disturb themselves when they insist that they must have their desires satisfied rather than merely wanting whatever it is that they desire. In our society the demands are so common that Ellis can within a few minutes guess at many of the irrational beliefs which each of the family members are saying to themselves. By a similar method, Adlerians can readily predict the behavior of children based on the common child-rearing mistakes made in our culture (Dreikurs, Grunwald, & Pepper, 1971).

COMPARISON OF THE BEHAVIOR CHANGE MODEL OF IP AND RET FAMILY THERAPY

Since the time of Adler's separation from the Vienna Psychoanalytic Society to the present, IP (Orgler, 1965) and later RET (Ellis, 1975) have been accused of being ego psychologies. The implication of being an ego psychology is the lack of depth attributed to the two schools. The assumption is that little more than guidance is offered because without consideration of the unconscious the therapies do not go deep enough (Freud, 1963). RET and IP focus on the purpose of behavior. They do not believe that behavior is caused, let alone caused by a great unconscious psychic energy. In fact they are ego psychologies.

Model for Behavior Change

1. *Learning theory.* Adler and Ellis would fit comfortably with Edward Chase Tolman's learning theory, which sees the organism as purposive and goal directed (Tolman, 1932). People are motivated by expectations, and reinforcement merely confirms or does not confirm expectations. This fits clearly with Dreikurs' remark that "reward and punishment no longer work" (Dreikurs, 1957). RET and IP see negative and positive reinforcers as somewhat unpredictable, aimed at symptom removal and not attitudinal change, lacking in generalization, furthering irresponsibility, time limited in their effectiveness, and seldom working outside of a controlled laboratory setting (Mosak, 1971).

Ellis, unlike Adlerians, does use both positive and negative reinforcement but believes that they are limited in value as indicated above. Ellis (1979) focuses on the individual family member's self-reinforcement. For example, a wife complains that she wants more sex. The husband claims that he too wishes to have a more active sex life. Ellis would determine what is rewarding to the husband—for example, listening to the 11 P.M. news—and what is punishment—say, painting the fence. Every time the husband initiates sex with his wife, he can then watch the 11 P.M. news. If he does not initiate sex before 10 P.M. on any given day, he must go outside and paint three slats in the fence regardless of the weather. Ellis sometimes arranges for other family members to offer rewards; for example, the wife might agree to shining her husband's shoes each time that he initiates sex.

Additionally, Ellis (1968) would use reciprocal inhibition advocated by Wolpe (1958), but he would be much closer to the cognitive-behavioral therapists such as Bandura (1969), Mahoney (1977), and Meichenbaum (1977) in combining the reinforcement ideas of Skinner (1938) and Eysenck (1964) with the cognitive theorists including Adler (1956), Rogers (1961), and Frankl (1966). To reiterate, however, Ellis (1972) would spend the bulk of time in therapy concentrating on changing the irrational beliefs (basic mistakes) of the family members. This cognitive restructuring would be seen as more time efficient and more effective in producing long-lasting and beneficial changes within the family members.

2. *Correcting basic mistaken beliefs.* The agreement of Adler and Ellis is clear in their views and emphasis on correcting mistaken beliefs. Both schools operate from the premise that mistaken beliefs are indigenous to neuroses, psychoses, and personality disturbances of any variety. Even though they agree on the central role of mistaken beliefs, they disagree with respect to apperception and behavior that follows from apperceptions.

Adler (1964c) posits that once people develop their distorted views of themselves, others, and the world, they tend to arrange conditions, interpersonal relationships, and circumstances to confirm their biased apperceptions. As Mosak (1954) says, "believing is seeing." The biased apperceptions are always in line with the fictive goal to which the individual is striving. If a particular behavior no longer works for maintaining the apperceptive schema and moving toward the fictive goal, the individual drops that behavior. RET theorists Ellis and Blum (1968) do not agree with the IP position of loss of behavior if it is no longer effective in the view of the individual. RET claims that the human condition is characterized by a proclivity to think and behave irrationally. This is furthered by the child's early conditioning in irrational thinking by his family and others. The tendencies become self-defeating behavioral *habits* irrespective of their current effectiveness. The family member's wishful thinking and demands that other members be different continues independent of the no longer or, frequently, never effective behavior.

IP and RET actively work on mistaken beliefs. IP uses children's mistaken goals of behavior and life style assessments to identify the mistaken beliefs and to begin the reeducation process (Mosak, 1972). IP therapists show the family members that their own family of origin constellations, as well as the present family dynamics, have aided and supported their basic mistakes. Ellis directly attacks the beliefs as unscientific and irrational. He tells the family members that their wants are not universal laws that others are required to obey. It is a fantasy, not a law. Others will continue to behave as they choose.

3. *New options.* Adler (1964a) notes that neurotic behavior is characterized by the antithetical mode of apperception: Situations are black or white, with no middle ground or shades of grey. Similarly, Ellis (1957) indicates that neurotic behavior is characterized by exaggeration and overgeneralization. Symptoms become "awful" rather than merely inconvenient or unfortunate. Additionally, the overgeneralization misconstrues the undesired behavior to always be present, rather than realistically present sometimes.

IP asks the family for suggestions to correct antithetical modes of apperception as well as directly pointing out that extreme statements such as never and always are inaccurate and cannot be supported by the complaining family member. The therapist will also indicate that the behavior is not occurring during the session. Asking the complaining member to indicate specifically the behavior and when and where it occurred will quickly show the overgeneralization as well as exaggeration. Ellis (1975) presents the unchallengeable evidence that people are too complex and multifaceted in their actions to ever be characterized by labels.

IP family therapy works toward consensual agreement to try on new forms of behavior for a week, at which time reevaluation occurs. This is an active method for the engagement of new options. Ellis works with the irrational thinking and behavior of each family member and elicits as well as suggests specific new behavior as a method of identifying new options.

4. *Power plays.* Adlerian therapists will observe as many power plays within the family as RET therapists. However, Adlerian therapists are more likely to work to disengage the struggles within the family than is Ellis. Ellis works with the individual family members and their complaints. He accepts at face value the individual's perception of other family members. He then shows the person that regardless of the unfair or unreasonable behavior of the others, it is the complaining person who is upsetting himself or herself. He further challenges the assumption that just because it would be better if the family behaved differently, they must behave differently. For example, he might ask, "Why must your daughter come in by curfew time?" Whatever the reasonable reply

from the parent, Ellis would say, "Those are good reasons, but where is it written that just because it would be better if she did come in on time, she must come in on time?" Where is the universal law that we must always do what is in our best interest and the best interest of our family? If there is such a law, then your daughter would be coming in by 11:00 P.M.

5. *Social interest.* Mental health according to RET is best achieved by each family member giving first consideration to himself or herself. The result may be the same as Adler recommends because when the individual considers his or her own best interest in the long-range hedonistic conception, he or she will no doubt do that which is best for the family (Ellis & Abrahams, 1978). Ellis believes that social interest will not improve family dynamics unless the individual members rid themselves of the "shoulds," "oughts," and "musts" (Corsini, 1973). Social interest is the heart of family well-being in IP (Croake & Hinkle, 1983). Adler (1958) conceives of mental health improvement as a decreasing distance between the self-ideal—that which we would be if we were perfect—and the self—that view we presently hold of ourselves. The more realistic our goals, the more likely will be the concordance between the self and the self-ideal.

RET does not discuss concepts such as the self and the ideal self, but does speak of beliefs, behaviors, tendencies, and traits. Mental health is an ongoing, lifelong challenge of the human condition to overcome the tendencies toward procrastination, underemoting or overemoting, wishful thinking, intolerance, short-range hedonism, irrational beliefs, and self-damning (Ellis, 1977c).

6. *Negotiation of differences.* The difference between social interest and self-interest can also be seen in the negotiating process within the family. IP believes that family conflict and family dysfunction can be resolved only through negotiating differences based on mutual respect (Dreikurs, 1963). RET suggests that family conflict is best resolved when each of the members has complete acceptance of himself or herself. When we fully accept ourselves, we are free of mistaken beliefs. This allows us to solve family conflicts in a problem-centered, rather than a self-centered manner. Like Adlerian theory, when emotional health is present people are free to work on the problem without having concern about winning or losing, dominating or submitting, personal triumph or defeat.

Adlerians are going to emphasize mutual respect: neither dominating nor submitting (Dreikurs, 1971). Ellis (1962) believes that mutual respect may be an outcome of acting in one's self-interest, but it is certainly not a goal. He would not hold that mutual respect is a requisite to the negotiation of differences, and those families which hold such a myth are placing a roadblock in the way of solving problems.

7. *Agreements.* IP sees agreements as indigenous to any democratic setting. The family orientation provides the most propitious time for the individual to learn the importance of keeping agreements. Agreements teach responsibility with freedom. The family members are free to enter into agreements and learn that satisfactory resolution can come from an agreement which is based on mutual respect. They also learn the natural and logical consequences which follow from broken agreements (Dreikurs & Grey, 1968).

RET does recognize the importance of individual family members learning to cooperate together. Cooperation results in less stress, enjoyment, and family efficiency. Agreements are one effective method for promoting cooperation. Paramount would be the individual family members learning to tolerate and accept themselves and other family members. It is lack of acceptance which fosters noncooperation (Ellis, 1979).

STRATEGIES AND TECHNIQUES COMMONLY USED IN IP AND RET FAMILY THERAPY

It has been said that Adlerian family therapists appear like reinforcement theorists when doing therapy, and the philosophy upon which their therapy is based resembles that of Carl Rogers (Dreikurs, 1960). RET shares many common philosophical beliefs with IP. It readily employs reinforcement and other techniques used in behavior therapy. Both approaches to psychotherapy assume that the family's interpretation of events is more important in dysfunction than the event itself.

The ABC Model

RET is a highly systematized approach to psychotherapy (Ellis & Whitely, 1979). Family members are taught, using a structured model, that they upset themselves. The behavior of other family members can only provide possibilities. Another's behavior will not emotionally affect us. Similarly, Dreikurs (1954) states that we make of the situation that which will fit our purposes.

The structured RET model begins with the activating event A. A is the stimulus which prompts our belief system, B. B contains two parts: the rational beliefs, rB, and the irrational beliefs, iB. Rational beliefs are accurate assessments of the situation. They neither underevoke nor overevoke emotion. The consequences, *C*, of *B's* are both emotions and behaviors in Ellis' system (Ellis, 1980). Adlerians are in agreement with this model, although they don't express it in *ABC* terms. *C* is a regular focus of Dreikurs' (1972) therapy: "And then what did you do?" This statement is made to parents in reaction to the child's misbehavior. It provides a clue as to the child's purpose in evoking *A* to which the parent responds with *C*. Adlerians will spend more time teaching methods for coping with *A*, and RET will spend more time challenging *iB's*.

The next step in the *ABC* model is disputing, *D*, each *iB*. Irrational beliefs are magical because they cannot be proven. Because RET is essentially the application of the scientific method to the therapeutic process, the therapist challenges the *iB's*, by saying, for example, "Where is the evidence that the *A* is awful rather than undesirable?"

Cognitive effect, *cE*, is the rational answer that results from disputing the *iB's*; for example, "It is unfortunate that *A* occurred, but it is not catastrophic." Behavioral effect, *bE*, follows from successfully disputing the *iB's*; for example, "I reduced my level of tension on a subjective scale from near 90 down to 10."

Beginning the Process of Psychotherapy

Adlerian psychotherapy has the aim of changes in the life style of the individual or changes in the life style of the family. Ellis (1969) emphasizes that when family treatment is correctly conducted, it is psychotherapy. Because Adlerians view the family as a system, in theory, seeing the family together would be the modality of choice. Unlike family counseling, which frequently interviews the parents separately from the children unless the children are of adolescent age or older, family therapy usually involves all members being present for each session, though the therapist may choose to work with parts of the family at any given time.

Ellis (1979) prefers to interview the entire family at least once when he or the patient determines that there is a family problem. The purpose for seeing all of the family members together is similar to that of IP. It gives the therapist an opportunity to observe the family dynamics. Ellis (1978) notes the dyadic conflicts and supports. He does not, as noted earlier, treat the system. Hence he will choose to see dyads, individual family members, or the entire family on various occasions. RET recognizes that individuals living in a family setting will be intimately involved with one another and will have interpersonal conflicts. That notwithstanding, it is the intrapsychic conflict for each troubled member to which Ellis attends.

Goal Alignment

Both therapies commence with treatment after there is goal alignment. This is more readily accomplished in RET because the therapist is making separate alignments with each family member. The IP therapist takes much longer in arriving at a family consensus. Goal alignment with the family group is seen as a major therapeutic step in IP, but only as an initial step in RET. Both approaches continue to realign goals as therapy proceeds.

Homework

The *ABCDE* steps previously discussed constitute the essentials of RET (Ellis, 1971b). RET routinely gives the family members homework forms to be completed before the next session. The *ABCDE* steps are learned in the first session with the therapist. The *ABCDE* constitutes the first part of each homework assignment. The sections that follow give the family members a specific frame in which to work through their demanding and condemning attitudes (Ellis & Grieger, 1977).

F is completed *if* the person did not challenge the *iB*'s with an explanation for the lack of completion. *G* is a statement by the person which indicates the activities that the person would most like to end. *H* indicates the activities in which the individual would like to engage. *I* is a statement of the emotions and ideas which the individual would most like to change. *J* represents the specific assignments given by the therapist, self, or other family members. *K* is a report of the activities which met the assignments. *L* is a Likert-type self-rating indicating the degree to which the person worked at completing the homework assignment. *M* indicates the number of times the family member challenged his or her *iB*'s. *N* is an opportunity for the member to state the other activities in which he or she engaged as a method of changing *iB*'s and *C*'s. *O* is a three-level response indicating the amount of RET reading completed. *P* represents the topics which the person would like to discuss at the next session.

This homework sheet is given frequently to all family members who are emotionally upset by the family situation. The sheet can be used by anyone who is able to read and write at a minimal level. The formal procedure for completing the homework helps the family overcome tendencies to procrastinate and prompts individuals to actively work on their beliefs in a more effective manner.

The *iB*'s are immediately attacked by the therapist. For example, in the situation noted earlier, it might be asked of the 16-year-old daughter, "Why must you feel that you should be able to determine when you will return home? How is it awful that you are given a curfew by your parents?" The daughter might state, "It's unfair. I'm responsible, and it ruins the evening if I have to come in just as activities are getting started." Ellis might respond, "Those are good reasons. But how is it awful that you are given a curfew? How is it more than inconvenient or unfortunate?" Ellis is showing the daughter and the others present how to dispute iB's, change iB's to rB's, observe that iB's rather than A cause C, not overgeneralize, and assume responsibility for their own feelings.

The therapist identifies for the patient and the other family members the A. In the example we've been using it is the incident of staying out past curfew. Also identified for each family member is his or her particular C. Mother and father feel angry. Father is saying that his daughter is irresponsible and notes at the same time an upset stomach. Mother has tense muscles in her neck and is angry with her daughter and her husband. The daughter feels flushed and notes a constriction in her chest and anger toward her parents. The son at C is dysphoric, his limbs feel heavy, and he believes that he is being unfairly treated. It is important in the RET model to learn to identify C, as it is often this cognitive-emotive response that first alerts the individuals that an A has taken place, and they are evoking iB's which result in C. It also gives the therapist an opportunity to illustrate that C results from B and not from A. The RET therapist does not check with other family members as to the accuracy of someone's A. The particular family member may have misinterpreted the A. From Ellis' phenomenological theory, the accuracy of A is irrelevant.

Once Ellis (1983b) has shown the family members how they are upsetting themselves through their iB's, he further requests the degree to which each member has reduced his discomfort at C. If individual family members are still reacting strongly at C, there are probably additional B's to be uncovered and probably each member has a second A that accompanies the B's.

Adlerians also give homework tasks, but they are created more to benefit the specific relationships and life styles of the family.

Self-Downing

In most instances there is a second A, and it is the self-condemnation that is not verbalized and often not in the patient's awareness until indicated by the therapist (Ellis, 1973a). Invariably when we evoke iB's about others we put them down; for example, "My parents are worthless, inconsiderate creatures." The daughter in the example puts her parents down, diminishes their worth, and overgeneralizes from the particular situation. Ellis (1970b) argues that humans are much too complex to rate as to their worth as human. Obviously one cannot just rate another's value based on one action, and it would be an impossibility to add all of the plus and minus actions over the course of one's life to come to a sum total of one's worth. If one could do all of the summing, then who is to say whether the actions were a plus or minus? Perhaps more obviously, it is not possible to change a human being into anything but a human being. One does not turn into a shit for acting in a shitty way (Ellis, 1982b). Neither does one always act in a shitty way. Even Hitler did some kind deeds and was not always acting in a dastardly manner.

When family members put others down for a given behavior, they tend to damn and down themselves in an even more stern manner for subsequent similar actions by themselves. They also damn themselves for their own involvement in the situation in which they are downing another family member (Ellis, 1981). In the example, the daughter might consider herself worthless for being incapable of convincing her parents that she should be able to stay out later. The father might be damning and downing himself believing that he has raised an irresponsible daughter, and he therefore must be an inadequate father. The mother-wife might be downing herself for not standing up to her husband, and thus considering herself a useless marshmallow. The son could be denigrating himself for not protesting the trips to the grocery store when others his age are out playing. He might consider himself a milksop for being the family doormat.

Because these feelings of inferiority are so common in our culture, it is relatively easy for the RET therapist to guess the self-downing *iB*'s correctly. These self-devaluations are very much like Adler's (1925) theory of "masculine protest" and neurotic responses of the inferiority complex. The Adlerian therapist would also confront the client with these maneuvers. However, she would probably add the purpose to the interpretation presented.

Antithetical Mode of Apperception

Antithetical apperception appeared early in IP (Ansbacher & Ansbacher, 1956). By 1912 Adler was describing neurotic thinking as lacking in elasticity (flexibility), seeing the world and people in dichotomized boxes. The antithetical mode of apperception encompasses both over-generalization and exaggeration of symptoms. This is what RET focuses on when attacking each family member's *iB*'s. Hence the two theories are in strong agreement concerning this major conceptualization of neurotic thinking. Regardless of the type of problem presented, Ellis (1981), within a few minutes of meeting and listening to the individual, begins attacking the *B*'s (basic mistakes), which are usually characterized by overgeneralization and overexaggeration (antithetical mode of apperception).

Eliminating the Verb "To Be"

Ellis (1980) extends the antithetical mode of apperception idea beyond that which IP has considered. He emphasizes the irrational logic of human beings in their use of the verb form "to be." This challenges such concepts as someone *being* schizophrenic. People with this diagnosis, for example, have many traits and schizophrenic behaviors, but they do not *always* act in a schizophrenic fashion. Frequently their thinking and behavior are realistic and appropriate to the situation. Adler did use descriptive terms like a "getting personality," indicating simultaneously that we were not to take such labels too seriously. Yet they do provide a useful handle for heuristic discussion. The implication is that no one could be a "getter," even if one frequently or almost always acted in a getting manner. Similarly, Dreikurs (1947) admonished those making use of his four descriptive goals of misbehavior that there was no such person as a "goal I, II, III, or IV child," per se.

In practice IP therapists label family members by type, such as martyr, rescuer, or prince. Ellis firmly believes that this use of "to be" is more than an academic argument. For the past decade he has written, lectured, and conducted therapy in an attempt to eliminate all forms of the verb "to be." He teaches the family members that use of terms like "good person" imply above human, superhuman. Such a being obviously would sit at the right hand of God and would be capable of judging all the worms about them who are masquerading as family members and human beings.

Eliminating this overexaggeration gives the family hope for change (encouragement). It is relatively easy to decrease the number of times that one stays out past curfew, but it is very difficult to change from a delinquent to a dependable person. Similarly, "bad" behavior can be decreased, but it is impossible, and very discouraging to consider, changing from a bad person to a good person.

Immediate Reduction of Tension

RET makes a direct, and usually successful, attempt to reduce the level of discomfort in each family member during the therapy hour. In addition to the previously mentioned methods of therapy, particularly attacking the irrational thinking, RET uses fantasy in several ways to reduce *C*. Two of the most frequently employed methods are changing exaggerations and scaling. By having each family member change the "awful" and "can't stand" to merely inconvenient, unpleasant, and undesirable, there is an immediate reduction in discomfort. Again the RET therapist accepts without question each family member's interpretation of *A*. This builds rapport between therapist and patient, promotes unconditional acceptance of the patient by the therapist, and reduces conflict between family members because "who is right" is not a question at any time. Returning to the philosophical bases of RET, "awful" and "can't stand" are two common basic mistakes which cannot be proven. Whatever the situation about which the individual family member is getting upset, it cannot be proven to be full of awe, and obviously the person can stand the circumstance because he or she is standing it; he or she is alive and can even stand. Thus RET is showing the family members that when they exaggerate to "awful" and "can't stand," they tend to behave "as if" that were the case and then become extremely upset. The comparison with Adler's (1956) teaching the patient about "as if" is obvious.

Scaling

This technique involves having the individual family member fantasize the upsetting *A* and the *C*, rate the *C* on a scale from 1 to 99, then think of a fantasy which reduces the intensity of *C* to a lower level, such as discomfort. The family member states a fantasy which reduces the level. The RET therapist asks for the fantasy. If it is an *rB*, the therapist contracts with the family member to practice fantasizing the *A* paired with the *C* so that *C* now feels inconvenient or unfortunate and less and less disconcerting. The family member with each practice session uses this method of reducing *C* in the face of *A* and each time records the level of emotional upset. The idiosyncratic nature of each family member's fantasy is unpredictable. However, the observation by the other family members of these individual fantasies creates a better understanding of the uniqueness within the family. This paired with the nonjudgmental and nonquestioning attitude by the therapist of each family member's perception of the situation promotes a noncritical, more accepting attitude within the family.

Not Caring Versus Not Demanding

As family members are taught in turn the method of disputing their *iB*'s, reducing their emotional upset, they are also questioned as to whether whatever it was that they desired in the situation is still a desire, and not a demand, that it be different. If the desire is still present, and if it is not short-range hedonism, the RET therapist asks the family members what they might do to secure whatever it is that they desire. This is a time when other family members might make helpful suggestions. If other than helpful suggestions are forthcoming, the therapist cuts off the offending party and asks for further suggestions.

Specific Methods

The use of RET methods for tension reduction, scaling, and caring versus demanding is not in conflict with IP per se; however, when they are applied within the family therapy context they promote intrapsychic rather than interpersonal problem solving and defocus the family life style in favor of independent life styles. They do, however, increase social interest as each listens to the others and withdraws from the power play by taking charge of oneself.

Shame attacking is a popular method within RET (Ellis, 1975). Like Adler's (1972) notion that all neurotic behavior is a form of vanity, Ellis believes that it is difficult to become very disturbed by any *A* if one stubbornly refuses to feel ashamed. Once the therapist determines the area (fictive goal) where the individual family member is most vulnerable to embarrassment, suggestions for a homework assignment in shame therapy are offered by the other family members, the therapist, and the member in focus. The family member contracts to practice for the coming week a specific assignment designed to reduce the tension associated with the vulnerable area. For example, if the area is wanting to be intellectually humble (intellectually superior in Adlerian terms), the homework might entail bragging about one's intellect to at least three different people each day.

Role playing and psychodrama are used by both theories, but the emphasis in RET is helping the individual family member. In IP the emphasis is on better understanding the family dynamics and developing cooperative interaction among all of the family members.

Humor

Role playing and psychodrama with either system often produces strong emotions and new insights. They can also bring forth much humor. Shame attacking usually produces laughter in everyone. Both RET and IP use humor liberally. Both see humor as helpful in putting situations into realistic perspective, teaching the family members to not take themselves too seriously, promoting family fun, relieving tension, diverting attention when anger or other nonbeneficial emotions are interfering with cooperation, and opening the way for more cooperative attitudes and behaviors.

SUMMARY OF SIMILARITIES AND DIFFERENCES

Practical Differences

IP uses affirmation to encourage. RET would find affirmation in opposition to theory. RET recognizes only human existence, not worth or value. This was discussed earlier. One exists in this world as a human being. One is not a worthless human, only human.

Adler (in Ansbacher & Ansbacher, 1956) educated patients in broadening their life style. When one sees the implausibility of the antithetical mode of apperception, then seeing the family situation in a new light (reframing) is possible. RET does not work with the family system, so reframing for the family is not a valid concept. Since the RET therapist never questions the perception at *A*, but only at *C*, reframing is of little value. Antisuggestion is not used in RET.

Similarities

Both RET and IP track behavioral patterns and themes. These are the *iB*'s and basic mistakes. Both look for new options that are free of demands and realistically plausible. Both actively teach new skills, although IP focuses on family skills such as the family council. RET and IP see irrational beliefs (basic mistakes) as the foundation for most disturbed behavior. Both theories emphasize education and see therapy as reeducation. Open forum is a common setting for both approaches to the family.

Philosophically the two theorists cite different sources, but their essence is the same. The phenomenological view of behavior is shared by both theories as is the emphasis on the conscious, or ego psychology. Both see behavior as purposive and goal-directed with humans having a proclivity toward kindness, helpfulness, happiness, joy, and rational behavior.

Horney's "tyranny of the shoulds" is accepted by RET and IP. Emotions are a form of thinking within both theories, and working with the intent of emotions is an area of agreement. Similarly, both agree with the idea that people have choice over their emotions and behavior. Thus the parental model is important, but it is not viewed as causal by either theory. Early childhood experiences are seen as very important.

The third force of S-O-R psychology is the base for their approach to therapy. Routine and order, rational thinking, and freedom from basic mistakes characterize well functioning. Chaotic and disorderly behavior, irrational thinking, and lack of self-acceptance are noted in dysfunctional families. Both RET and IP promote family problem solving without personal ego involvement. RET and IP therapists are very active and directive. They are not uniform in their attitudes or manner, but both seek cooperation from the family members. Neither ties the member's own worth to the family's behavior.

IP and RET therapists seek goal alignment and contracts, and both employ the stochastic method to ascertain irrational beliefs (basic mistakes). They attend to exaggerations and overgeneralizations (antithetical mode of apperception) in an educative manner. Role playing, psychodrama, homework assignments and liberal use of humor characterize both therapies.

Differences

The differences between IP and RET begin in the theory and practice since a general concordance in philosophy is apparent even if the references and terminology differ. The one notable exception in philosophy is the view of human nature, with RET agreeing with IP on proclivities which are positive, but Ellis goes on to add that human nature is lazy, selfish, procrastinating, self-damning, and prone to short-range hedonism. The hedonistic premise further separates the two theories with Adler positing *Gemeinschaftesgefühl,* (social interest) and Ellis being in the *Gesellschaftsgefühl* (self-interest) camp.

Ellis accepts the teleological nature of behavior but does not hold with the unifying function of a fictive goal, and he strongly disagrees with Adler on the concept of logic. Ellis believes that humans not only form incorrect premises, but they also proceed illogically from these premises. This position would seem to negate the concept of holism.

Equality and worth are basic to IP and are seen as irrational and scientifically invalid concepts by Ellis. As such they are deleterious to family functioning. Life tasks are not seen as a need in RET. The fact that RET does not recognize a family system leads to intrapsychic problem solving as opposed to interpersonal problems and family consensus in IP. The RET therapist works with each family member separately. IP works with the family system, but it also attends to the individual's needs.

Adler believes that the therapist must be genuinely interested in the family in order to help them. Whether the therapist in RET likes the family or not is irrelevant. Furthermore, life style assessment, including early recollections and dream interpretation which are so important in IP, are viewed as unnecessary in RET. Ellis uses techniques with which Adlerians are not in agreement. These are the techniques that have evolved from reinforcement and social learning theory. Ironically, Ellis believes that some behaviors continue in spite of lack of reinforcement, while Adler believes that behavior is discarded when it is no longer effective.

IP therapists attempt to sidestep power struggles, but they are probably more prone to them than RET therapists. RET therapists accept without challenge the individual family member's view of the situation, and unconditionally accept all of the family members while stubbornly refusing to condemn them regardless of their behaviors. Furthermore, RET therapists place each family member's selfish interests in advance of the family's group interest. While working separately with each family member, the RET therapist takes a more structured approach to problem solving than does the IP therapist.

Perhaps most noticeable in therapy is RET's emphasis on eliminating all forms of the verb "to be," which is an idea not usually practiced in IP. Additionally, Ellis uses several methods of fantasy to reduce discomfort in the individual while Adlerians are striving for family harmony. Ellis' methods for attacking shame are also unique.

Conclusions

In conclusion, there are probably more similarities than differences between IP and RET. Differences are most obvious in theory and therapy. A few of these differences can be accounted for by differing terminology and possibly a few are caused by a lack of understanding, but major differences remain. RET places the individual in advance of the family group, and the therapist works with each member in turn. RET's emphasis is clearly intrapsychic rather than interpersonal. The emphasis upon the individual and intrapsychic processes would not be so obvious in IP, and they are most apparent in family therapy.

ANNOTATED REFERENCES

Ellis, A. (1962). *Reason and emotion in psychotherapy.* New York: Lyle Stuart.
    This text is the most complete presentation of the philosophy and theory of Rational Emotive Therapy. Ellis cites those from whom he has borrowed,

including Adler, and ties these references into his coherent approach to psychotherapy.

Ellis, A. (1971). *Growth through reason: Verbatim cases in Rational-Emotive Therapy.* Palo Alto, CA: Science and Behavior Books.
Through the use of six case presentations, Ellis makes editorial comments at key points in each of the cases to illustrate the theory and method of Rational Emotive Therapy.

Ellis, A. (1978, 1979). A Rational-Emotive Approach to family therapy: I and II. *Rational Living, 13:* 15-20; *14:* 23-27.
In these two articles Ellis provides the theory, philosophy, and psychology for his work with families. He differentiates his method from others and is particularly critical of the systems approach. These articles provide the reader with a clear differentiation between Rational Emotive Therapy and other forms of family therapy.

Ellis, A., & Abrahams, E. (1978). *Brief psychotherapy in medical and health practice.* New York: Springer.
The value in this text is the tailoring of Rational Emotive Therapy for physicians and other workers in the medical setting.

Ellis, A., & Grieger, R. (Eds.) (1978). *Handbook of Rational-Emotive Therapy.* New York: Springer.
Of the 28 chapters, by different authors, in this book that attends to various facets of Rational Emotive Therapy, the first chapter is the most valuable. Ellis here makes the clearest statement of the basic principles and procedures of Rational Emotive Therapy.

Goodman, D., & Maultsby, M. (1978). *Emotional Well-being through Rational Behavior Training.* Springfield, IL: Charles C Thomas.
Ellis writes the introduction to this text and states that Rational Behavior Training is the best description of the process of therapy using Rational Emotive Therapy. The authors show how behavioral therapy is integrated into basic Rational Emotive Therapy. The text serves as self-help guidance and as a text for Rational Emotive Therapy in graduate courses in psychotherapy.

Walen, S., DiGiuseppe, R., & Wessler, R. (1980). *A practitioner's guide to Rational-Emotive Therapy.* New York: Oxford University Press.
The text, as the title indicates, is designed for therapists. It is most useful for those unfamiliar with Rational Emotive Therapy, but it also brings fresh approaches which the experienced Rational Emotive Therapy therapist will find helpful.

Wessler, R., & Wessler, R. (1980). *The principles and practice of Rational-Emotive Therapy.* San Francisco: Jossey-Bass.
This book has a foreword written by Ellis in which he commends the authors for presenting so clearly the ideas of Rational Emotive Therapy. This text is

particularly useful when teaching Rational Emotive Therapy to graduate students or others at a similar level of training.

ADDITIONAL REFERENCES

Adler, A. (1917). *A study of organ inferiority and its psychical compensation. Nervous and mental disease monograph.* New York.

Adler, A. (1925). *The practice and theory of Individual Psychology.* London: Kegan Paul.

Adler, A. (1927). *Understanding human nature.* Greenwich, CT: Fawcett Publications.

Adler, A. (1931). *What life should mean to you.* New York: Putnam.

Adler, A. (1958). *The practice and theory of Individual Psychology.* Paterson, NJ: Littlefield, Adams.

Adler, A. (1964a). *Problems of neurosis.* New York: Harper and Row.

Adler, A. (1964b). *Social interest: A challenge to mankind.* New York: Capricorn Books.

Adler, A. (1964c). *Superiority and social interest.* Ed. H. L. Ansbacher. Evanston, IL: Northwestern University Press.

Adler, A. (1969). *The case of Mrs. A.: The diagnosis of a life style.* Chicago: Alfred Adler Institute.

Adler, A. (1972). *The neurotic constitution.* New York: Arno.

Ansbacher, H. L. (1965). Sensus privatus versus sensus communis. *Journal of Individual Psychology, 21:* 48-50.

Ansbacher, H. L., & Ansbacher, R. R. (1956). *The Individual Psychology of Alfred Adler.* New York: Harper & Row.

Bandura, A. (1969). *Principles of behavior modification.* New York: McGraw-Hill.

Corsini, R. (Ed.). (1973). *Current psychotherapies.* Itasca, IL: Peacock.

Croake, J. (1983). Adlerian parent education. *Counseling Psychologist, 11:* 65-73.

Croake, J., & Hinkle, D. (1983). Adlerian family counseling. *Individual Psychology, The Journal of Adlerian Theory, Research and Practice, 39:* 247-258.

Croake, J. W., & Myers, K. M. (1984). Holistic medicine and chronic illness in children. *Individual Psychology, The Journal of Adlerian Theory, Research and Practice, 40:* 462-475.

Croake, J., & Rusk, R. (1980). The theories of Adler and Zen. *Journal of Individual Psychology, 36:* 219-227.

Dollard, J., & Miller, N. (1950). *Personality and psychotherapy.* New York: McGraw-Hill.

Dreikurs, R. (1946). *The challenge of marriage.* New York: Duell, Sloan & Pearce.

Dreikurs, R. (1947). The four goals of children's misbehavior. *Nervous Child, 6:* 3-11.

Dreikurs, R. (1948). *The challenge of parenthood.* New York: Duell, Sloan & Pearce.

Dreikurs, R. (1950). *Fundamentals of Adlerian psychology.* Chicago: Alfred Adler Institute.

Dreikurs, R. (1951). The function of the emotions. *Christian Register, 130*(3): 11-14, 24.

Dreikurs, R. (1953). *Fundamentals of Adlerian psychology.* Chicago: Alfred Adler Institute.

Dreikurs, R. (1954). The psychological interview in medicine. *American Journal of Individual Psychology, 10:* 99–122.

Dreikurs, R. (1957). Perspectives of delinquency prevention. *Journal of Correctional Psychology, 2:* 1–9.

Dreikurs, R. (1959). Early experiments with group psychotherapy. *American Journal of Psychotherapy, 13:* 82–91.

Dreikurs, R. (1960). *Group psychotherapy and group approaches: Collected papers.* Chicago: Alfred Adler Institute.

Dreikurs, R. (1961a). The Adlerian approach to therapy. In M. I. Stein (Ed.), *Contemporary psychotherapies.* Glencoe, IL: Free Press.

Dreikurs, R. (1961b). *Prevention and correction of juvenile delinquency.* St. Louis: Metropolitan Youth Commission.

Dreikurs, R. (1962, August). Can you be sure the disease is functional? *Consultant* (Smith, Kline & French Laboratories).

Dreikurs, R. (1963). Individual Psychology: The Adlerian point of view. In J. M. Wepman & R. Heine (Eds.), *Concepts of personality.* Chicago: Aldine.

Dreikurs, R. (1967). *Psychodynamics, psychotherapy, and counseling.* Chicago: Alfred Adler Institute.

Dreikurs, R. (1968). *Psychology in the classroom.* New York: Harper and Row.

Dreikurs, R. (1969). Social interest: The basis of normalcy. *Counseling Psychologist, 1*(2): 45–48.

Dreikurs, R. (1971). *Social equality: The challenge of today.* Chicago: Henry Regnery.

Dreikurs, R. (1972). *Coping with children's misbehavior: A parent's guide.* New York: Hawthorn.

Dreikurs, R. (1977). Holistic medicine and the function of neurosis. *Journal of Individual Psychology, 33:* 171–192.

Dreikurs, R., Corsini, R. J., Lowe, R., & Sonstegard, M. (1959). *Adlerian family counseling.* Eugene: University of Oregon Press.

Dreikurs, R., & Grey, L. (1968). *Logical consequences.* New York: Meredith.

Dreikurs, R., Grunwald, B., & Pepper, F. C. (1971). *Maintaining sanity in the classroom.* New York: Harper and Row.

Dreikurs, R., & Mosak, H. H. (1966). The tasks of life: I. Adler's three tasks. *Individual Psychologist, 4*(1): 18–22.

Dreikurs, R., & Mosak, H. H. (1967). The tasks of life: II. The fourth life task. *Individual Psychologist, 4*(2): 51–55.

Dreikurs, R., & Soltz, V. (1967). *Children: the challenge.* New York: Hawthorn.

Ellis, A. (1953). Marriage counseling with couples indicating sexual incompatibility. *Marriage and Family Living, 15:* 53–59.

Ellis, A. (1956). A critical evaluation of marriage counseling. *Marriage and Family Living, 18:* 65–71.

Ellis, A. (1957). *How to live with a "neurotic."* New York: Crown.

Ellis, A. (1962). *Reason and emotion in psychotherapy.* Secaucus, NJ: Lyle Stuart.

Ellis, A. (1963). Toward a more precise definition of "emotional" and "intellectual" insight. *Psychological Reports, 13:* 125–26.

Ellis, A. (1968). What *really* causes therapeutic change? *Voices, 4*(2):90–97.

Ellis, A. (1969). *The art and science of love.* New York: Lyle Stuart.

Ellis, A. (1970a). The case against religion. *Mensa Journal,* No. 138, September.

Ellis, A. (1970b). Humanism, values, rationality. *Journal of Individual Psychology, 26:* 37–38.

Ellis, A. (1971a). *Growth through reason.* Palo Alto: Science and Behavior Books.

Ellis, A. (1971b). *Homework report.* New York: Institute for Advanced Study in Rational Psychotherapy.

Ellis, A. (1971c). Reason and emotion in the Individual Psychology of Adler. *Journal of Individual Psychology, 27:* 50–64.

Ellis, A. (1972). *Executive leadership: A rational approach.* New York: Citadel Press.

Ellis, A. (1973a). *Humanistic psychotherapy: The rational-emotive approach.* New York: McGraw-Hill.

Ellis, A. (1973b). Rational-emotive group therapy. In G. Gazda (Ed.), *Group therapy and counseling.* Springfield, IL: Charles C Thomas.

Ellis, A. (1975). Does rational-emotive therapy seem deep enough? *Rational Living, 10:* 11–14.

Ellis, A. (1976). Techniques of handling anger in marriage. *Journal of Marriage and Family Counseling, 2:* 305–316.

Ellis, A. (1977a). *Fun as psychotherapy.* Cassette recording. New York: Institute for Rational Living.

Ellis, A. (1977b). *How to live with—and without—anger.* New York: Reader's Digest Press.

Ellis, A. (1977c). Rational-emotive therapy: Research data that supports the clinical and personality hypotheses of RET and other modes of cognitive-behavior therapy. *Counseling Psychologist, 7*(1): 2–42.

Ellis, A. (1977d). *Rational self-help form.* New York: Institute for Rational Living.

Ellis, A. (1978). A rational-emotive approach to family therapy. *Rational Living, 13:* 15–20.

Ellis, A. (1979). A rational-emotive approach to family therapy: II. Emotive and behavioral therapy. *Rational Living, 14:* 23–27.

Ellis, A. (1980). The fact of mental illness. *Rational Living, 15:* 13–20.

Ellis, A. (1981). Is rational-emotive therapy ethically untenable or inconsistent? A reply to Paul E. Meehl. *Rational Living, 16:* 10–12.

Ellis, A. (1982a). Rational-emotive family therapy. In A. M. Horne and M. M. Ohlsen (Eds.), *Family counseling and therapy.* Itasca, IL: Peacock.

Ellis, A. (1982b). Self-direction in sport and life. *Rational Living, 17:* 27–34.

Ellis, A. (1983a, February). *Sex therapy.* Lecture, Toronto, February.

Ellis, A. (1983b). How to deal with your most difficult client—you. *Rational Living, 1:* 3–8.

Ellis, A. (1984). Sex therapies. In R. J. Corsini (Ed.), *Encyclopedia of psychology.* New York: Wiley.

Ellis, A., & Abrahams, E. (1978). *Brief psychotherapy in medical and health practice.* New York: Springer.

Ellis, A., & Blum, M. (1968). Rational training: A new method of facilitating management and labor relations. *Psychological Reports, 20:* 1267–1284.

Ellis, A., & Grieger, R. (1977). *Handbook of Rational-Emotive Therapy.* New York: Springer.

Ellis, A., & Harper, R. A. (1961). *Creative marriage.* New York: Lyle Stuart.

(1971). Paperback edition, retitled *A guide to successful marriage.* Hollywood: Wilshire Books.

Ellis, A., & Harper, R. A. (1975). *A new guide to rational living.* Englewood Cliffs, NJ: Prentice-Hall.

Ellis, A., & Knaus, W. (1977). *Overcoming procrastination.* New York: Institute for Rational Living.

Ellis, A., & Whitely, J. M. (1979). *Theoretical and empirical foundations of rational-emotive therapy.* Monterey, CA: Brooks/Cole.

Eysenck, H. J. (Ed.). (1964). *Experiments in behavior therapy.* New York: Pergamon.

Frankl, V. (1966). *Man's search for meaning.* New York: Washington Square Press.

Freud, S. (1963). *Collected papers.* New York: Collier Books.

Fromm, E. (1963). *Sigmund Freud's mission.* New York: Grove Press.

Horney, K. (1951). *Neurosis and human growth.* London: Routledge & Kegan Paul.

Jacobsen, E. (1942). *You must relax.* New York: McGraw-Hill.

Mahoney M. (1977). Reflections on the cognitive learning trend in psychotherapy. *American Psychologist, 32:* 5-114.

Maslow, A. H. (1963). *Religious value and peak experiences.* New York: Viking Press.

Meichenbaum, D. (1977). *Cognitive behavior modification.* New York: Plenum.

Mosak, H. H. (1954). The psychological attitude in rehabilitation. *American Archives of Rehabilitation Therapy, 2:* 9-10.

Mosak, H. H. (1958). Early recollections as a projective technique. *Journal of Projective Techniques, 22:* 302-311.

Mosak, H. H. (1965). Predicting the relationship to the psychotherapist from early recollections. *Journal of Individual Psychology, 21:* 77-81.

Mosak, H. H. (1967). Subjective criteria of normality. *Psychotherapy, 4:* 159-161.

Mosak, H. H. (1971). Strategies for behavior change in schools: Consultation strategies. *Counseling Psychologist, 3*(1): 58-62.

Mosak, H. H. (1972). Life style assessment: A demonstration based on family constellation. *Journal of Individual Psychology, 28:* 232-247.

Mosak, H. H. (1977). *On purpose.* Chicago: Alfred Adler Institute.

Mosak, H. H. (1979). Mosak's typology: An update." *Journal of Individual Psychology, 35:* 192-195.

Mosak, H. H. (Ed.). (1973). *Alfred Adler: His influence on psychology today.* Park Ridge, NJ: Noyes Press.

Mosak, H. H., & Dreikurs, R. (1967). The life tasks: III. The fifth life task. *Individual Psychologist, 5*(1): 16-22.

Orgler, H. (1965). *Alfred Adler: The man and his work.* New York: Capricorn Books.

Rogers, C. R. (1961). *On becoming a person.* Boston: Houghton Mifflin.

Sicher, L. (1955). Education for freedom. *American Journal of Individual Psychology, 11:* 97-103.

Skinner, B. F. (1938). *The behavior of organisms: An experimental analysis.* New York: Appleton-Century-Crofts.

Terner, J., & Pew, W. (1978). *The courage to be imperfect.* New York: Hawthorn.

Tolman, E. (1932). *Purposive behavior in animals and men.* New York: Appleton-Century-Crofts.

Vaihinger, H. (1965). *The philosophy of "as if."* London: Routledge & Kegan Paul.

Wessler, R. A., & Wessler, R. L. (1980). *The principles and practice of rational-emotive-therapy.* San Francisco: Jossey-Bass.

Wolpe, J. (1958). *Psychotherapy by reciprocal inhibition.* Stanford: Stanford University Press.

Woodworth, R. S. (1929). *Psychology.* New York: Holt.

11

Adlerian Family Therapy Techniques

INTRODUCTION AND GOALS OF THERAPY

The therapist demonstrates respect for the family and thereby helps the family develop a mutual respect. The therapist is nonjudgmental and noncritical, regardless of the behavior and relationships presented. He accepts, listens, understands, and then helps family members question the way they are currently relating. There is no attempt to find scapegoats to blame for what is happening in the family relationships.

The techniques are used to help the therapist achieve the major goals of the therapy. Although these goals are always unique to each family situation, there are some general goals of therapy that the therapist strives toward.

1. *Work to effect movement and change.* Everything that is done, active or passive, is done with the hope that it will promote active/constructive behavior. The therapist watches closely for any movement, progress, or attempts to relate more effectively. These are encouraged.

For example, the therapist notes that the family now talks together at dinner instead of watching television. She acknowledges the new activity.

2. *Family members are taught to accept personal responsibility.* They must first change themselves before there is any attempt to change other members of the family. Family therapy works on the premise that self-change will facilitate relationship change. The question is, what will you personally do differently?

3. *Jointly evaluate goals and means of achieving them.* The therapist assists the family and each member to become aware of their goals, and the effects or consequences of their behavior, and to evaluate both.

Then they refine or change their goals to more suitable ones and identify appropriate means for achieving the new or refined goals.

4. *Helps the family learn effective methods and problem-solving techniques.* Family therapy has an educational component. One of the tasks for the family therapist is to determine the skills, techniques, and processes which the family appears to be lacking, and to help family members develop more effective methods of relating. The best goals and intentions will fail without the knowledge and skill to implement them.

5. *Reorganize family roles and relationships in a more effective, appropriate, and satisfying structure.* The therapist assists the family members to shift positions and take on new reciprocal role behaviors and new rules to support the behaviors. The roles and rules will appropriately support the new or one final goal of the family system. The family may also be helped to take on new positions and roles in relation to other systems and a revised world view.

Therapeutic techniques employed are to accomplish these five goals.

The techniques described next are general in nature. They need to be refined and adapted for use with a particular family and situation. Further, ethnic and cultural factors of the client and community will influence if and how a given technique can be ethically and profitably utilized.

COMMON TECHNIQUES INCLUDED IN ADLERIAN FAMILY THERAPY

1. *Focus on understanding and influencing psychological movement.* Adlerian psychology operates on the basis of giving considerable attention to the pattern of relationships in the family, the goals that have been verbalized, and those that are revealed by behavior. It is important to be aware that although some people express their goals orally, the therapist will often learn most from the nonverbal communication (facial expression, recognition reflex, grins, and body posture).

The therapist's knowledge of the purposive nature of behavior and the role of belief systems and priorities in determining and influencing relationships is used in understanding movement. We believe that you can trust only movement. Examples of the kinds of movement that we look for may be movement to be superior, to get power, to be excused, to get even, or to please.

2. *Work with the family communication system.* It is important to understand how family members currently communicate with each other. Early in the session it is often most effective to introduce a general topic on relationship to the group and see how family members work with each other. At this point the therapist would be trying to determine whether communication is horizontal (talk to each other as equals) or whether most communication is from a superior position to an inferior position, vertical communication; whether the family system is one that is open, with mutual trust, where it is safe to share openly any feelings, or if people intrude upon one another without respect for individuality, or if it is instead a closed system in which people dare not share what they believe or think for fear of retaliation or punishment.

The counselor observes for patterns of miscommunication: misperception of what is said or done; lying or withholding of information; inconsistent double messages; double-bind messages; and magical thinking (you should know what I want without being told).

When analyzing family communication systems, bear in mind that there may be a difference between the words that are stated and the literal meaning of those words. For example, the therapist asks, "What do you mean by 'closeness'?" At the same time, nonverbal communication is observed to see whether this contrasts with the oral statements.

One of the ways that therapists can learn to interact more effectively with families is to sometimes do an analysis of their own communication behavior. Allred has developed some material called Phrases for Allred's Interaction Analysis for Therapists (AIAT) (1983). The categories he developed with the AIAT include the following:

Encouraging: Focusing on the positive, designed to build self esteem.
    Ex: I really think you can do it.
    I appreciate your. . . .
Evaluating: Involving family members' evaluation of their progress and sharing therapist's perception of progress or lack of it.
    Ex: It seems to me you are being more consistent.
    I feel you are being less directive expressing anger.
Educating: Sharing observations, tests, opinions in general.
    Ex: Children will often use crying to get parents to give in.
    Many people are afraid to offend those they love.
Discovering Behaviors: Asking questions for information regarding behavior.
    Ex: And then what happened? Please be more specific.
Interpreting: Clarifying meanings, hypothesizing, and guessing the purpose of members' behavior.

Ex: What do you think that feeling you have means?

Could it be you wanted to get even with . . . ?

Confronting: Respectfully challenging behavior, feelings, thoughts and showing incongruencies.

Ex: How come you don't deal with him when he puts you down?

I get the feeling your clinched hands are expressing what you really feel.

Exploring Alternatives: Exploring alternative ways of acting, feeling, thinking.

Ex: Is there another way?

If that doesn't work, what else could you try?

Prescribing Change: Asking clients to commit to assignments or tasks.

Ex: Will you stop doing that for one week since you recognize it doesn't help?

Provide three encouraging statements each day for one week and make a record each time you do it.

This is only a partial list of ways in which the therapist communicates with the family. Through an analysis of your communication and interaction style, you can become more aware of how you are experienced by the family. It can also help you to see additional ways to be more facilitative.

In family therapy, the therapist needs to introduce some simple rules that are established early in the relationship. They are watched closely since they are basic to improving communication and relationships. These rules include the following:

1. Each person speaks for himself. Don't suggest what somebody else believes or thinks.

2. Speak directly to each other, not through the therapist or some other person in the family.

3. Do not scapegoat or blame.

4. Listen and be empathic.

3. *Work on your own communication skills.* Frequently the family not only has interpersonal relationship difficulties, but lacks basic communication skills as well. The therapist can teach these skills by modeling in his transactions with the family. However, at other times it may be necessary to directly intervene in teaching skills.

Often the feeling and emotions of family members are not being communicated to each other. Mother feels sad and unappreciated, the son is angry about restrictions on his activity, and the daughter feels unloved; until they learn to share perceptions, feelings, and beliefs it is extremely difficult to work on solutions to problems in the relationship. They need to learn to identify what they are feeling and to share it directly. They are taught to communicate in ways that should indicate that they are taking responsibility for their feelings and actions.

Instead of avoiding open, honest communication by saying "it's ok," "it doesn't bother me," or any other responses that remove a family member from the status of a person, the therapist helps family members to be in touch with what they are experiencing and feeling. They are helped to constructively express anger and any other emotions as they learn that this does not end relationships but may improve them when expressed in an "I" position rather than by attacking. "I *feel* very small when you criticize me like that. It would be better for me if you just tell me what you prefer and I will share my opinion." Withdrawing or revenge behavior creates increasing hostility and distance. As family members learn to say in a nonblaming way "I feel angry when I'm avoided for two weeks because I feel like you don't care about me," honest caring and sharing occur. There is a greater feeling of belonging and common goals.

At the same time, family members need to attend closely to the feelings that are being communicated by other members of the family. The process is one of paying attention to each other, becoming aware of how other members feel, being empathic, and accurately reflecting the feeling to the person.

Sometimes communication within the family needs to be very direct and perhaps even confronted. This can be done in terms of an "I" message which states briefly how the person feels when a particular thing is occurring and why. Delivering an "I-message" is a most effective way of making certain that your feelings are understood without attacking.

I-messages focus on your feelings about the other person's behavior. You focus on the actions, not the person. For example, using the wording "When . . . " conveys you are upset with a particular behavior: "When you are an hour late . . . "; "When you leave the kitchen in a mess . . .," you identify the behavior without blaming. Then describe how you feel when the behavior occurs: "I feel concerned . . ."; "I worry . . . ." Recognize it is the consequence for you or that person that concerns you. Your concern is usually that something may have happened to the person.

The I-messages communicate clearly through three steps:

1. They describe the behavior without blaming: "When I see the kitchen is a mess . . ."

2. They state your feelings about the possible consequences of the behavior: "I feel angry and disrespected . . ."
3. They clearly state the consequence: "because I have to get breakfast and get to an appointment, and there is no time to get it all done."

Another skill is that of processing feedback. When you process feedback to another family member you state what you are experiencing but make no demand for change. This creates a feeling of mutual awareness. Feedback, of course, can be positive or negative, but the challenge is to share the feedback in a way that is neither critical nor blaming, but instead is merely a sharing of how the person is being experienced.

Feedback's intention is to make the communication process more open and honest. It is done tentatively and in a caring manner: "When you do none of your chores I get the feeling you don't care about helping the family."

The family also needs to affirm each other if they are to increase the members' self-esteem and feeling of belonging. By affirming what is positive in other family members, the members communicate acceptance and concern. The positive statement provides feedback and builds self-esteem. When we affirm we focus on the positive and are ready to note any asset or positive movement.

Affirming indicates you value the family member and want to share positive feelings:

"I liked your bringing your friends home. I can see why you enjoy them."

"I appreciate your taking time to bring your dirty clothes to the laundry room. I know I can count on you to help."

"I enjoyed your concert. Your solo was very well done."

"I'm very pleased with how you are responsible for yourself."

Affirming builds the self-esteem of the one being affirmed. Uniquely, the one affirming also feels better about himself as he becomes a more positive person.

4. *Focus on the real issue.* Family therapy presents a challenge because of the many and varied symptoms that may appear to be present in individual members and the family system. It is the therapist's challenge to observe transactions and interactions for the purpose of discovering

beliefs and priorities. Then it is important to identify which pattern of these goals, beliefs, or priorities appears to be most influential in determining the behavior of the family.

On the surface the issue may be staying out late, when the real issue is power or deciding for oneself. Other examples are:

The Surface Issue	*The Real Issue*
Getting homework done	Control, being in charge
Fighting with sibling	Revenge, getting even

When the family can cut through the surface issue and work on the underlying issue, it is possible to solve more problems in a more efficient manner. Instead of hassle over lateness, schoolwork, and being un-cooperative, a bigger issue like self-control or power can be discussed.

Usually more than one issue is involved. In that case, it is sometimes more important to identify the real issue, not the symptom, and to have the family work with the real issue. The symptom is seen as a symbolic representation of the real issue. Sometimes it is more efficient to begin with a less difficult issue that the therapist thinks may be readily resolved and hence be encouraging to the family in terms of their progress in tackling the more intense ones.

In considering the issue, the therapist of course is concerned with stimulating the family to increase social interest and cooperation. This may be done by providing tasks that involve sharing, being engaged in a give and take between family members and in a dialogue about plans to cooperate.

5. *Encouragement.* Encouragement is focused on increasing self-esteem and the feelings of worth of the members of the family. Encouragement is first demonstrated by the therapist's interest in identifying assets and strengths instead of investigating problems, pathology, and weaknesses. The therapist also encourages as he is empathic to the feelings of all members of the family from the scapegoat to perhaps the youngest or oldest member of the family. There is a definite attempt to develop mutual respect.

The therapist can also redefine the reported symptomatic behavior in positive terms. Changing negative meanings into positive ones is a major focus of Adlerian therapy. A situation in which the wife complains her husband just sits in a chair and vegetates and the husband complains that his wife nags him constantly can be redefined: "I see that you, sir, really know how to relax, and that you, madam, are a good initiator who sees opportunities to do and change things. Is it possible that you would like to help your wife to slow down a bit and enjoy some leisure while you would like to stimulate your husband to enjoy more excitement?"

Family therapy utilizes the encouragement process when it embraces some of the following characteristics:

1. Each person in the family feels he or she is listened to.
2. Members of the family intentionally are empathic and are understanding. They not only hear feelings but they indicate that they hear feelings.
3. There is a focus on strengths, assets, and resources. Adlerian family therapy places an emphasis on identifying some strengths that can be used to foster family and individual growth.
4. Development of perceptual alternatives first by the therapist and then by members of the family is a vital resource. Members learn to recognize there are positive ways to look at any negative situation.
5. A sense of humor helps members of the family see themselves in perspective and enables them to laugh at some of their mistakes, foibles, and attempts to overpower each other.
6. Families who are encouraging focus on efforts, contributions, and any attempt to move in a positive direction. See the section on encouragement in Chapter 3 (pp. 50-51) for additional discussion of this process.

6. *Confrontation of private logic, beliefs, and purposes.* Private logic consists of the goals, ideas, attitudes, and reasons used to justify behavior. Confrontation is the procedure by which the therapist in a sensitive and perceptive manner enables members of the family to be aware of the discrepancies between their behavior and their intentions, their feelings and the feelings they reveal, their insights and their actions.

Shulman (1973) indicates that confrontation is the combination of a challenge and a question which is designed to evoke the feeling that an immediate response is required. It is used to stimulate therapeutic movement by mirroring to family members their mistaken goals. The choice of which of a variety of techniques to use depends on the object of the confrontation. Shulman lists several types of confrontation:

1. Confronting clients with their subjective views, sometimes called revealing the hidden reason or private justification the client

gives to himself to make the behavior acceptable in his eyes. For example, "It's because I had so little sleep" or "I'm just nervous."

2. Confronting clients with their mistaken beliefs. The beliefs to which this type of confrontation refers are the person's basic convictions about himself, the world, and the meaning and requirements of life. Shulman has said, "These basic convictions fill in the following blanks: I am . . . ; Life is . . . ; Therefore. . . ."

3. Confronting clients with their private goals may be used when a family member attempts to deny a feeling you suspect is there.

All this confrontation is usually done with a tentative hypotheses, such as "Could it be you want to show them they don't make you do it?" or "Is it possible you are interested in upsetting them?"

When you are dealing with young children you would confront them with the four goals. The four goals of misbehavior are attention getting, power, revenge, and the display of inadequacy. These categories are called goals because the misbehavior achieves something for the child. Misbehaving children are discouraged. They seek to belong through misbehavior. However, this needs to be done with caution in the presence of their parents. We do not believe that parents can be effective in confronting their own children with the four goals. When the confrontation is effective, it usually results in improved rapport. Confrontation actually helps the person feel understood.

7. *Paradoxical intention.* The paradoxical intention or antisuggestion often persuades the person to produce the symptom he appears to be complaining about. The symptom is actually prescribed. The person is encouraged to become even more "symptomatic." In simple terms, it helps to reframe the symptom. Reframing involves changing the entire meaning given to a situation. The family member comes to learn that he has the capacity to initiate or stop the symptom. This is often introduced by saying, "Would you be willing to try something which may be strange to you at first, but may help?" This is followed by suggesting that they practice some symptom that they are complaining about in some systematic, regular fashion. For example, if the fight is with a spouse, fight systematically at a specific time for two minutes.

According to Mozdzierz, Macchitelli, and Lisiecki (1976), Alfred Adler was the first modern therapist to use and write about paradoxical strategies. Adler's nonspecific paradoxical strategy was to avoid power struggles with the family. He believed the use of paradoxical strategies shifted the person's uncooperative behavior to cooperative behavior. Adler suggested going with or accepting the patient's resistance. See also the discussion on paradox in Chapter 3 and the description of many paradoxical techniques in Chapter 6 of Sherman and Fredman (1986).

8. *Role Reversal.* Very often in the family, members do not understand how their behavior is perceived by others. This may be true of husband and wife as well as between parents and children. In role reversal, we ask each person to act as if he or she was the person with whom they are in conflict. Then they are asked to express as clearly and honestly as possible how they believe that person perceives the relationship, themselves, the family, and how people are working together. The persons who are reversing roles then have an opportunity to react by indicating which parts of the role reversal were accurate and which parts are not in line with their own thinking, feeling, and beliefs. They can also experience what it feels like in the other person's shoes.

9. *Structure and promote direct interaction.* Family therapy is obviously an aspect of the group process. It is important that members in family therapy learn to interact directly with each other. At times family members will talk to each other through the therapist. They will make complaints about Billy, Suzy, Mom, or Dad. The therapist must be certain to avoid the role of "translator." The therapist will simply say "Please tell . . . directly." As the therapist does this consistently, the family learns to speak directly to each other without the coaching. This type of interaction will be useful to them in all their relationships.

10. *Teach the family specific skills and how to conduct family meetings and encouragement meetings.* Skills to be taught could include the family or couple meeting, encouragement meetings, how to deal with anger, and the communication process. These are skills which the family can practice between sessions and thereby improve the communication process within the family.

We believe that families are often helped best when they are taught skills and specific procedures they can use outside the session in the daily challenges of living.

(a) Family meetings

Family meetings provide an opportunity to children and parents to participate in decision making and then taking responsibility for their behavior. The family meeting is a regularly scheduled meeting of all family members to make plans, solve problems, and encourage. The meeting as described by Dinkmeyer and McKay (1983) is an opportunity for each family member:

(A) To be heard.
(B) To express positive feelings.
(C) To give encouragement.
(D) To agree on a fair distribution of chores.
(E) To express concerns, feelings, and complaints.
(F) To help settle conflicts and deal with recurring issues.
(G) To participate in planning family recreation.

Effective family meetings adhere to the following guidelines:

(A) Establish a specific weekly meeting time.
(B) Rotate the offices of chairperson and secretary.
(C) Establish and stick to time limits.
(D) Be certain all members have a chance to offer ideas.
(E) Encourage everyone to bring up issues.
(F) Don't permit meetings to become gripe sessions.
(G) Distribute chores fairly.
(H) Plan family fun.
(I) Use the skills of communication and encouragement.

(b) Encouragement meetings

Encouragement meetings are briefer than family meetings. They provide a regular, systematic way to strengthen individuals and the relationships in a family. The purpose is to allow two persons, or as many as want to participate, to share the positive things they see in each other and the relationship.

The guidelines include:

(A) Meet in a place that is free of interruption.
(B) Face each other.
(C) One person begins by saying "The most positive thing that happened today was . . ." or "Something I appreciated about you today was . . . "
(D) The first partner may take three or four minutes. The listening partner maintains eye contact and does not interrupt.

(E) At the end of this time period the listener briefly feeds back the ideas, beliefs, feelings, or values heard, not challenging but accepting.

(F) After the partner has given feedback, the process is repeated with the other partner using the same sentences (Dinkmeyer & Carlson, 1984).

(c) How to deal with anger

When family members are angry, it is important to process the anger in a nonblaming, nonattacking manner. As described earlier, we believe this can be accomplished most effectively in the form of an I-message which shares

"I feel . . .

when . . . (describing the behavior that appears to initiate anger)

because . . . (describing the consequence experienced by the behavior and the feeling)."

Example: I feel angry when you take me for granted because I feel you expect too much of me.

Then the persons involved in the anger incident agree they will not attack but respect each other. They share their thoughts and feelings, asking for feedback and empathic listening so the messages are clear and communication and understanding are achieved.

The person listens to the person first experiencing anger and feeds back clearly until there is agreement that the angry person is understood. The listener then shares how he feels about the situation while the first person provides feedback and empathy.

Finally, options for dealing with the issue are discussed. They agree on an option that they can both act on. They check with each other at a set time to assess their progress.

(d) The communication process

The communication process is basic to all of family therapy. We believe that communication can be modified through the model that the family therapist provides. As the therapist listens, is empathic, and reflects feelings, the behavior may be transmitted to the family members.

We have learned that often it is both necessary and more effective to didactically teach the skills. We ask family members to speak to each other, asking them to be empathic and reflect back the feelings they hear. The person sharing feelings then has an opportunity to indicate whether the feelings were heard accurately or not. Then there is an opportunity to exchange roles. Therapy provides an opportunity to model, teach, practice, and evaluate progress in the development of communication skills.

11. *Resistance and goal alignment.* Resistance in family therapy is usually best understood as a lack of common goals between the therapist and the family. Aligning goals so all are moving towards the same purposes is basic to effecting constructive change. Family therapy is complicated when mother is concerned about the children's academic achievement, while father pushes athletics, and the son and daughter are just interested in being with their peers. In this set of apparently confused purposes, the therapist helps the family find areas of agreement and compromise so they can live together more cooperatively. All of the goals reflect ways of achieving significance as seen from varied perspectives. For a further discussion of techniques to deal with resistance see Chapter 4.

12. *Tentative hypotheses.* Tentative hypotheses are made by the therapist concerning the purpose of a family member's behavior in the session. They are tentative—"Could it be . . . ? " or "Is it possible . . . ?"—so the person does not feel accused. The hypotheses help the person and the family investigate what is happening at the moment. The goal is to create insight into behavior by understanding its purpose.

Disclosure through tentative hypotheses is not concerned with the causes of behavior but with its purpose.

13. *Setting tasks and getting commitment.* The therapist with the family sets tasks and works to obtain commitment to specific changes which the family or individual members indicate they desire. The establishment of tasks begins at the first session when each member is asked to state his or her goals and what should be changed. The more specific the task, the more readily it can be accomplished. Family members make specific contracts and are expected to share progress made at the next meeting. The tasks are methods to achieve the changes desired and agreed upon.

14. *Conflict resolution.* All conflicts are interpersonal. Problems in families are problems in the relationship. The therapist needs a specific process for dealing with the conflicts that occur in the session as well as outside the session.

The steps in conflict resolution which were originally set forth by Dreikurs include the following principles:

(a) Show mutual respect by neither fighting nor giving in. The principle is that you neither overpower nor give in. Instead, it believes that the resolution of conflict is based on understanding and respecting each other's point of view.

(b) Pinpoint the issue. This identifies the issue behind the complaint. Those issues may be a threat to status or prestige, a feeling that your superiority is being challenged, your control is being challenged, or you are being treated unfairly.

(c) Seek areas of agreement. Instead of looking to another member of the family, concentrate on what you are willing to do. Make no demands that your partner change. Agree to cooperate rather than bicker.

(d) Mutually participate in decisions.

15. *Summarizing.* Summarizing is a way of getting at the perceptions of the members of the family and looking at the themes in the session. At times it occurs during the session when the therapist wants to look at the meaning of what has been happening. The therapist may decide to have a summary at the close of the group where family members summarize what they have been learning and the therapist also summarizes and perhaps clarifies commitments and tasks.

16. *Follow-up.* Any tasks committed to are checked on in the following session. Who did what? What was each person's reaction? What were the consequences? Are the tasks in need of refinement? Are they worth continuing? Nonperformance of a task committed to is a unilateral decision and a refusal to cooperate. The effects of the prior lack of cooperation are explored. Excuses are, in general, not accepted. The goal and task need to be reexamined until agreements are made which will secure cooperation.

EXAMPLES OF ADDITIONAL TECHNIQUES AVAILABLE

There are, of course, hundreds of other techniques developed by Adlerians and other family therapists that can be used to effect behavior change. A few are briefly listed below to illustrate the breadth of possibilities. They are described in greater detail in Sherman and Fredman (1986) and in other sources.

1. *Family photographs.* Clients select three to six photographs. They discuss them in terms of why they were selected, who is in them, how the people in them have been arranged, the circumstances surrounding the pictures. Patterns of family relationship over time are revealed, family myths can be corrected, and misperceptions can be changed.

2. *Dream a drama.* A client describes in family session a dream or daydream he has. The family enacts the dream together. Life style and family interaction patterns are expressed and modified as the enactment progresses with coaching by the therapist. Goals are identified and clarified.

3. *The genogram.* Based upon interview data, a multigenerational map is prepared showing the family constellation, history, and dynamics. Relationships, nodal events, values, and family guiding lines are identified to describe and explain what is currently happening and to point the direction for change. Mistaken ideas can also be discovered and clarified.

4. *Sculpting.* Clients symbolically and nonverbally portray family organization and relationships around the symptom, a specific event, a period of life. One person asks each other member to assume and hold a prescribed physical position in relation to the others which best represents the relationships. There are many variations of the technique. Intimacy, power, boundaries, and feelings about one another and each one's perceived place in the system are dramatically revealed. Past, present, and ideal patterns can be sculpted.

5. *Caring days.* On prescribed days clients agree to perform a fixed number of specific activities on behalf of other family members or say encouraging, positive things to show their caringness. It creates a positive, cooperative climate in the home and enhances social interest.

6. *Pretending to have the symptom.* Clients are requested to enact the symptom (which they believe is out of their control). By controlling the enactment they demonstrate that they can both start and stop the symptom.

7. *Role restructuring.* Family members assume positions in the family that provide them with some significance, but also contribute to the symptom. Suggesting that members each assume a new role approximately opposite their typical one opens up many new possibilities for

behaving: the peacemaker becomes more assertive, the dominating one seeks to please, and so on. They are asked to act as if they were this kind of person and have some fun with the new role.

Any technique selected is based on the therapist's understanding of what is going on in the family and their interacting systems and how desired changes are likely to be brought about. Techniques used properly within a theoretical frame are not a bag of tricks. They are the professional tools to get the job done. The administration of a technique in cooperation with the family needs to be performed with sensitivity, skills, artistry, and a good sense of timing. It is adapted and refined for use with this particular family under these specific circumstances at this time. The therapist anticipates the consequences of using the technique both for the family members and for their circle of interacting systems.

Techniques are not standardized instruments. Therefore, even though they are typically invented by proponents of a given theory, they often can be redesigned to fit the requirements of many other theories.

REFERENCES

Allred, H. (1983). Phrases for Allred's Interaction Analysis for Therapists (AIAT). Personal communication.

Dinkmeyer, D., & Carlson, J. (1984). Training in Marriage Enrichment (TIME). Circle Pines, MN: American Guidance Service.

Dinkmeyer, D., & McKay, G. (1983). Systematic Training for Effective Parenting of Teens (STEP-Teen). Circle Pines, MN: American Guidance Service.

Dreikurs, R. (1971). *Social equality: The challenge of today*. Chicago: Henry Regnery.

Mozdzierz, G., Macchitelli, F., & Lisiecki, J. (1976). The paradox in psychotherapy: An Adlerian perspective. *Journal of Individual Psychology, 32:* 169–184.

Shulman, B. H. (Ed.) (1973). Confrontation techniques in Adlerian psychology. In *Contributions to Individual Psychology*. Chicago: Alfred Adler Institute.

Sherman, R., & Fredman, N. J. (1985). *Handbook of couple and family therapy techniques*. New York: Brunner/Mazel.

12

Adlerian Family Therapy:
An Educational Component

INTRODUCTION

When a family is dysfunctional, family therapy is the helping modality of choice. There is a need to reorganize the thinking, feeling, behavior, goals, and organization of the family. However, if we focus on health, wellness, development, and growth, then we seek means of helping families avoid dysfunction by learning effective functioning.

It is evident that such activities will be most successful if they involve both an individual family and the families who make up a community. We generally think of education as the method of choice to promote growth and development before serious dysfunction occurs. Adlerians, with their focus of attention on health, growth, and community interest, have taken a leadership role in prevention strategies.

It is also an objective in therapy to teach the family new ideas and skills in communication, understanding of personal goals and expectations, goal setting, problem solving, conflict resolution, and social interest. Participation in one of the educational groups described in this chapter is an effective way to help the family learn those skills as an adjunct to or as a follow-up of the therapy.

This chapter summarizes the history of educational models, procedures, and materials available.

HISTORY

Alfred Adler was a social psychiatrist more concerned about educational approaches and prevention than in the treatment of sick people. Adler had a high interest in the reeducation of individuals, as he believed that through this process we might best transform society and its values. He was concerned with helping people live together as equals.

Adler believed that most of the problems that parents and children were having were a direct outgrowth of poor relationships. He believed that the disintegration of family was largely a result of the changes in society which had moved us from a traditional, autocratic posture to a democratic base. The major problem was that while society had shifted, parents did not have democratic methods available to work with their children. As a result, the traditional methods for raising children had become outdated and ineffective because of the shift to a democratic society and the diversity of values and goals in such a society with its respect for the individual and the group.

After World War I Adler became very aware that teachers were also having more problems with their students than ever before. He recognized that the problems of parents and teachers were interrelated. At the same time, it was for all practical purposes an impossible task to help the many parents and teachers who needed assistance on an individual, one-to-one basis. It was from this thinking that Adler's idea for an open child guidance center originated. He felt from there he could reach parents, teachers, and parents-to-be. Many of the problems in families were similar and they were generally the result of a lack of education of adults in the understanding of children. Adler felt that counseling in public would be helpful to many people at the same time that he could help just one family.

In 1922 Adler organized his first Child Guidance Center in the community. This center was received enthusiastically and was so successful that the movement grew to 31 such centers. Primarily located in public schools and conducted by psychiatrists whom Adler trained, the centers became very popular. They were observed by not only parents and teachers, but by a great variety of people interested in childhood education.

Adler invited audience members to participate and to share their own experiences, successes, or failures and their methods of dealing with the problems to help encourage the family. This removed any stigma or shame that parents might have felt working with Adler in front of the group. They were no longer alone and they were aware that the people in the audience were interested in encouraging them. These centers were closed in 1934 when the Nazis came to power in Austria.

Adler had hoped that someday these centers would be established in the United States. His hopes were realized when one of his most energetic and enthusiastic followers, Rudolf Dreikurs, emigrated to Chicago in 1937. In 1938, working with the Abraham Lincoln Center in

Chicago, a neighborhood house, Dreikurs arranged to conduct a class for staff workers in the dynamics of child behavior. It was at these meetings that the group leaders first learned about the goals of the misbehaving child and were told what they could do to help redirect the behavior into more healthy channels. Dreikurs had a strong impact on the staff as he was able to not only help them diagnose but to provide specific suggestions for correction of misbehavior. Dreikurs was able to provide the specific suggestions because of his experience with Adler, who had dealt with the same problems in the Vienna public schools shortly after the close of World War I.

The class at Abraham Lincoln Center decided that this technique could be applied in their own situations. They then planned to invite the parents of the most difficult children to come to a special afternoon session once a week along with an identified problem child and his siblings. In February 1939 the first session was held. Attendance at the open counseling sessions proceeded slowly at the start. After three years, in February 1942, social workers reported that 40 families had been enrolled and received the usual counseling at intervals of two or three weeks. Of these families 17 were white and 23 were black, which represented the racial proportion residing in that area at the time. Thus it was felt that the center had established itself and was an excellent base for a child guidance clinic.

In 1947 the Individual Psychology Association of Chicago, after a number of years of theoretical discussion programs, accepted the practical responsibility for the extension of the child guidance movement into other areas of Chicago. They were interested in whether this method of counseling would be accepted by families in higher socioeconomic levels than the original group.

In 1941 Dreikurs conducted a center for the Mary Crane Nursery of the Hull House on Halsted Street. At this time another worker trained by Adler in Vienna began to work with Dreikurs in these programs. Eleanore Redwin, who had formerly conducted nursery schools and guidance centers in Vienna, started a unit at Mercer Center with Dreikurs and conducted another at the University of Chicago settlement.

In 1948, with two centers in successful operation, the time seemed appropriate to establish a separate organization. This became The Community Child Guidance Centers of Chicago. From this step the centers' movement expanded to a variety of areas in the United States.

Rudolf Dreikurs at this time was also training counselors from many parts of the United States and the world in the methods of Adler in family counseling. Today we find many Adlerian-Dreikursian Family Counseling Centers spread over the United States, Canada, Israel, and countries in Europe.

RATIONALE FOR FAMILY COUNSELING

Oscar Christensen, a student of Dreikurs and an internationally recognized proponent of Adlerian family counseling, has helped in the establishment of methodology throughout the United States and Canada. Christensen believes that the American child-rearing practices were basically derived from a European model which was autocratic. Regardless of the status in society, someone was always more than someone else and someone was always less (Christensen & Schramski, 1983).

As Christensen has clearly illustrated, if a parent attempts to speak down to the child from a position of superiority, while at the same time a child listens and reacts from a position of equality, there is no reception of the message or understanding, and the communication basically is ineffective. It is only as parents recognize the equality of youth that they can begin to understand the complications in parenting. Adlerians believe that mutual respect is a necessary component for a relationship as equals. However, at the same time, very few of us understand the meaning of equality.

Equality is not sameness. Sameness is actually a violation of the concept of individual differences. Equality means equal in worth and equal as a person. "By accepting the concept of equality of value rather than sameness, it is possible to define different roles for parent and child without violating your child's respect. The parent is the leader and not the boss. The child may then become the learner without being expected to act or feel inferior. Respect, the parents' desire from children, can be taught by modeling the same respect toward the children" (Christensen & Schramski, 1983, p. 5).

EDUCATION AND THERAPY

Therapists frequently think of therapy as a process to be clearly differentiated from education. They have not considered, as Adlerians have, that therapy is an educational process. The therapeutic process is one in which the person (or family) learns more about himself, understands the options available, and initiates a course of action based on this information.

When a family comes for counseling, it is sometimes apparent that they lack a large amount of information about how to function more effectively as a family, and the parents lack parenting skills. It is important early in the contact to identify what it is the family needs. There may be problems in the system or in the relationships, and certainly in the beliefs that both parents and children hold. However, at the same time, it is important to identify whether the family lacks information about how to motivate, discipline, encourage, or develop cooperation.

It is important to assess the skills the parents have for communicating effectively, encouraging, utilizing logical consequences, holding family meetings, and dealing with the myriad of details in family relationships.

Before determining that the family has only a need for family therapy, the therapist should determine the level of skill and information available to the parents. We have found that in some instances, supplying the family with a book describing the practices and relationships recommended in family therapy accelerates the progress of the family. In instances where such a lack of information and skills has been identified, we immediately encourage the family to begin to read materials relevant to our approach. Part of the session, perhaps the closing period of the session, is spent in determining how these ideas are being applied. Thus we believe that the family therapist must clearly identify the need for skills and information, and not merely assume that the problem is best solved by a family therapy process without utilization of educational materials.

DIFFERENTIATING ADLERIAN FAMILY COUNSELING FROM ADLERIAN FAMILY THERAPY

Adlerian family therapy is a different process from Adlerian family counseling. Historically, Adlerian family counseling preceded Adlerian family therapy. The family therapy that Adlerians do is different from the traditional Adlerian family counseling insofar as:

1. All members are usually seen at the same time. If there is a major marital problem, the procedure is modified.
2. The session may take from one to one and a half hours.
3. The therapist focuses on the psychological movement and the transactions among family members.
4. The therapist has an opportunity to model more constructive and effective behaviors.
5. There is a greater focus on such psychological dynamics as roles, place, rules, expectations, priorities, family guiding lines, superiority and inferiority motives, and others described in preceding chapters (Dinkmeyer & Dinkmeyer, 1983; Okun, 1984).

ADLERIAN PARENT EDUCATION

The first Adlerian book for parents which was widely received was

The Challenge of Parenthood (1948). This text began a series of Adlerian parenting publications. It was used in parent study groups as well as being read individually. Dreikurs took up the revision of this book by working with Vicki Soltz on *Children: The Challenge* (1964). This book received even wider acceptance than Dreikurs' original work, *The Challenge of Parenthood*. It continues to be a popular book that can be found in bookstores throughout the country. It is a classic text in the sense that it sets forth the ideas of a seminal thinker, Rudolf Dreikurs.

Raising a Responsible Child, written by Don Dinkmeyer and Gary McKay (1973), helped to extend the Adlerian child training movement. This book dealt with many of Dreikurs' basic concepts about understanding behavior and misbehavior, encouragement and logical consequences. However, it added the facet of the communication process by suggesting certain listening skills for parents and methods of exploring alternative solutions. The book also dealt with games children play and approaches to working with children on school problems.

Perhaps the major popularization of Adlerian parenting education ideas occurred with the development of *Systematic Training for Effective Parenting* (STEP) by Dinkmeyer and McKay (1982). STEP produced a handbook or guidebook, which is available in bookstores throughout the country and internationally. More important, it provided a systematic training program. This program is available in a kit that includes a leader's manual, tapes, cassettes, and a systematic way to approach each lesson. The STEP program is a systematic sequence of instructions in which parents and the group are asked to:

1. Discuss the last week's previous activities assignment.
2. Discuss the assigned reading in the parents' handbook.
3. Discuss the charts.
4. Respond to the tapes and exercises.
5. Deal with specific problem situations.
6. Respond by summarizing what they had learned from the specific section.

STEP captured the interest of the American public. At this time it is believed that about 2 million parents have been involved with Systematic Training for Effective Parenting. The program has been translated into Spanish and Japanese, and has been used in several South American countries and Mexico.

Systematic Training for Effective Parenting of Teens was developed by Dinkmeyer and McKay (1983) specifically to help parents deal with the difficult teen years. The program extends itself to meet the particular challenges of personality development during the teen years and how to work with emotions at that time in life. Extensive attention is given to the process of encouragement, communication, and discipline, as well as family meetings. A specific session is devoted to dealing with special challenges in parenting the teenager. There has been a high level of interest by the parents of teens in the STEP/Teen Program.

All of the Adlerian parenting education programs focus on the importance of understanding behavior utilizing encouragement, applying consequences, and developing a method of meeting as equals, titled the family meeting.

Two other former Dreikurs' students, Raymond Corsini and Genevieve Painter, wrote *The Practical Parent,* which sets forth their view of how Adlerian principles can be applied to parent education (Corsini & Painter, 1975).

Some additional brief booklets have been developed which help set forth the Adlerian parenting education approach. These are often used by psychologists and marriage and family therapists as bibliotherapy to accompany their work with the family. The pamphlets which are particularly applicable to family work include the following:

- *The Basics of Adult-Teen Relationships* by Don Dinkmeyer (1976)*
- *The Basics of Parenting* by Don Dinkmeyer, Jr. and Jim Dinkmeyer (1980)*
- *The Basics of Encouragement* by Gary McKay (1976)*
- *The Basics of Discipline* by Jon Carlson (1978)*
- *Winning Teenagers Over in Home and School* by Francis X. Walton (1980)†

Family education groups have been sponsored throughout the United States for a number of years. Adlerian approaches have attracted special interest because they teach an understandable and practical theory of human behavior which is directly applicable in the home. It is based on understanding human behavior as purposive. Children are disciplined in terms of the social consequences of behavior.

Dreikurs made this particular significant contribution to parent education when he formulated the four goals of misbehavior: attention getting, power seeking, revenge, and the display of inadequacy. This

---

* Available from CMTI Press, Box 8268, Coral Springs, FL 33075.
† Available from Child Care Books, Columbia, SC 29210.

look at purpose of clue *

distinguished the Adlerian approach from other methods in that it does not seek to explain behavior by determining its cause but instead focuses on the purpose and the goal of the behavior.

THE PARENT "C" GROUP

The Adlerian parent education methods that we have mentioned up to this point have generally been based on the study of a book or other materials with the focus on learning basic concepts so that they might be applied to child-training situations. This has been a very successful approach. However, there have been frequent inquiries about ways in which people might go beyond the basic child study to the actual application of the concepts to their specific children. In other words, they would begin focusing on their child and then see how the concepts are applied.

The parent "C" group is based on the assumption that parents have already been enrolled in Adlerian parent education groups before joining the "C" group. The parent "C" group then was developed to present knowledge about human behavior in a group setting. The group permits people to share ideas and procedures. It also helps members become more aware of how their own feelings, attitudes, and beliefs may affect their relationships with their children. A major feature of the "C" group is that it helps parents understand how their own beliefs—such as "I must be in control" or "Disobedience is a personal challenge and must be met with force"—keep them from functioning more effectively with their children. This is contrasted with discussion groups that do not consider how the parents' personal beliefs keep them from putting the principles into practice.

* Premise
* a belief

The parent "C" group provides a unique opportunity to deal with the affective, cognitive, and behavioral domains. It goes beyond involving the "whole child" to involving the "whole parent." Parents are helped to consider how their beliefs may be blocking more effective relationships with their children. The approach has been titled the "C" group because the factors that make it effective begin with a "C." The specific components of the "C" group include:

1. *Collaboration.* Working together on mutual concerns is emphasized. The leader and the group work as equals.
2. *Consultation.* Consultation is both received and provided by the parents. The interaction that occurs in the group helps members become aware of new approaches with children.
3. *Clarification.* The group clarifies for all members their belief

systems, their feelings, and the congruence or incongruence between their behaviors, beliefs, and their feelings.

4. *Confrontation.* More realistic and honest feedback allows each individual to see his or her own purposes and beliefs and be willing to confront other members with their belief systems.

5. *Concern.* The group is concerned and shows that it cares. This concern leads members to collaborate, consult, clarify, and confront.

6. *Confidentiality.* The group is confidential. Whatever is discussed within the group stays within the group.

7. *Commitment.* The group helps individuals develop a commitment to change. Participants in the group become involved in helping members recognize that they can really change only themselves. They may come to the group expecting to change children, but they soon learn that they must develop a specific commitment involving the action they will take in order to change their approach to the problem (Dinkmeyer, 1973).

"C" groups enable people to become aware of how their own beliefs and perceptions influence the parenting process. Those interested in more detailed information about how a comprehensive parent education program might encompass both parent education and parent "C" groups will be interested in obtaining "Systematic Parent Education in the Schools" (Dinkmeyer & Dinkmeyer, 1976).

MARRIAGE ENRICHMENT

Marriage enrichment is a relatively recent addition to methods utilized to facilitate family relationships and enrich families. Historical roots of marriage enrichment generally go back to Barcelona, Spain, 1962, for the site of the first weekend marriage-enhancement retreat. The worldwide network of Marriage Encounter resulted from this original group developed by Father Gabriel Calvo.

In October 1962, David and Vera Mace began leading weekend enrichment sessions for married couples in the United States. In 1973 the Maces founded the Association of Couples for Marriage Enrichment, ACME, an organization whose slogan is "To work for better marriages beginning with our own."

The first specifically Adlerian enrichment program was developed by E. Clair Hawes. The couple enrichment groups she advocates are not therapy groups. Participation by couples with serious difficulties is always discouraged. The best facilitators are generally couples who play a fully participative role in the enrichment group. The study group is not an encounter group. There are various procedures which can help make the couple learn more about themselves and their relationships. Details on this program can be found in the material developed by Hawes titled "Couples Growing Together" (1979).

Training in Marriage Enrichment (T.I.M.E.) is an educational program that addresses the special challenges facing married couples. The principles and philosophy are developed by Dinkmeyer from other programs (Systematic Training for Effective Parenting, STEP, and Systematic Training for Effective Parenting of Teens, STEP/Teen).

T.I.M.E. primarily reflects Adlerian psychology, although it is influenced by other schools of thought which are congruent with the social psychological approach to improving human relationships. The goals of a T.I.M.E. course are to help couples understand their relationship by developing skills that will make the marriage more effective, rewarding, and satisfying. Couples learn how to align their goals, be mutually encouraging, communicate more openly and honestly, understand their relationship, and make choices that support their relationship, solve conflicts, and deal with their feelings.

T.I.M.E. was developed primarily to be used as a ten-session marriage enrichment program. Each session focuses on specific skills and activities which are presented in the book, *Time for a Better Marriage* (Dinkmeyer & Carlson, 1984). T.I.M.E. can be used in an intensive weekend by modifying the reading and activity assignments. It can also be used in a special meeting or workshop where one of the topics is discussed by a leader, for example, encouragement or conflict resolution. Marriage therapists can also effectively use *Time for a Better Marriage* as a resource in their marriage counseling and therapy. The book will provide resource reading on the various skills of marriage.

The T.I.M.E. program is presented in a kit and includes:

- A couple resource book
- A four-color cartoon-illustrated book
- A leader's guide which contains an introductory overview of the program along with information on organizing and leading each session
- Six audio cassettes, five of which are provided for use in a T.I.M.E. session
- "Time to Relax and Imagine" cassette, which is for the couple's private use

- Leader outline cards that provide the leader with an outline for each session and a publicity packet

Topics in *Time for a Better Marriage* are:

1. A Good Marriage Begins With You
2. Encouragement in the Marriage Relationship
3. Understanding Your Relationship
4. Honesty and Openness: Being Congruent
5. Communication: Basis for an Effective Relationship
6. Communication Skills
7. Choices in Marital Relationship
8. Conflict in Marriage
9. Conflict Resolution: Applying Your Skills
10. Self-Help Procedures for Maintaining Your Marriage

Each session in the T.I.M.E. program is systematically arranged so that the group is exposed to a variety of developmental experiences. A typical sequence for each T.I.M.E. session includes:

1. Building communication. Couples develop more effective methods for improving their communication process. Activities generally are done as couples but occasionally may involve some group interaction.
2. Discussion of the activity for the week. Each week couples are expected to do one or more activities that reinforce the skill introduced in the previous session. At this point, couples share their experiences in working with the activity of the week, followed by a group discussion that provides additional support and encouragement.
3. Discussion of the reading. Group members express their ideas and feelings. Answers emerge as the result of the reading assignment.
4. Presentation of the audio tape for each session which focuses on the skill presented in the session. Participants practice this skill by responding to the situations presented on the cassette.
5. Application. The skill or concept introduced in the session is experienced and practiced through an activity.
6. My plan. A form is found at the end of each chapter of *Time*

for a Better Marriage. Partners confidentially write their concerns and commitments and assess their progress each week.

7. Summary. The summary in the central part of each section that each member is expected to contribute. The summary gives the couples the time to identify what they have learned during the session. The summary may deal with the content or participants' feelings. This is usually followed by giving the activity and reading assignments for the ensuing week.

FAMILY THERAPY: USING AN EDUCATIONAL COMPONENT

We have found that family therapy which uses an educational component provides an opportunity to expand the potential of the family therapy process. For the practitioner in private practice, parent education provides an opportunity for the therapist to do preventive and developmental work while at the same time gaining visibility in the community as a resource for families. Many families who are reluctant to present themselves to a family therapist may develop the courage for such a contact from original exposure in the parent education format. The family therapy which is assisted by the educational components provides the opportunity to accelerate the process.

It has been our experience that in utilizing educational materials by providing parents with a book and discussing with them the concepts of the book as they apply to their specific situations, there is an opportunity for considerable growth in a relatively limited period of time. To illustrate briefly, in seeing a family with an adolescent, we typically make the STEP/Teen book and The Basics of Adult Teen Relationships available to the family. We have found in a situation in which the parents were too demanding, too autocratic, and far too discouraging, sometimes in a period of several sessions we have been able to change the parents' attitude by the process of reading and discussion. In a typical session we will see parents the first time to go over the concepts of the book and make the assignment.

We have found in dealing with younger children where a child is obviously displaying one of the goals of misbehavior, helping the parents learn specific ways to encourage and apply logical consequences has been extremely efficient in both use of time and therapeutic effectiveness.

REFERENCES

Carlson, J. (1978). *The basics of discipline.* Coral Springs, FL: CMTI Press.

Christensen, O., & Schramski, T. (1983). *Adlerian family counseling.* Minneapolis, MN: Educational Media Corp.

Corsini, R. & Painter, G. (1975). *The practical parent.* New York: Harper and Row.

Dinkmeyer, D. (1973, December). The parent "C" group. *Personnel and Guidance Journal, 52*(4). 252–256.

Dinkmeyer, D. (1976). *The basics of adult-teen relationships.* Coral Springs, FL: CMTI Press.

Dinkmeyer, D., & Carlson, J. (1984). *Time for a better marriage.* Circle Pines, MN: American Guidance Service.

Dinkmeyer, D., & Carlson J. (1984), Training in Marriage Enrichment (TIME). Circle Pines, MN: American Guidance Service.

Dinkmeyer, D., and Dinkmeyer, D. Jr. (1976, June). Systematic parent education in the schools. *Focus on Guidance, 8*(10).

Dinkmeyer, D., & Dinkmeyer, J. (1983). Adlerian family therapy. *Individual Psychology, 39*(2).

Dinkmeyer, D., & and McKay, G. (1973). *Raising a responsible child.* New York: Simon & Schuster.

Dinkmeyer, D., & McKay, G. (1982). Systematic Training for Effective Parenting (STEP). Circle Pines, MN: American Guidance Service.

Dinkmeyer, D., & McKay, G. (1983). Systematic Training for Effective Parenting of Teens (STEP/Teen). Circle Pines, MN: American Guidance Service.

Dinkmeyer, D. Jr., & Dinkmeyer, J. (1980). *The basics of parenting.* Coral Springs, FL: CMTI Press.

Dreikurs, R. (1948). *The challenge of parenthood.* New York: Duell, Sloan & Pearce.

Dreikurs, R. & Soltz, V. (1964). *Children: The challenge.* New York: Hawthorn.

Hawes, E. C. (1979). *Couples growing together.* Sechelt, British Columbia: R.C.C.S. Associates.

McKay, G. (1976). *The basics of encouragement.* Coral Springs, FL: CMTI Press.

Okun, B. (1984). *Family therapy with school related problems.* Rockville, MD: Aspen Systems Corp.

Walton, F. X. (1980). *Winning teenagers over in home and school.* Columbia, SC: Child Care Books.

Appendix

SUMMARY OF PRINCIPLES OF
ADLERIAN FAMILY THERAPY

The major principles of Adlerian family therapy derive from the concepts of human behavior described in Chapter 1. The principles are to be seen in the context of (1) the development and self-determined behavior of individual members; (2) the interactions and dynamics of the family system as a holistic unit; (3) the social context of other institutions of which the family and its members are a functional part; and (4) the goals that they all individually and collectively strive for.

The following list of twenty principles guide the therapeutic enterprise.

1. All persons are socially embedded and seek personal significance through belonging in social systems. Most problems in therapy reflect some form of alienation or feeling of lack of worth and acceptance among members.

2. The power drive is generated by the need of both the individual and the family to complete, improve, or protect themselves by initiating a line of movement or action in accord with their idiosyncratic beliefs. It encompasses the methods used to achieve their goals. In turn the direction of the movement helps us to better identify and understand the goals.

3. Social interest directs that power drive toward caring for others and behavior whose means and ends will be constructively useful for both the individual and the family. Conversely, undeveloped social interest or antisocial feeling is likely to direct the power against or away from others. Our mutual interdependence requires that we be concerned about one another and that we learn to cooperate and work together to live together. Developing social interest and overcoming alienation form a major focus of therapy.

4. Behavior and personality are created and defined in the group

---

The principles discussed in this Appendix are described more fully in Chapters 1 and 2. The behavior change principles are described more fully in Chapter 4.

interaction and one's place in the group, which leads to development of individual and family life styles. The multigenerational legacy of the family also influences the life style of the current family and its members. The life style includes beliefs, values, goals, and the means used to attain those goals. Therapists assist the family to understand and evaluate its life style.

5. Differences between people provide opportunities for growth through the presentation of a thesis followed by the other's antithesis leading to the negotiation or discovery of a new synthesis (Dreikurs, 1970). The opposite is a tension-producing test of power, each trying to overcome the other through power plays or ploys. A repeating pattern of conflict represents a standoff since neither is able to overcome the other. Therapists model and teach the negotiation of differences.

6. The family is a separate dynamic entity created by the interaction among its members. It is a unit different from any and all of its members.

7. The family interactions are guided by the goals, life style, and private logic of each member and the family as a unit. We need to work with the family as a unit and with its individual members who create the family.

8. The family interactions are mediated by values held in common, the negotiation of differences, and the interdependency among members for survival, development, and significance.

9. Members hold both biological and assumed roles and places in the system. Examples of biological places are birth order, gender, and generation. Examples of assumed roles are good child, initiator, peacemaker, and scapegoat.

10. Assumed roles are created by each person based on his subjective perceptions, personal goals, and achievements. He tries to elicit reciprocal behavior in others which conforms to his perceptions and goals. The family as a unit also assigns roles to members based on its goals. The actual roles arise as a result of cooperation, conflict, and negotiation.

11. The dynamic family system constantly evolves out of the interactions just mentioned with its own characteristic private logic, life style, goals, and methods of striving toward those goals—its unique line of movement.

12. Characteristic ways of pursuing the challenges of life and solving problems evolve as part of the family's life style through the development of rituals, myths, and rules. They are expressed over time as continuing patterns and themes in behavior. An example of a ritual is we all gather at grandma's house for Sunday dinner every week. A common myth is that blood is thicker than water and you depend more on family than

strangers. A typical rule accompanying such a myth is that we must stick together. The symptomatic behavior will involve ritual, myth, and rules that need to be modified or changed.

13. Assumptive values and expectations fuel the demands made upon the members. They also serve as criteria in measuring how satisfying the relationships are and what improvements are occurring. An example is that my child is very bright and should be in an honors class. If he doesn't keep up I will be very disappointed and punish him. The therapist helps the family to identify, clarify, negotiate, or change those expectations.

14. The family is organized as a unitary whole. Each member contributes as a functionally subordinated part of that whole. If one person contributes more or differently than the system requires, the system is disrupted and must obtain conformity or reorganize. For example, if one person with a fertile mind insists that everyone else act upon his constant flow of ideas and demands regardless of their wishes, the family will either acknowledge that member as boss and leader or act to place some limits on him so that the family can pursue other needs as well. The therapist assists the family to reorganize so that each person contributes to the whole in a meaningful way and that the family contributes to the development of each member.

15. The family constellation describes the place occupied by each person multigenerationally, and each person's roles and relationships. The subjective view of their family and world varies with the places occupied. It is different to be the oldest or the youngest child, a parent or a child, employed or economically dependent. Knowing the place gives the therapist important clues about behavior and relationships. Reorganizing places in the family will change behavior and relationships.

16. The family interacts around nine dynamic qualities: (a) power and decision making; (b) boundaries and intimacy; (c) coalitions; (d) roles; (e) rules; (f) similarities; (g) complementarities and differences; (h) myths; and (i) patterns and styles of communication.

17. Behavior makes sense within the private logic of the family no matter how it appears to an objective observer. Since behavior is purposive and goal directed, the therapist carefully examines the goals and the subjective perceptions that support them and the unique meaning of the behavior to the participants.

18. Treatment is based upon helping the clients observe their behavior, understand its purpose and discover goals, or means of attaining goals, which are in error. New options for behaving are then identified or created and implemented.

19. The therapist creates a new system that includes the family and

himself. The new system is organized according to democratic principles, with the therapist assuming the role of the initial leader of the group based upon her expertise. All of the above principles will also apply to this new group. Similarly, if a supervisor is involved, still another system is created.

20. Therapeutic change takes place in the system as a result of new subjective perceptions, goals, information, skills; improved communication patterns; and the reorganization of places and roles in the system.

REFERENCES

Dreikurs, R. (1970, February 21). Unpublished address. Nanaimo, British Columbia.

Author Index

Subject Index

306